Economics and Politics
in the USSR

About the Book and Editors

Soviet scholars have apparently stayed clear of meaningful analysis of such touchy subjects as interdependence and conflict in the relationship between economics and politics. Very little has been published on this issue—no surprise in a system that controls centrally both politics and the economy, with an emphasis on rapid economic development.

The absence of meaningful Soviet research led the Federal Institute for East European and International Studies in Cologne to sponsor an international interdisciplinary conference on the subject. Contributions to the resulting book cover three main areas. The first includes the impact of traditional Russian political culture on contemporary Soviet economic thinking and behavior, the rank of economic aims in the priority system of Soviet politics, and the function of economic institutions in the implementation of political aims. The second concerns the role of political lobbies in the economy and repercussions of economic change for Soviet politics. Foreign economic relations and the USSR's foreign policy make up the third area. The concluding discussion reviews the state of international research and identifies areas for future study.

Dr. Hans-Hermann Höhmann is senior economist at the Federal Institute for East European and International Studies in Cologne. Dr. Alec Nove is professor emeritus of economics at the University of Glasgow. Dr. Heinrich Vogel is the director of the Federal Institute for East European and International Studies.

Published in cooperation with
das Bundesinstitut für ostwissenschaftliche
und internationale Studien/
the Federal Institute for East European
and International Studies

Economics and Politics
in the USSR
Problems of Interdependence

edited by Hans-Hermann Höhmann,
Alec Nove, and Heinrich Vogel

Westview Press / Boulder and London

We are grateful to the Federal Institute for East European and International Studies for its contribution to the cost of publication.

This Westview softcover edition was manufactured on our own premises using equipment and methods that allow us to keep even specialized books in stock. It is printed on acid-free paper and bound in softcovers that carry the highest rating of the National Association of State Textbook Administrators, in consultation with the Association of American Publishers and the Book Manufacturers' Institute.

Published in 1986 in the United States of America by Westview Press, Inc.; Frederick A. Praeger, Publisher; 5500 Central Avenue, Boulder, Colorado 80301

Library of Congress Cataloging-in-Publication Data
Economics and politics in the USSR.
   1. Soviet Union—Economic policy—1976–
—Addresses, essays, lectures. 2. Soviet Union—Politics
and government—1953–   —Addresses, essays, lectures.
I. Höhmann, Hans-Hermann. II. Nove, Alec.
III. Vogel, Heinrich, 1937–   .
HC336.25.E28 1986   338.947   86-1534
ISBN 0-8133-0334-6 (soft : alk. paper)

This book was produced without formal editing by the publisher.

Printed and bound in the United States of America

The paper used in this publication meets the minimum requirements of the American National Standard for Permanence of Paper for Printed Library Materials Z39.48-1984.

6   5   4   3   2   1

Contents

Preface ix

1   History, Political Culture, and Economics in the
    Soviet Union, *Alec Nove* 1

2   The Role of Economics in Soviet Political
    Ideology, *Helmut Dahm* 17

3   The Place of Economic Policy Objectives on
    the List of Soviet Political Priorities,
    Hans-Hermann Höhmann 41

4   Economic Institutions as Instruments of
    Political Rule, *Georg Brunner* 58

5   Economic Activities and the Intermediate and
    Lower Levels of Party Organisation,
    Peter Frank 77

6   Economic and Political Aspects of the
    Military-Industrial Complex in the USSR,
    Christopher Davis 92

7   The Political and Social Implications of
    Economic Reform in the USSR, *Ronald Amann* 125

8   The Political Economy of Soviet Nationalities
    and Regions, *Hans-Jürgen Wagener* 146

9   Inflationary, Political, and Social Implications
    of the Current Economic Slowdown,
    Gregory Grossman 172

10 Political and Moral Aspects of the Two
    Economies, *Peter Wiles* 198

11 Economic Relations as an Instrument of
    Soviet Hegemony Over Eastern Europe?
    Klaus von Beyme 214

12 Economic Reform and Soviet Foreign Policy,
    Jerry F. Hough 232

13 Developing Countries in the Foreign Economic
    Relations and Foreign Policy of the USSR,
    Heinrich A. Machowski 252

14 The Politics and Economics of
    Soviet Arms Exports, *Roger E. Kanet* 274

About the Contributors 303

Preface

Since 1979, the pattern of Soviet economic performance, which had produced relatively high (though declining over the long run) growth rates over previous decades, turned into a veritable recession. The downward trend levelled off in 1984, but even on the eve of the 12th Five-Year plan economic developments in the USSR are better described by stagnation than by any other term used in capitalist economic analysis. Several attempts to reverse the long-term trend by rearranging annual economic plans have failed; the signals set for the rest of the decade are still too vague to be interpreted as a grand design. The task is to raise significantly the levels of productivity by means of a mix of economic, administrative, and technological initiatives, resulting in steady and sufficient, but not necessarily high, rates of growth, to be based on qualitative change in all sectors of the economy.

Western observers have recently been fascinated by this unprecedented development in Soviet history, speculating about its impact on Soviet politics at home and abroad. How is the situation perceived by the Soviet elite and by the leaders themselves? With a growing sense of urgency, if not of impending crisis? As a situation to be managed by piecemeal engineering, combining measures of economic policy with political-psychological campaigns, or by waging "real reform"? What about the undefinable knife-edge: If problems seem not too serious, nothing need be done; if too serious, nothing can be done? What range of options is open to decisionmakers who face an increasing burden of the empire and, at the same time, the growing power of the main challenger to their foreign policy? Who promotes fundamental change (restructuring or major reform) in the economic system, i.e., who are the modernizers and what is their motivation? What, on the other hand, are the forces that sabotage fundamental change: the blinders of ideological heritage, vested interests of *apparatchiki* in party and state, structural inertia entailed in hypertrophic bureaucracies, or good reasoning and mature consideration of unacceptable political risks for the communist party's power monopoly?

Western media have been mesmerized by the question of to what extent charisma and vitality in a secretary general of the Communist Party of the Soviet Union are decisive for any major change. At the end of 1985, the question is still unanswered. A more systematic (and system-related) approach remains necessary in order to evaluate developments in the USSR and their impact on Soviet foreign policy. Will the Soviet superpower's crumbling economic base induce a more contemplative mood, maybe even restraint (if only temporarily) in foreign policy?

Obviously, a differentiated analysis of economic developments is indispensable for assessing the objective latitude for movement in Soviet policies. Without due regard, however, for the revealed spectrum of Soviet perceptions and for imponderabilities in decisionmaking processes (still a black-box for external analysts), the results of economic research will remain academic and open to overinterpretation in many directions.

On the other hand, the most sophisticated analysis of Soviet institutions, functional elites, professional or regional pressure groups and their revealed motivations and visibly conflicting preferences would be useless without consideration of economic potentials and constraints. Recent changes in political leadership were accompanied by changes in the style and language of public controversies over a number of issues, most of which are closely tied to the faltering dynamism of the economy. Despite open acknowledgment, from Brezhnev to Andropov, Chernenko, and now Gorbachev, of the growing urgency of major corrections, the outline of reforms in the economic and political system remains to be seen. The extreme schools of thought in Western interpretation of Soviet affairs have been disproved: The USSR neither lost critical economic vitality altogether, nor did it continue an openly expansionist confrontation in foreign policy. The realistic scenarios are somewhere in between—for political and economic reasons. Any attempt to develop more plausible patterns of interpretation will have to rely on more differentiated analysis than the usual monocausal and monodisciplinary analytical shorthand.

In any country of the world, economic and political phenomena can be understood only by explicitly addressing interdependencies and conflicts between the various spheres of complex societies. In most cases, however, "interdependence" is hardly more than a synonym for absence of empirically relevant strategies in research. Even more when it comes to interpreting trends in the USSR, interdependence turns out to be a more elegant statement of aporia, aggravated by the scholastics of Soviet writing or by its reticence. Conventional Soviet literature has not been helpful in its insistence on inherent fundamental harmony within socialist society. This has changed recently, but the open (not too esoteric) controversy over the antagonistic and non-antagonistic contradictions of socialism may hardly be more than just an interlude in an extremely slippery area. The bold statements from Novosibirsk, however, in favour of a macro-sociological approach to organizational reform—nothing less than an adapted theory of vested interests—appear to have a more lasting impact. There seems to be a growing awareness that old taboos may have to be traded for higher efficiency. The exchange of personnel on high and intermediate levels is a necessary, but not sufficient, precondition for modernisation. And the stakes are high.

The literature on these dilemmas of contemporary Soviet politics is voluminous. Typical volumes of collected papers that cover different segments of Soviet development, however, address the problem of interdependence between economics and politics only implicitly. In an international conference, organized by the Bundesinstitut für ostwissenschaftliche und internationale Studien in November 1984, participants tackled the problem in detail. The authors of various papers were asked to contribute expertise drawn from their respective disciplines (history, political science, philosophy, economics) to deal with traditions of Russian political culture and ideology, economic thought, the role of institutions, various groups and subgroups in the Soviet elite, the political and social implications of economic slowdown and of parallel economies, the political risks of economic reform, and the interrelationship between foreign economic and foreign political relations.

This book presents slightly updated and expanded papers from this conference, which produced a number of valuable insights into rarely discussed issues. The editors are greatly indebted to all the active contributors to the conference, primarily the discussants of papers: Hannes Adomeit, Wolfgang Berner, Heinz Brahm, Horst Herlemann, Peter Hübner, Gyula Jósza, Jiri Kosta, Gail Lapidus, Gert Leptin, Christian Meier, Friedemann Müller, Gerhard Simon, Karl-Eugen Wädekin. All three editors particularly wish to express their thanks to Roger Clarke (Glasgow) and Barbara Langer (Bundesinstitut) for competent and expeditious editing of the manuscripts.

Hans-Hermann Höhmann
Alec Nove
Heinrich Vogel

1
History, Political Culture, and Economics in the Soviet Union

Alec Nove

Some Methodological Remarks

Man is a cause-seeking animal. All events, institutions, and systems, do of course occur within chains of causation. But it is all too tempting to devise explanations that do indeed fit the facts, but that could with almost equal plausibility "explain" a totally different outcome. If I may begin with what might seem a trivial example: When Glasgow Celtic was defeated in the first round of the European Cup, one reason given was that there is insufficient high-level competition in the Scottish Football League. The next year, when Celtic won the Cup, one reason given was that because there is little high-level competition in the Scottish League, Celtic was able to concentrate its energies on the European cup. Or let us take a much less trivial example. If in 1981 there had been an anti-Soviet free trade union movement in Hungary and not in Poland, we would doubtless be tempted to seek an explanation in the events of 1956, the brutal suppression of the Hungarian reform movement by Soviet troops, while no such unpleasant things happened in Poland. It would sound very convincing. Unfortunately, as we know, what actually happened was the exact opposite.

National tradition is a tricky concept to handle. To deny its importance because it is not measurable would be foolish. But it is not measurable, and it cannot be isolated from other factors. Several contradictory strands may be present. Thus, while few would deny that the causes of Hitlerism are to be found in

1

Germany's past, this same past contains elements that—had Hitler failed to gain power in 1933—would be advanced as a convincing explanation of his failure. It would be a foolish historian who tried to account for Japan's remarkable economic achievements since the war without reference to the peculiarities of Japan's social structure with its roots deep in history. But there is no evident connection between the characters and behaviour patterns of the Samurai and the modern Japanese businessman (or is there?).

Turning to Russia, few doubt that today's Soviet Union has been influenced by Russia's historical experience, and so any argument would turn on the relative importance of the past (and which elements of the past) in explaining the present. Some try to ride two horses at once. Thus Richard Pipes argues both that the USSR is aggressive because of the essence of its Marxist-Leninist ideology, and that its expansionism and aggression follow centuries-old tsarist tradition.

Political Culture

Stalin was said to have been conscious of the people's need for a substitute *batyushka-tsar*. He most certainly sought to have history written and films made to show the line of succession stretching back to Ivan the Terrible and Peter the Great. The historian-politician Milyukov traced the power of the autarky and the weakness of the landed nobility back to the poverty of the land and sparse population of mediaeval Russia: The nobility derived little income from the land and often had to take service with the Grand Duke. As Pushkin pointed out in his historical notes, they "did not fortify their estates," they were not a countervailing power, and Ivan IV had little difficulty in cutting off their heads. Russian feudalism, if that label is applicable at all, was very different from its Western counterpart. True, in the West also strong monarchs reduced substantially the political power of the landed nobility (e.g., Louis XI and later Richelieu and Louis XIV in France), but the nobility (and the growing towns) did have some real social standing and influence, and rights of property were—much of the time—

respected. Ivan IV went far to enforce his claims to own the bodies and properties of all his subjects. Peter was able to eliminate the remaining vestiges of hereditary *boyar* status, and treated all *dvoryane* as a mobilisable service class, serving him and the state for life. Even in the nineteenth century the differences from Western Europe remained deep. Pushkin, in the already-cited historical notes, asserts that there was no real aristocracy in Russia, since positions depended on rank and rank on the tsar. He was interestingly ambivalent as to the desirability and the consequences. On the one hand, the failure of the nobility (in the reign of Anna Ioannovna) to secure a share in state power was a good thing, since otherwise it would have made of itself a closed caste and prevented the promotion of talented persons from below. But on the other, it meant a "despotism surrounded by devoted stipendiaries, and the snuffing out of any opposition and independence of spirit." A hereditary high nobility is a guarantee of its independence. *"Le contraire est nécéssairement moyen de tyrannie ou plutôt d'un despotisme lâche."*[1]

The poet Maksimilian Voloshin wrote: *"Velikii Petr byl pervyi bol'shevik"*. Writing in 1926, he must have had in mind both the despotic methods and the mobilizing role of the state, its claim over the lives and property rights of the citizenry. He could hardly have foreseen collectivization, but, if he had, he would surely have drawn the parallel with the attachment of the peasants to the land, their duty to deliver produce and labour for the state's needs, to catch up to the more advanced West by barbarous methods.

Much has been written about the power of the autocracy and the weakness of "unofficial" social forces, the one both justifying and causing the other. This needs to be linked both with the behaviour patterns of authority and the reactions to them on the part of the ruled. Parallels between the specific characteristics of tsarist and Soviet bureaucracy were made already by Lenin. Trotsky deplored the passivity of the masses (when he ceased to be "the prophet armed"). Lermontov, a hundred years earlier, wrote of the *"zhandarmy golubye, i vy, poslushnyi im narod"*, Chekhov of the need to "squeeze the slave out of ourselves drop by drop". Through the centuries people have been accustomed to internal passports, *propiska* and its tsarist equivalent, and arbitrariness. Not even the educated classes had much time for the notion of Rechtsstaat, as can be seen in the attitude to law and laws on the part of Gogol, Tolstoy and Dostoevsky.

Much has been written too about the specific features of the Russian intelligentsia. Among recent works on the subject in *samizdat* and in emigration I would note those of Shragin (*Protivostoyanie dukha*) and "Klenov" (in *Sintaksis*, No. 12). The tsars needed an educated service elite, to run the country and officer the army, they needed scientists, specialists, educators, but they wished them to be obedient servants. However, a part of the educated strata developed a critical and independent mind, which soon brought them into conflict with authority. At the same time their outlook separated them also from the masses. The peasantry retained, along with tendencies to passivity and obedience, a tradition of rebellion.

Stenka Razin and Emelyan Pugachev are also part of Russian history and folk memory. I have just been reading a fascinating dissertation on the peasantry in Saratov province, by O. Figes, in which he shows that a kind of cult of Razin was still influencing peasants in 1905 and 1918. Peasant violence sometimes took totally destructive forms, and an important difference between bolsheviks and mensheviks was their attitude to this aspect of peasant rebellion: Martov was fearful of and dismayed by the prospect of a twentieth-century version of *Pugachev-shchina*, while Lenin was ready to ride the storm (though it came close to sweeping him away too in 1921).

Fear of revolt from below, fear of anarchy, of *bezporyadok*, was—perhaps still is—an important factor explaining the acceptance of authority on the part of a large segment even of the critically-inclined intelligentsia. This was noted already by Herzen. Today also some are "prepared to wear their chains for fear of what would happen if the people were unchained."

It should also be noted that the Bolshevik revolution had the quite unintended effect of disrupting the process of "social Europeanization" which was in process at least since the reforms of Alexander II. It did so above all by physically destroying or driving into exile the bulk of the bourgeoisie and professional men, along with landlords and officials.

Shragin made the very interesting point that many who supported the Bolshevik revolution did so for conservative motives: capitalism in town and village was resented as destroying the old ways of life. A contemporary example is that of Iran: the Shah's modernization programme led to conservative revolt. Obviously, the Bolsheviks themselves were not conservative, but, for example, many of the peasant rebels of 1917–1918 sought to destroy the Stolypin reform in the name of a return to older communal forms of tenure. However, Vasili Grossman, in his *samizdat* work *Vsye techet,* points quite explicitly at the effects of Lenin's own doctrine and methods in reinforcing and restoring age-old Russian despotic traditions. "Vast was the break-up of Russian life which Lenin carried through. . . . And yet the centuries of Russian history determined, incredible as it may seem, that Lenin preserved Russia's curse: the link of its development with unfreedom, with serfdom (*krepost'yu*). . . . It so turned out that his revolutionary fanatical belief in the truth of Marxism, total intolerance towards those who thought otherwise, caused Lenin vastly to strengthen that aspect of Russia that he himself hated. . . . Lenin's victory turned into his defeat" (p. 180). (I strongly recommend anyone who does not know them to read pp. 153–183 of this remarkable book.) It may well be that this was Lenin's tragedy, which others, Lewin and Deutscher, for instance, have described in the context of his "last struggle" to try to cope with the twin dangers of bureaucracy and of Stalin; but quite clearly Lenin understood neither the cause of the disease nor any method of curing it.

Evidently, the rise of Stalinism is not to be explained solely as the outcome of Russian political tradition and culture. There are other important elements involved: cultural backwardness, the dreadful experience of civil war, isolation in a hostile world, the real or imagined imperatives of industrialization, and, finally, Marxist-Leninist ideology. To the last of these we must now devote some attention.

Marxism-Leninism and Russia

The obvious counter-argument that might be deployed against the stress on Russian tradition would be to stress the "alien" ideology of Bolshevism. This would most certainly be the position of Solzhenitsyn and of some neo-slavophile in Russia itself. Throughout the nineteenth century the radical Russian intelligentsia followed various Western philosophical fashions, and by 1900 it was Marxism which attracted many. In its Leninist version it triumphed in 1917. The revolutionary intelligentsia, much of it non-Russian, imposed this ideology and form of government on the people, having first used popular discontent to overthrow the tsar and the provisional government. There is no Russian precedent for the party, and its political theory and practice ("democratic centralism") can be dated from 1903. "Diamat," the Comintern, the denigration of Russian history, proletarian internationalism, can be regarded as novelties, lacking any roots in national culture.

Yet the contrary view has, in my opinion, more to commend it. Marxism-Leninism was not only Marxism adapted to Russian conditions, but itself developed a strong Russian accent. Many books and articles have traced the influence on Lenin of some elements of Russian populism. The alleged link with Tkachev seems tenuous, but he acknowledged the influence of Chernyshevsky. While it is true that there was no precedent in Russian history for Lenin's concept of the party, there was none in Marxism either. German social democracy was a model to all socialist parties before 1914, but in the end it had much more in common with the menshevik concept of the role and organization of a party than with Lenin's bolshevism.

As for the influence of Marxism as such, probably the most satisfactory discussion of this complex question is to be found in the contributions of Leszek Kolakowski and Mihajlo Marković to the symposium on Stalinism, edited by Robert Tucker. While they differ in some of their interpretations, both would certainly agree that Stalinism cannot be explained or be "caused" by what Marx had written: It would indeed be extreme idealism to attribute the emergence of a new social order, which Stalinism surely was, to the power of ideas alone. Marxism contained evolutionary as well as revolutionary elements, and has inspired both moderate social democratic and several kinds of bolshevik ideas (orthodox Leninism, workers' opposition, real or imagined Trotskyism, etc.). The relationship between "dictatorship of the

proletariat" and parliamentary democracy, as this may or may
not have been seen by Marx and Engels, has been a matter of
dispute for many decades. The Marxist tradition no doubt made
some contribution, some of it negative. I borrow from Marković
the notion that Stalin advanced through gaps in Marx's argument.
Marx had really very little to say about the politics of transition
to socialism, or for that matter about the politics (if any) of
socialism itself. Similarly, Marx wrote very little on the economics
of socialism, but implied that it would be a simple matter to
replace the law of value and the market by some undefined
form of control of production and distribution by "the associated
producers." Despite some percipient criticisms by Bakunin, Marx
did not take seriously the possibility of abuse of power by his
workers' representatives and the Marxist tradition has been
opposed to "separation of powers," an independent judiciary.
It seemed enough to provide for the recall of unworthy representatives. Nothing of substance was said about how power
was to be exercised, or how a complex industrial economy was
to be run. It seems to have been believed that, given the facts
and freed from the distortions of class interest, people would
unanimously agree to do the right thing. Lenin's concept of the
party was one attempt to fill the "political" gap, no doubt
influenced (as argued above) by the specific circumstances of
tsarist and revolutionary Russia. As for the economy, Marx
never saw the connection between centralization, the elimination
of the market mechanism, bureaucracy and hierarchy. Soviet
practice had somehow to find a way of coping with the gaps
and contradictions in Marx's thoughts about socialism. The
process of necessary improvisation was inevitably greatly affected
by the specific situation of Russia, but it would be misleading
to assert that Marx's vision was in some way distorted by his
followers. They could not follow Marx's guidelines, partly because
they were absent and partly because they were contradictory.
Bureaucratic centralization was a functional necessity in a nonmarket economy, but it also fitted the "Peter the Great" model
of state mobilization of material and human resources.

To return for a moment to the Kolakowski-Markovic debate,
it would not be unfair to summarize their different conclusions
as follows: for the former, Stalinism was one possible progeny

of Marx, for the latter it was an illegitimate child of Marx. Both
agree that, in the unlikely event of his coming back to life in
(say) 1950, Marx would have been rather shocked at what he
saw.

Some Further Remarks About Stalinism

This is not the place to debate the controversial issue of
whether or not Stalinism is a natural outcome of Leninism.
Personally, I tend to the view that Lenin and Leninism facilitated
the rise of a Stalin, but that it was no coincidence that he
systematically exterminated Lenin's comrades when he had the
chance to do so. More to the point in the present context is
what could be called Stalin's cultural counter-revolution of the
1930s. In his anxiety to show the non-Russian nature of Bolshevism, Solzhenitsyn has to play down the extent of the changes
that took place at this time.

One was the extermination of cosmopolitan bolshevik intel-
lectuals, their replacement (in the main) by Russian men-of-
the-people. Another was the elimination of avant-garde art,
architecture, educational methods. Traditional values were ex-
tolled, similar to Pétain's later slogan of "Travail, famille, patrie".
History of the Pokrovsky type was denounced, the new histories
that were published after 1935 were of a type that older Russian
nationalists could find acceptable. Films like "Alexander Nevsky"
and "Ivan the Terrible" were consciously devised to reconnect
Stalin's Soviet Union with traditional Russia. The process was
partly explained by the imminence of war, but was then speeded
up because of the exigencies of war. *"Rodina-mat' zovet"*. Stalin
soon called up the spirits of Alexander Nevsky, Suvorov, Kutuzov.
In his speech in 1946, after the dearly-bought victory, he singled
out the Russian people, the elder brother. As in most countries,
ordinary people and ordinary party officials hold rather conventional views. The difference was (and is) the Soviet party's
belief in its right to impose these tastes. As for the doctrine of
"socialist realism", in one of its aspects it can be seen as a
perversion of the sort of attitude which led to attacks on Turgenev
for writing novels carrying no political or social message. There

was a tradition opposed to art-for-art's-sake, asserting the author's duty to society. Lenin stressed similar ideas in his frequently misquoted article *"Partiinaya literatura"*—misquoted because when he wrote it, he referred to the duty of party litterateurs in a situation when there were other parties and other (including non-party) literatures. The Stalin-Zhdanov version of *Partiinost'* totally distorted both Lenin and the earlier traditions, perhaps another case of an illegitimate child.

The Nakaz of the Empress Catherine begins like this: *"Rossiya est' evropeiskaya derzhava"* (Russia is a European country), and "the proof of this is as follows". The "proof" was that, when Peter the Great introduced Europeanizing reforms, their success was such that even he was astonished. Suppose we were to say, *"Rossiya est' polu-aziatskaya derzhava,"* and the proof of it is as follows: that when Stalin established a form of oriental despotism, his success exceeded his own expectations. It turned out that the mass of the Russian people accepted an autocrat, shed tears when he died, and now look back with a kind of nostalgia to the days of Stalin, when the great ones in the land trembled and were fearful. Even some critical spirits were caught up in this mood, which was well expressed in Alexander Zinoviev's recent work *Nashei yunosti polet.*

Economic Strategy Under Stalin

When Peter the Great developed *manufaktury*, it was to serve the state's purposes. The factories made guns, ammunition, sailcloth, uniforms, also paper for the state bureaucracy to write on. Plans were imposed by the only customer, the state. A large part of the labour force was serf or slave. Not until the nineteenth century was there a sizeable segment of industry producing for the civilian market, notably textiles, and some enterprising serfs succeeding in making themselves millionaires. Much has been written about the large role of the state in railway building and promoting industrial development in the period following 1890, a policy associated with the name of Count Witte. One of his remarks comes to mind: "I have been accused of artificially fostering industry. This is clearly absurd. How else can one foster industry?"

Some see in Witte a sort of follower of List, believing in protectionism as the basis for a national development strategy. But in fact he had a Russian predecessor who was arguing on these lines seventy years earlier, in memoranda submitted to Tsar Alexander I, and ante-dating List. This was the remarkable Admiral (he was that as well!) Mordvinov. Already then he was arguing that free trade leads to excessive dependence on other countries' industries and so to military weakness: He instanced Spain's decline as an example of what happens if a nation's industries are allowed to go under.

With the rapid development of military technology since Mordvinov's time, the strategic arguments for industrialization, with special emphasis on heavy industry and the railways, were obviously reinforced. It would be misleading to see Witte as a precursor of Stalin, but certain similarities there are. Relevant here is an acute remark by Alexander Gerschenkron: When, in the 1870s, the problem of Russian industrialization was debated, many argued that the biggest obstacle was the poverty of the peasantry. It could not provide a big enough internal market for Russian manufactures. Yet when, in the 1890s, industrialization was under way, and foreign investment and imports of capital goods were being encouraged, the problem became one of burdening the peasants with the fiscal consequences. Gerschenkron concluded that while "spontaneous" industrial development did indeed need an internal mass market, state-sponsored industrialization was a quite different matter. Tugan-Baranovsky's picture of a possible growth of producers' goods without any increase in final consumption actually fitted Stalin's strategy better than Witte's: though heavy industry was indeed encouraged under the latter, aggregate consumption also rose, even among many of the peasants, which certainly cannot be said of the peasantry in Stalin's time.

Two other observations may be relevant. One relates to "primitive socialist accumulation." In Preobrazhensky's mind it was an adaptation of Marx's "primitive capitalist accumulation" to the situation of the Soviet Union in the 1920s. Yet if its purposes were explained to Peter—to mobilize capital to modernize and strengthen Russia—he would surely have understood. Primitive accumulation by the methods of Genghis Khan, "military-feudal exploitation", were terms used by Bukharin to describe what Stalin actually did, casting doubt on the socialist or Marxist lineage of Stalin's industrialization and collectivization drive.

A second remark concerns an interesting theory advanced by Hans Raupach, to the effect that the geographic handicaps from which Russia suffered—notably huge overland distances, e.g. between iron ore and coking coal—made capitalist profit-orientated industrialization more difficult than in Western countries, and so involved a much greater role for the state as an investor.

A Few Remarks on Foreign Policy

Given the facts of geography and the nature of great-power politics, some similarities of pre- and post-revolutionary foreign policy should occasion no surprise. Here too there was a period, coinciding with Lenin's rule, when differences seemed much more important. The priority of "world revolution" was all the more present in Lenin's mind because he, like most of his comrades, believed that the fate of Soviet Russia depended on revolutions in Western Europe. When, in 1920, he advocated an advance by the Red Army into Poland, it may be reasonably surmised that, apart from suffering from the delusion that the Polish workers would welcome the Soviet troops, he hoped to link up with German revolutionaries. Clearly, such aims were wholly alien to the tsars.

But Lenin can also be credited with preserving the bulk of the old Russian empire. It was in process of dissolution, with claims to independent status from the Ukraine, Georgia, Azerbaidzhan, Armenia, and actual independence gained by Finland and the Baltic states, while nationalist groups sought power in Central Asia. Lenin, it is true, inveighed against "great-Russian chauvinism". Nonetheless he put the Ukraine firmly back under central control and sent troops to subdue menshevik Georgia in 1921. It was only the failure of local communists to hold on to power, plus outside support, which preserved the independence of the three Baltic states until 1939.

Finland was different. Finland was always different. The tsars allowed the Finns their own constitution, laws, elected Diet, even their own currency and stamps. Later, in 1940 and 1944, although the Finns had fought against the Soviet Union, relatively mild peace treaties were imposed and Finland is still an independent non-satellite country. Contrast the very different relationship with the Poles, both under the last tsars and in Stalin's time. It is surely only partly explicable by Poland's strategic situation. Poland was an ancestral enemy. I am sure it would never have occurred to Stalin to kill Finnish officer-prisoners (nor, to do them justice, would the tsars have thought of killing Polish officers; probably not even Ivan the Terrible).

But to return to the 1920s. Historians will long discuss precisely when the change took place. Some place it at the adoption of the slogan "socialism in one country". But whatever the date, the transformation of the Comintern into a branch of the Soviet foreign office was far advanced before the end of that decade, and the 1930s saw the killing in Moscow of most foreign Comintern officials, with the Poles (again!) hit harder than anyone else: hardly a single member of the party who resided in Russia survived, and the party itself was dissolved (surviving Polish communists had the good fortune to be in Polish jails).

This is not the place to discuss the actual policies pursued, only the motives in pursuing them. Is there any sense in asserting, as some do, the continuity of Soviet foreign policy from Lenin through Stalin to Chernenko? Did the post-war spread of Soviet power into Central Europe demonstrate the desire to spread communism or increase Russian power? If both, then, so to speak, in what proportions? Does the fact that Chernenko has to repeat Lenin's slogans mean that he shares Lenin's objectives, giving them the same degree of commitment and priority? Books are still being written—for instance *This War Called Peace*, by Brian Crozier and others, just published—that assert that world conquest for communism is the operational aim, and prove it by appropriate quotations from the present leaders' ideological pronouncements. Yet the split with Tito demonstrated, if any such demonstration was necessary, that any communist ruler who did not obey Moscow was regarded as a dangerous enemy. The thought that the gerontocracy, or the little Stalins who are provincial first secretaries, have the messianic inspiration to convert the world to communism is, for me, rather far-fetched.

"The new tsars" of Chinese propaganda seem to fit the bill somewhat better than the "new Lenins." "There is no one in the politbureau who cares about what Marx said about any subject," remarked a percipient emigre. Which does not in any way make it simpler to deal with the USSR. But that is another story.

To cite a very old anecdote, it is said that, at the Congress of Vienna, a senior Russian delegate died. Whereupon Metternich (or was it Talleyrand) said: "I wonder what his motive was". It seems to me that, as a working hypothesis, it is useful to analyze Soviet behaviour in foreign affairs as explicable in terms that would be understood by Count Gorchakov, Alexander II's foreign minister. Only when such an approach becomes clearly inadequate should other explanations be sought. Certainly Gorchakov, in trying to expand Russian power, would not call it "proletarian internationalism". Neither should we.

But this theme requires book-length analysis, and has indeed been the subject of books.

The Soviet Union Today

Whatever may have been the parallels between Stalin's political style and economic strategy and that of Peter, Stalin died over thirty years ago, and none of his successors has resembled him: to treat Brezhnev or Chernenko as a species of oriental despot would surely be absurd. Some perhaps far-fetched historical parallels could nonetheless be attempted. Peter, like Stalin, was highly active as a builder and as a warrior; the nobility had to do his bidding, was mobilized to carry out his civil and military projects. Soon after he died they were able to free themselves of compulsory service and to become a privileged estate. Stalin played a major role in creating the Soviet privileged estate, the *nomenklatura* officials, even while he made their lives individually extremely insecure. They are secure today. Many books and articles (some by this author)[2] have tried to discuss the nature of the system: Is it a class society? Is the word "class" appropriate to describe a universal service state, in which what matters is rank? As in the case of the nineteenth century *dvoryanstvo*, promotion from below was possible: Anyone who achieved high civil or military rank became a *dvoryanin*. True, *nomenklatura* status is not formally speaking hereditary, whereas Lenin was a hereditary *dvoryanin* because his father had been promoted in the education department to the appropriate rank. But in practice, while no specific *nomenklatura* post can be inherited (except perhaps in Romania), sons of high officials are extremely likely to be given some *nomenklatura* post. So perhaps the word "estate" (*soslovie*) is a better one than class to designate the nature of the Soviet ruling stratum. Its existence would occasion no surprise to a resurrected Peter the Great. It would surely greatly astonish Marx, and probably Lenin too.

A problem with such a system is that its dynamism depends on pressure from above. This is also of vital importance for the economy. One recalls the title of an article by Gregory Grossman: "Routine, Inertia and Pressure". In the absence of the stick of competition and of the carrot of profit-making, inertia is a major problem. True, terror has its own high economic costs, but its absence, in the absence of effective alternative stimuli, leaves the system short on dynamism. Of course the slowdown in growth has a whole number of other explanations: demography, the military burden, the exhaustion of easily accessible natural resources, and, last but not least, the growing complexity of the economy, which "has long surpassed the level at which it could be controlled from a single centre", to quote from the leaked "Zaslavskaya" memorandum.

Alvin W. Gouldner, in one of his last articles, made the point that oriental despotisms were inherently prone to stagnation, as indeed Marx himself had noted. Soviet leaders are well aware of the need to overcome inertia, imbalances, shortages, and the corruption that accompanies shortages. What can they do about it? Here historical parallels are of little use to us. In the nineteenth century private enterprise, Russian and foreign, was gradually developing, and after 1890 the process speeded up with government encouragement. The close link which existed earlier between the state and the economy was being broken. The revolution, by destroying private capital and capitalists, reestablished that link. This in turn led to the merging to political and economic. It has been pointed out that there are three kinds of power: political, economic and ideological or religious. In the West, they are usually in different hands, even if there are links between them. In the USSR they are, both in theory and in practice, in the same hands. It is this which justifies the use of the often misunderstood label "totalitarian". It seems to be an essential part of the ideology of the regime that they must remain in the same hands. Hence continued opposition to religion, which was once based upon an enthusiasm for atheism and enlightenment, an enthusiasm now conspicuously absent. Hence insistence on ideological purity based on disciplined dogmatism, which has done much to extinguish not only any real belief in Marxism but also its life as a set of ideas (all developments of Marxism now occur only outside the USSR). Hence also a major obstacle to necessary economic reform. It is hard to believe that loss of political power would follow from allowing management to produce what its customers need. Indeed, plans imposed from above are supposed to ensure that what is produced is what the customers need. What is threatened is the unity of political and economic power, just as the weakening of censorship, allowing greater intellectual freedom, threatens the unity of political and ideological power. Here we are in a territory where reference back to Russia's past is of little help in either understanding or anticipating what might happen. After this paper was written, the long-awaited generational change in the Soviet leadership occurred, and Gorbachev lost no time in stressing the vital importance of making major organizational and structural changes to correct the economic deficiencies of which he showed himself to be acutely aware. Perhaps the following sentence from his speech to the central committee reported in *Pravda*, 24 April 1985, can demonstrate this clearly in his own words: "We must, comrades, deeply and fully take cognisance of the existing situation and draw from it the most serious conclusions. The historical fate of our country, the position of socialism in the contemporary world, largely depend on how we will now proceed. Fully utilizing the achievements of the scientific-technical revolution, bringing the forms of socialist management into conformity with today's conditions and needs, we must attain a substantial acceleration of social and economic progress. There just is no other way."

So to conclude: Russia's past and her political traditions have evidently played a significant role in shaping post-revolutionary history, as would be agreed by most historians of the most diverse schools, from Pipes and Szamuely to Carr and even Bettelheim. But this is not a reason for adopting a viewpoint of rigid determinism, as if the weight of Russia's past led inexorably to Stalin and Brezhnev. Better might be a sort of "negative determinism," that is to say, the exclusion of what might in other countries have been viable alternatives, such as a stable parliamentary democracy. It seems equally far-fetched to argue, as Pipes seems to do, that a combination of tsarist and Marxist-Leninist expansionism somehow compels the Soviet leaders to try to achieve world domination and risk a nuclear holocaust.

Perhaps I could end with a quotation from E. H. Carr's "What is history?": "No historian has ever said that anything is inevitable until after it has happened."

Notes

1. Pushkin wrote this in French. *Sobranie sochinenii*, 1887 edition, Vol. 7, p. 87.

2. My first essay on the subject, which discussed the parallel between the *nomenklatura* and the *dvoryanstvo*, was published in *Soviet Studies*, Vol. XXI, No. 1 (July 1969), pp. 71–92.

2
The Role of Economics in Soviet Political Ideology

Helmut Dahm

Clarification of Concepts

First of all, I should like to clarify the concepts used below. In contrast to "economy" as the general term for the sphere of material production, "economics" means political economy. In its widest sense this is the science of the laws of social production, distribution and exchange of material goods on the distinct developmental levels of human society. Strictly speaking, it designates the science of a system of economic laws working in a certain determined mode of production.

According to Marxism-Leninism, the political economy of the working class is the economic theory not of property, but of labor. Its real subject is the so-called relations of production in their contradictory unity with the so-called productive forces. The totality of the relations of production for a given society constitutes its economic order of infrastructure.

As the economic theory of the working class, the political economy of socialist society must be understood as a component of Marxism-Leninism. As such, it forms an ideological unity with dialectical and historical materialism, and scientific communism. From this it follows that socialist political economy or economics has to fulfill two essential functions: that of political ideology and that of production. First of all, the political economy of socialism is an essential foundation of ideology, because it is said to serve the development of the collective consciousness of all members of the socialist society. Secondly, the political

17

economy of socialism is the decisive scientific groundwork for the building up of the new mode of production, for the direction and planning of the economy itself, for the improvement and optimal outcome of the processes of reproduction, and for the founding and establishment of the economic and social policies of the Communist Party. So, the political economy of socialism provides the theoretical foundations for the particular branches of economics in order to use the productive function of all economic sciences and to employ the newest knowledge, especially of the theory of the economic planning.

Thus, socialist political economy or economics is partly in itself a political ideology. But even its other essential functions in production are, strictly speaking, ideologically founded, too, because it has to guarantee the building up of the new mode of production within the economic formation of the socialist communist society.

As is well known, in his *Economic-Philosophic Manuscripts* of 1844 Marx stated that religion, family, state, right, morality, science, art, etc., are only special modes of production and are, therefore, to be put under the general law of production. Fifty years later, Engels added: "We see the economic conditions as what, in the last instance, determines historical development. The political, legal, philosophical, religious, artistic, literary, etc., development depends on that of the economy."

If this were the whole truth, the role and influence of economics—that is to say of socialist political economy according to Marx, Engels, and Lenin—in Soviet political ideology would be not only imposing, but also completely and uniquely determinant. Actually, however, this aspect of economic necessity or "law-boundness" is only half of the truth. The other half consists in the theoretical guidance of the class struggle and of the social—meaning 'socialist' or 'proletarian'—revolution. The main set of theories dealing with such questions within Soviet social science today is the so-called scientific communism. As one of the four essential parts of the disciplines of the total world view system of Marxism-Leninism, scientific communism presents the Soviet political ideology in the most literal and strictest sense of the word.

This second aspect, namely class struggle and social revolution, refers to the subjective factor, which contains the element of intellectual judgement, choice and freedom. So, a wide bow of tension stretches between the two possibilities for explaining historical development and the succession of several social-economic formations. In other words, there are, from the Marxist-Leninist viewpoint, two binding interpretations of human history: first, that of political economy with regard to the objective factor in the sense of material necessity, where the contradiction between the productive forces, on the one hand, and the relations of production, on the other, is predominant; and, second, that of political ideology strictly speaking—encompassing the subjective factor in the sense of intellectual freedom—where one finds things such as class struggle, proletarian revolution, the building up of a socialist and, later on, of a communist society, etc.

Because of the clear ambivalence in the thought of Marx, Engels, and Lenin, the Soviet political leadership of today also continuously oscillates and even sometimes flutters between these two ideologically founded positions. Just for this reason there exists, and essentially must exist, an unstable equilibrium of partial truths. From this, however, it follows that in case of need either of them can be criticized as one-sided. For instance, the objective factor of political economy can be said to misunderstand material necessity by giving free play to its driving forces and motive powers, while the subjective factor in the political ideology might be accused of misunderstanding intellectual freedom by making the mistake of voluntarism.

It is of great importance to emphasize here that dialectical and historical materialism, as the obligatory philosophy of Leninist Marxism, is by nature a causal monism of matter. This is the true reason why intellectual freedom is and can only be defined as insight into necessity. Whence it follows inevitably that the room for praxis-oriented action if not very large and that ideology in both sets of problems—economy as well as politics—cannot leave a very large margin for change and modification of an extensively defined and fixed social system, composed of stipulating principles, purposes, aims and values.

So, if one takes all this seriously, one cannot but concede that in the final analysis the role of ideologically founded economics—that is, of socialist political economy—is, or at least ought to be, decisive for Soviet political ideology in the sense of scientific communism. But, in order to avoid serious misunderstanding, I should like to emphasize here, once more, that this argument is valid for the ideological discipline of political economy and not for the economy itself.

Evidence for the above can be found in the relevant articles in the Soviet *Philosophic Encyclopedia* or in the *Political Dictionary* (e.g. 'economy', 'political economy', 'production', 'relations of production', 'forces of production', 'mode of production', 'social-economic formation', 'political sciences', etc.). One might also consult Martin Seliger's book, *The Marxist Conception of Ideology* (Cambridge, 1977), as well as my own *The Failed Escape from Ideology*.[1]

The Question of Method

My next basic point has to do with the question of method. The so-called 'unity of opposites', which has intruded into the foregoing relation of the two fields (political economy and political ideology) obviously compels us to deal with the subject of the dialectic. It is clear that nearly all scholars and scientists have become accustomed to using the term 'dialectic', but few of them (and maybe few of us, too) have a clear idea as to what the 'dialectic' really is. In a study by Marx, 'Critique of Hegelian Dialectics and of all Philosophy' (from the *Economic-Philosophic Manuscripts*) and in Engels' *Ludwig Feuerbach* both communist thinkers state that in the final analysis Hegel's dialectical system, in its method and content, represents nothing but materialism turned upside-down and stood on its head. Therefore, in the opinion of Marx and Engels, it was only necessary to set that upside-down dialectic of ideas and concepts back on feet of genuine materialism. But, this conversion or reversion of Hegel was one of Marxism's gravest mistakes for the following reasons:

First, Hegel's monism of spirit as substance means that nature is not only a product of the absolute idea, but it also is this absolute idea itself, if only in its differentness *(Anderssein)*.

Second, the method of Hegel's *Logic*—according to which thinking and being are identical by way of self-reflection—is that of dialectic and not that of linear causality. The meaning of this is that, following Hegel's monism of spirit as substance, the absolute thus conceived (as well as personal mind) is able to reflect not only upon itself—or to relate not only to itself in the sense of pure identity (A is equal to A)—but also upon or to its own other by means of its own negation (A is equal to non-A). In this way the spiritual absolute or the personal mind comes to the distinction of itself from itself, in order to return by means of a second negation (e.g. non-A is equal to B) to itself, in the dialectical sense of mediated identity or identification, i.e., of raised, removed or thought contradiction. For this reason, identity in the Hegelian understanding is to be determined as negative relation to itself or as distinction of itself from itself.

This intellectual movement does not depend on the relationship between cause and effect, but is founded on the ability to self-reflect or to self-posit. This is why Hegel asserted that spirit is only what, being free in itself, exists by itself, and this means that it posits itself. Therefore, the unity of identity and difference, or of reflection upon itself and upon the other, is the posited contradiction *(der gesetzte Widerspruch)* or the posited essence *(das gesetzte Wesen)*. In other words: according to Hegel, the dialectic presupposes something extremely universal, like thought, idea, notion, concept, because only in this way is multiplicity in unity (namely in universal idea, general concept or simply in form) conceivable and possible.

All this cannot be asserted in regard to philosophic materialism. For, Marxist monism of matter as substance is based on the sensible *(das Sinnliche)*, and that means concrete, distinct, individual things, which in their change and development are determined not by themselves, but by others. For this reason, the connection, correlation and interrelation of all these sensible, concrete, separate, individual things, of which matter consists according to dialectical materialism, must be causal, and can by no means be dialectical. Only thus, namely by cause and effect, is matter (unity in multiplicity) as distinct from spirit (multiplicity in unity) ontologically possible and conceivable. From this, however, it follows that arguments in favor of the existence of God are unconditionally valid with regard to the philosophy of Leninist Marxism because they rest on causality, while this is not true in Hegel's spiritual philosophy of identity.

Moreover, the dialectic in the speculative thought of Hegel is in truth an illusive appearance, a mere semblance, a deception and a real mistake for the following reasons: Hegel asserted in his *Logic* that "intrinsic, genuine self-movement. . . . means nothing other than that something in itself, and the deficiency, its negative, exist in one and the same regard . . . (or) that the positive in itself is the negative".[2] Now, opposites which exist in one and the same regard at the same time are contradictory, and therefore really impossible. The one is and cannot but be the actual negation of the other, and only one of the two in this relation can be true and remain valid. Since this is necessary and indisputable in universally binding logic, Hegel makes his dialectical method applicable to it by alternating the negation of the subject and of the predicate. In this way, the contradiction, A is equal to non-A, changes to the contrariety, A is not equal to A, because only in this way could Hegel reach a B, C, D, and so on. As we have indicated, by this change of the negation from the subject to the predicate, the relation between the two opposites becomes a contrary one. Such opposites can exist on or in one and the same thing at the same time, even if not in one and the same regard.

In order to re-examine these matters, it will come as no surprise that we have to distinguish between contradiction (*protivorechie, kontradiktorischer Gegensatz*) and contrariety (*protivnost', konträrer Gegensatz*). The former is 'dialectical' in the false sense of actually existing contradiction, but clearly impossible in a reality of matter. The latter is 'analectical', meaning formally logical and causal, and therefore consistent with a reality of matter.

All these items and particulars can be filled out from Helmut Ogiermann's *Materialist dealectic* (1958) or G. A. Wetter's *Conversion of Hegel* (1963) or the present author's *The Untenability of Marxist Philosophic Atheism* (1984).[3] All of these subjects have also been frequently discussed—sometimes very critically—by Soviet and East European thinkers and theorists of Leninist Marxism, like A. Deborin, M. Rozental', S. Tsereteli and S. Dudel' who favored the Hegelian dialectic, or M. Mitin, N. Kondakov. K. Bakradze and V. Borodkin, who leaned rather toward an Aristotelian formal logic.

Analagous to the continuous oscillation between the objective and subjective factors with regard to political economy and political ideology, there is a similar situation with regard to the method of dialectic and of formal logic, periodically over two or three decades. Thus, the dispute between Deborin and Mitin took place in the late 1920s: those between Rozental' and Kondakov and between Tsereteli and Bakradze date from the 1950s; and that between Dudel' and Borodkin occurred in the early 1980s.[4] I should like to confine myself here to the Tsereteli-Bakradze dispute, and to contrast it with the Borodkin-Dudel' discussion.

In his voluminous book, *On the Dialectical Nature of Logical Relations*,[5] Tsereteli tried to interpret the analysis of the connection of production and consumption, as well as that of capital and circulation, produced by Marx in his *Introduction Toward a Critique of Political Economy* (1857), using the dialectic. Tsereteli asserts: "Production is consumption. But consumption is the negation of production and vice versa: production is the negation of consumption".[6] In this way, production is both itself and its own negation at the same time: similarly, consumption is both itself and its own negation at the same time. A bit later on in Tsereteli's book, we read: "Capital cannot arise from circulation" and "Capital cannot arise but from circulation".[7]

In his *The System and Method of Hegel's Philosophy*[8] Bakradze profoundly criticizes his fellow countryman, Tsereteli. To begin with, Bakradze notes that the forms which Tsereteli uses seem at first glance to be completely inconsistent with the principle of non-contradiction. Criticizing Tsereteli's samples of dialectical judgements, Bakradze calls them strange *(kur'eznye)*,[9] dubious *(somnitel'nye)* and ambiguous *(dvusmyslennye)*.[10] One finds that they are all related either not in the same regard or not at the same time. So Bakradze continues, "The main fault of authors who try to construct dialectical judgements and syllogisms, which nominally are not subject to the principles of formal logic, and in which there is assumed the truth of two contradictory judgements 'at the same time as well as in one and the same relation or regard', consists in the assumption that a thought which reflects a contradiction is a thought about contradiction, and that, therefore, such a thought must in itself be contradictory. But, it is impossible to attribute to a thought about reality all characteristics of reality. Nevertheless, the sole argument that comrade Tsereteli adduces in favor of his assertion consists in just this: If there is a contradiction in the appearances of reality, then this contradiction must exist in thoughts and judgements about reality, too, and that in the same way.[11] Tsereteli's conceptions are, therefore, untenable.

A quarter of a century later, a similar controversy recurred between Borodkin and Dudel, with just the same evidence, namely capital and circulation in Marx, movement in Engels, and the interpretation of movement as the unity of continuity and discontinuity in Lenin. But now there is a difference in the parameters of the dispute. As distinct from Kondakov's criticism of Rozental, as well as from Bakradze's criticism of Tsereteli— where the formal logicians were able to dominate—under the rule of Andropov it is the quasi-dialectician Dudel' who sets out to attack the representative of the universal validity of formal logic, Borodkin, a member of the Institute of Philosophy. The occasion was the latter's book, *Problems of Contradiction in the Materialist Dialectic,* which appeared in 1982 from the Nauka publishing house, under the editorship of Vladimir Tyukhtin, a well-known specialist in the field of philosophical questions of cybernetics.

In *Kommunist,* May, 1983, Dudel' wrote on Borodkin: "The author of *Problems of Contradiction in the Materialist Dialectic* maintains without any reserve that 'one and the same object cannot be in a certain place and not be in it at the same time, and in one and same respect'."[12] What is more, in his remarkable book, Borodkin also openly criticizes Lenin, asserting that "at the present-day level of knowledge, it is hardly possible to educe arguments which would allow us to qualify continuity and discontinuity as dialectical opposites. . . . The hypothesis that

. . . continuity and discontinuity are dialectical opposites (and, therefore, contradictions) is unlikely".[13] Dudel' goes on: "But the culmination of the replacement of dialectic by metaphysics is perhaps the author's conclusion that 'the logical structure of a well-constructed theory must not contain either logical or dialectical contradictions'."[14] Since Borodkin did not make the claim about non-contradictoriness in relation only to theories, but also to methods of thought, so Dudel' stresses that Borodkin would seem also to have to maintain that the theory and method of Marxist-Leninist philosophy must lack the status of 'good theory'.[15] The same would be, a fortiori, the case of Marxist-Leninist political economy. On the other hand, there is no reason to be surprised at Dudel' 's steady repetition of apparently dialectical judgements like "the individual is the collectivity", "man is society", "good is evil", "peace is war", "truth is lie", the "bourgeoisie is the proletariat", and so on. All these had appeared in previous discussions (especially in Tsereteli).[16] This quite misunderstood type of dialectic is, in fact, the legacy of Hegel to contemporary Marxist-Leninist philosophy.

For such absurdity, there is no cure after Kondakov's brave defense of formal logic but the re-establishment of correct thinking, such as Borodkin's affirmation of two basic truths—one ontological, the other epistemological: "The transition of contrary opposites into dialectical ones and vice versa in one and the same object is impossible. In knowledge, however, this transition is bound up with a change in the object of knowledge."[17] These statements have nothing to do with apparent dialectics, but are in complete accord with the analectical thought that is native to formal logic.

To put matters with perfect clarity, at the end of his book Borodkin uses three logical rules to show how lack of specificity about the types of opposites has to be compensated for in terms of "defects in knowledge":

Rule 1. If the subject accepts contrary opposites for dialectical ones, it falls into a logical contradiction.

Rule 2. If there is the further contention that the adequate form of reflection of dialectical opposites of the object would be their synthesis in various relations, then the subject does indeed avoid being involved in a logical contradiction, but therewith it loses all grounds for distinguishing between dialectical and contrary opposites.

Rule 3. If the subject accepts dialectical opposites in place of contrary ones, then it is not involved in a logical contradiction, but the ability adequately to recognize the correlation of such opposites.[18]

Findings of Analysis

Behind this quite faithful restatement of the modern methods of thinking stands an uncompromising certainty that all kinds of logical contradiction must be entirely excluded. For this reason, Borodkin over and over again repeats such declarations as: "Specifically logical problems of the dialectic as theory and method, can only be solved by means of formal logic. If the elaboration of the dialectic does not satisfy the requirements of formal logic, then this demonstrates that the logical form of the dialectic is imperfect."[19] Or, again: "The nature of logical contradiction excludes the possibility that it performs the functions of the dialectical contradiction."[20]

Unfortunately, although the universal validity of analectical thought and of formal logic is acknowledged in the Soviet Union from time to time for the political ideology, which decides in the final analysis, it remains only one side of the matter. It can be subordinated, recalled, and cancelled at any time, as it shown by the discussions mentioned above. This remains to the present day the actual and official state of affairs.[21]

The Political Debate on Contradictions

In February 1984, Anatolii Butenko, head of a section at the Institute for the Economics of the World Socialist System, came back to the debate on contradictions within socialism, suspended during the Andropov years, by asserting that there are now two different conceptions as to the possibility, causes and range of social crises in a socialist country.

According to the first position—old, familiar and Stalinist—contradictions within socialism are of a non-antagonistic character. Its theorists insist that the basic reason and motive for such non-antagonistic contradictions (which are precisely contrary opposition of contrarieties) consists in the fact that so-called remnants of the capitalist past still exist in the consciousness and behavior of people, remnants of an inherited social antagonism. This first and well-known group of ideologists and politicians seemingly tries to start from a materialistic viewpoint by respecting the objective factor of historical necessity and "law-boundness" expressed by continuous tension and conflict between the two main motive powers of human sociality: the productive forces, on the one hand, and the relations of production, on the other.

In actuality, however, this traditionalist group lives in fear of the terrible mechanism of a possibly contradictory opposition, discovered or invented, and described so graphically by Marx and Engels. For this reason, the representatives and spokesmen of this group prefer to banish the danger accompanying the terrible mechanism by terming its contradiction of productive forces and relations of production 'non-antagonistic'. These ideologists and politicians can on no account be expected to accept far-reaching and extensive reforms in the fields of economic organization and management. They hold that the relations of production must not be touched for fear of a possible rebellion precisely in the sense of the Marxian theory of social revolution. In place of this they put all their hopes on efforts to strengthen governmental power and control.

According to the other position, represented by Butenko, it is not enough to take into consideration only the objective causes for contradictions between the productive forces and relations of production in socialist society. The true reasons for the rise of social-economic crises and conflicts in the socialist countries, for this second group of ideologists and politicians, are and can only be faults, blunders, misjudgements, etc., on the part of the responsible political leadership. These, in turn, are due to the lack of a scientific approach to solving obvious social and economic contradictions which, for these theorists, are possibly antagonistic even while being produced by socialism itself. Clearly, this second position stresses the subjective or voluntaristic aspect.[22] Its representatives are no less afraid of that terrible mechanism of "contradiction between a certain social character of production, that is of productive forces, on the one hand, and the concrete social forms of socialist property, that is of the relations of production, on the other."[23] For this basic contradiction can possibly find its actual expression "in an open demonstration of the masses against the political level and its policies".[24] In this context, Butenko specifies: "The causes which generate a social-economic conflict, the compounding of its participants, but also the aims pursued by those who rise against the existing power, determine the character of the social-economic conflict: is there only a protest by the working people against existing policy, i.e., against faults in and mistakes of the socialist rulers, or is there a counter-revolutionary uprising which aims to overturn socialist power and to restore counter-revolutionary power?"[25] In order to meet this danger, the representatives of this second position are ready to adapt the relations of production, i.e., the political organization of society and its economic system, to the development of the productive forces, i.e., to the needs, the necessities of life, and the real interests of the working people.[26]

The Economic Debate on Reform
of the Relations of Production

In the *Novosibirsk Report*, prepared for a closed seminar of economic specialists in Moscow in April 1983, Tatyana Zaslavskaya, largely agrees with this view. Zaslavskaya, professor of economics at the University of Novosibirsk and head of the section on social problems of the Institute of the Economics and Organization of Industrial Production of the Siberian Division of the Soviet Academy of Sciences, has been a member of the CPSU since 1954 and a full member of the USSR Academy since 1981. She states that the general reason for the deterioration of the economic indices in the majority of sectors and regions of the Soviet economy consists in the lagging of the system of relations of production—and of the mechanism of state management of the economy which is its reflection—behind the level of development of the forces of production. "To put it in more concrete terms, it is expressed in the inability of this system to make provision for the full and sufficiently effective use of the labor potential and intellectual resources of society."[27]

Without going into too much detail, the most important features of the system of state management of the Soviet economy include:

- A high level of centralization in economic decisionmaking
- Production planning characterized by and based on direct indicators
- Weakly developed market relations
- Central regulation of all forms of material incentives for labor
- Prevalence of the branch over the territorial principle of management
- Lacking departmental liaison in the management of the economy by branch and sub-branch
- Restriction of economic rights
- Restrictions on the economic responsibility of enterprises for the results of their economic activity
- Restriction of all aspects of informal economic activity

All these features reflect the predominance of administrative (which means about the same as 'political' here) methods over economic ones, of centralization over decentralization.

The scientific basis of the system of economic management is the theoretical notion, developed by economic science, of the laws of social reproduction under socialism, especially the five main 'laws' which are, at best, goals yet to be achieved by the Soviet economy. They are:

1. The *Basic Economic Law of Socialism,* characterized by the 'steady expansion and improvement of production on the basis of advanced technology and socialist collaboration'
2. The *Law of Planned, Proportional Development of the National Economy*
3. The *Law of Value,* stipulating the necessity for producing and selling commodities on the basis of socially necessary labor outlays

4. The *Law of Distribution According to Work*
5. The *Law of Socialist Accumulation,* stipulating the systematic use of part of net income for continuous expansion of production and for increase in national wealth.

In his article 'Marxist-Leninist Ideology and Soviet Policy', in *Studies in Soviet Thought,* David Comey classified ideology as 'directive' when it serves as a guide for choosing and implementing policy, as 'masking' when ideological statements are made to deflect attention from current realities, and as 'authenticating' when policies or measures are justified by citing ideological doctrines and even 'classical' loci of Marx and Engels. According to this terminology,[28] the economic laws of socialism perform an 'authenticating', and perhaps a 'masking', rather than a 'directive', function. This is partially reflected in the textbooks on political economy and in specific economic disciplines, in dictionaries of philosophy, of scientific communism and of economics; and it can partially be inferred from the actual practice of management of the Soviet economy. The main elements in it are based on notions that not only correspond for the most part to the level of development of the productive forces of Soviet society in the 1930s, but also are nearly the opposite of what actually exists or is valid at the present time, including, for example, the following assertions:

• Socialist production relations 'outflank' the development of the productive forces;
• There are no deep, much less antagonistic, contradictions between individual, group and public interests under socialism, just as there are none among the interests of different classes and social groups;
• The labor of workers in socialist production has a directly social character;
• As a result, there is no need to affirm the social necessity for individual expenditure on the production of goods by means of the market mechanism, and so on.

As the *Novosibirsk Report* states in this connection: ". . . all this testifies to the fact that the present system of relations of production has substantially fallen behind the level of development of the forces of production. Instead of facilitating their accelerated development, it is becoming more and more of a brake on their progressive advancement. One outcome of this is the inability of production relations to provide modes of conduct for workers in the social-economic spheres that are needed by society."[29] Chapter 3 of the *Novosibirsk Report* ('A Strategy for Perfecting Relations of Production') asserts that the urgent need for reorganizing state management of the economy was realized by the party a long time ago. This can be seen in the numerous party resolutions over the past decade. So, when Andropov called in November 1982 for economic and organizational conditions that would stimulate top quality productive labor, initiative and enterprise, this was not news. These party documents, however, failed to inspire the people responsible for the actual running of the Soviet economy. There was a sort of 'silent opposition'.

The *Novosibirsk Report* divides the causes of this silent opposition into the ideological, the social and the scientific. The main or ideological reason has to do with the Marxian notion of the mechanism for perfecting relations of production. In the Soviet reference work, *Political Economy*, Yuri Vasil'chik notes that in every society the relations of production form a more stable and integral system in comparison with the productive forces which develop according to their own laws. At a certain point, these relations of production lag behind the productive forces and become a brake on the further progress of the workers and of the technological forms of production.[30] Hence it follows that "either there will be the beginning of a period of acute social-economic and political shake-up from the inside, of modification and accommodation of production relations to the new conditions of production, or there will be an era of general crisis in the present social formation and its destruction as a result of social revolution."[31]

Thus, the core of the problem of economics involves the following incompatible aspects of the ideologically binding official doctrine: according to the theories developed in political economy textbooks, the perfection of productive relations within a capitalist framework constitutes a social process which reflects the conflict between social classes and groups. In a socialist society, however, this process is essentially void of social content; it ceases to reflect the struggle of interests of any social group whatever; i.e., it acquires an almost 'technical' character. This viewpoint is expressed particularly well in the latest edition of the *Dictionary of Philosophy,* where the corresponding entry states baldly that under socialism no group is interested in the preservation of outmoded production relations and therefore their perfection takes place without social conflict.[32]

Here it is of the greatest importance to point out that analysis of the past few decades of Soviet economic development casts grave doubts on the view that perfection of outmoded production relations takes place without social conflict and therefore sees antagonistic contradictions as possible under socialism. In the present author's opinion, such an analysis shows that the process of perfecting production relations under socialism is more complicated than is commonly suggested. Above all, the reorganization of the existing system of production relations is given over to social groups that occupy a somewhat elevated position within this system and, accordingly, are bound to it through personal interest.[33]

Connection, Inter-Relation, and Association of Both Ideas

This is confirmed by the following noteworthy conclusion to the Report by Zaslavskaya:

Therefore, a radical reorganization of economic management essentially affects the interests of many groups, to some of which it promises improvements, but to others a deterioriation of their position. By virtue of this, attempts at improving production relations, bringing them into greater correspondence with the new demands of productive forces—attempts undertaken by the higher organs of power—cannot run their course without conflict. The successful resolution of this task is only possible on the basis of a well thought-out socialist strategy, a strategy that would simultaneously stimulate the activity of groups interested in changing present relations and block the actions of groups capable of obstructing this change.[34]

From all we have mentioned, it is now quite easy to see that there exists a connection, inter-relation, and association of ideas between the two main theoretical events we have described: namely, the political debate on contradictions in the field of scientific communism, and the discussion among experts in the field of political economy.[35] In the first of these we find the thesis that under certain conditions non-antagonistic contradictions, compatible with socialism, can take on certain traits of antagonistic contradictions.[36] Butenko names a number of examples of such contradictions:

- Between the moral foundations of socialism, on the one hand, and numerous offences against them in practice on the different levels of power and in many spheres of society, on the other
- Between the forcibly proclaimed thesis concerning the leading role of the working class, on the one hand, and the real weakening of its influence in social and economic life, on the other
- Between the officially proclaimed ideology of social justice, on the one hand, and the strongly increased differentiation of wages and incomes for the leading personnel of the economy, on the other
- Between word and action; i.e. between the presentation of reality in the mass media, on the one hand, and the actual state of affairs, on the other[37]

The second of these events, the *Novosibirsk Report*, expresses doubts about the viewpoint of those theorists who vehemently defend and maintain the exclusively non-antagonistic character of contradictions within socialist society, and uncompromisingly deny the possibility of deep, socially antagonistic, conflict within Soviet society.[38]

Concluding Remarks

In order to sum up the course and the results of these two internally linked social-economic discussions, we can now make the following concluding remarks.

Within a month of Andropov's death, the protagonists of the possibility of antagonistic contradictions under socialism, previously protected by Chernenko, started a new offensive to bring this view to official recognition.[39] Such an acceptance would have been the decisive confirmation of the conclusions of the *Novosibirsk Report*.

A fierce struggle between these protagonists and the traditionalists took place in 1984. The traditionalist stance of Kosolapov, editor-in-chief of *Kommunist*, first in *Pravda*, 4 March 1983[40] and then again on 20 July 1984, was decisive in this respect.[41] This last was followed by Kuz'menko's extensive critique of Butenko[42] and by Bugaev's firm and harsh rejection of the views of Ambartsumov, like Butenko a member of the Institute for the Economics of the World Socialist System.[43]

Voprosy filosofii also contained a series of articles on the subject, issuing from the pens of Butenko, Semenov, Dzhumadurdiev, Fedoseev, Il'ichev, Burlatsky, Sulimov, Medvedev, Kozlovsky and Stolyarov, in chronological order.[44] A twenty-page leading article in October 1984 provisionally ended the discussion by calling on the protagonists to wave the white flag.[45]

For the time being the Andropovians, led by Kosolapov and protected by Gorbachev, dominate the field. Even Chernenko had had to submit to the notions of Andropov.[46] The *Kommunist* editorial that followed the Plenary session in June 1983 advanced Andropov's suggestions for guide-lines for the future. These include "that, for all the importance of other questions, ideological work is coming more and more to the fore".[47] In August 1983 the head of the department of scientific communism at the Institute of Philosophy, Stepanyan, published 'On the Question as to the Unity and Contradictoriness of the Development of Socialist Society', in which Butenko is thoroughly criticised.[48] Finally, in October 1983, Chernenko referred in *Kommunist* to

Andropov's general line as "a matter of the whole party" and as the "duty of every communist".[49]

To be sure, there was no essential difference between the ideological positions of Chernenko and Andropov when one stated that all attempts to weaken the leading role of the party would open the door to restoration of capitalism, while the other stressed the possibility of 'serious collisions'. For, despite Andropov's seemingly resolute rejection of antagonistic contradictions within socialism, he was forced also to admit to 'serious collisions' which in fact mean antagonistic contradictions, as is clear from *The German Ideology*, where Marx and Engels hold that "all collisions of history have their origin in the contradiction between the productive forces and the form of communication *(Verkehrsform)*, i.e., the "relations of production" *(Produktions-verhältnisse)*, and "this contradiction must burst forth every time in a revolution".[50]

In view of all this, it is hard to be optimistic concerning a breakthrough for the strategy that would follow from the *Novosibirsk Report*, namely, a way of perfecting productive relations in the Soviet economy so as to avoid social rebellion in the future.[51] To my mind, this is a striking and impressive example of the decisive role played by economics (i.e., political economy as an ideological doctrine) in Soviet political ideology (i.e., scientific communism). Evidently, the role of economics is as alive and powerful as it was after the death of Stalin, when its central position was attacked during the discussion of Konstantinov's *Historical Materialism*[52] by Makarov and others,[53] using almost the same arguments as Butenko and Zaslavskaya. Unfortunately, however, this considerable role of economics is nonetheless fatal and disastrous for the Soviet economy. *Pozhivem, uvidim!*

Notes

1. See the relevant articles in *Filosofskaya entsiklopediya* (Philosophical Encyclopedia) vols. 1–5, Moscow 1960–1970; *Kleines politisches Wörterbuch* (Small Political Dictionary), Berlin (East), 1978; Martin Seliger. *The Marxist Conception of Ideology*, Cambridge, 1977; Helmut Dahm, *Der gescheiterte Ausbruch*, Baden-Baden, 1982. The sources for

the quotations from Marx and Engels above will be found on p. 552 of this book.

2. G.W.F. Hegel, *Sämtliche Werke*. Jubiläumausgabe, Vol. 4: *Wissenschaft der Logik I*.

3. Helmut Ogiermann, *Materialistische Dialektik*, Munich, 1958; G. A. Wetter, *Die Umkehrung Hegels*, Koln, 1963; Helmut Dahm, *Die Unhaltbarkeit des philosophischen Atheismus*, Vienna, 1984. Special edition.

4. A. Deborin, *"'Gegel' i dialekticheskii materializm"* ("Hegel and Dialectical Materialism"), in G.V.F. *Gegel*, Vol. 1, Moscow and Leningrad, 1929; *Vvedenie v filosofiyu dialekticheskogo materializma* (Introduction to the Philosophy of Dialectical Materialism), 7th edition, Moscow and Leningrad, 1931; M. B. Mitin, *Gegel' i teoriya materialisticheskoi dialektiki* (Hegel and the Theory of the Materialist Dialectic), Moscow, 1932; M. M. Rozental', *Materialisticheskaya dialektika* (The Materialist Dialectic) Moscow, 1951; and *Marksistskii dialekticheskii metod* (Marxist Dialectical Method) Moscow, 1951: and *Printsipy dialekticheskoi logiki* (Principles of Dialectical Logic) Moscow, 1960; N. Kondakov, *Logika* (Logic) Moscow, 1954; and *Vvedenie v logiku* (Introduction to Logic), Moscow, 1967; and *Logicheskii slovar'* (Logical Dictionary), Moscow, 1971.

Cf. S. Tsereteli, *O dialekticheskoi prirode logicheskoi svyazi* (On the Dialectical Nature of Logical Relations) Tbilisi, 1956; and *Dialekticheskaya logika* (Dialectical Logic) Tbilisi 1965 (Russian edition) 1971; K. Bakradze, *Sistema i metod filosofii Gegelya* (System and method of Hegel's Philosophy) Tbilisi, 1936, 1958, 1973; and *Logika* (Logic) Tbilisi, 1951.

Cf. S. Dudel', *Zakony materialisticheskoi dialektiki* (Laws of the Materialist Dialectic) Moscow, 1958; and 'Razvitie li eto marksistsko-leninskogo ucheniya o protivorechi?' ("Is There Development in the Marxist-Leninist Doctrine on Contradiction?") *Kommunist*, 1983 No. 7, pp. 111–115. V. Borodkin, *Problemy protivorechiya v materialisticheskoi dialektike* (Problems of Contradiction in the Materialist Dialectic) Moscow, 1982.

See also in German: *Die Sowjetphilosophie-Wendigkeit und Bestimmtheit*. Dokumente. Herausgegeben und eingeleitet von Wilhelm Goerdt, Darmstadt 1967; *Abram Deborin, Nikolaj Bucharin: Kontroversen über dialektischen und mechanistischen Materialismus*. Einleitung von Oskar Negt, Frankfurt/M. 1969, 2nd ed., 1974.

5. Tsereteli, *O dialekticheskoi prirode logicheskoi svyazi*.

6. *Ibid*. p. 506.

7. *Ibid.* p. 564. See also K. *Marks* and F. *Engels: Sochineniya.* 2nd edition, Vol. 12, Moscow 1958, pp. 716f. ('Proizvodstvo i potreblenie').

8. Bakradze, *Sistema i metod filosofii Gegelya;* 3rd edition (1973).

9. *Ibid.* p. 344.

10. *Ibid.* p. 349.

11. *Ibid.* p. 347.

12. Dudel', 'Razvitie . . .' p. 112. The reference there is to V. V. Borodkin, *Problemy protivorechiya v materialisticheskoi dialektike,* p. 186.

13. Borodkin, p. 245f.; Dudel', p. 112.

14. Dudel', p. 114; Borodkin, p. 224f.

15. Dudel', p. 114.

16. Tsereteli, *O dialekticheskoi prirode,* p. 506; Bakradze, *Sistemaimetod,* p. 348f.

17. Borodkin, *Problemy protivorechiya* . . . p. 186.

18. *Ibid.* p. 246.

19. *Ibid.* p. 59.

20. *Ibid.* p. 212.

21. Cf. also Horst Wessel, *Logik,* VEB, Berlin, 1984, *passim.* See also James P. Scanlan, *Dialectics in Contemporary Soviet Philosophy,* Occasional Paper of the Kennan Institute for Advanced Russian Studies Number 162, Washington, D.C., September 1982.

22. A. P. Butenko, "Eshche raz o protivorechiyakh sotsializma" ("Once Again on the Contradictions of Socialism") *Voprosy filosofii,* 1984, No. 2, pp. 124–129, especially p. 127.

23. V. S. Severnov, 'K teoreticheskomu uglubleniyu i konkretizatsii analiza problemy protivorechii v usloviyakh razvitogo sotsializma' ("On the Theoretical Deepening and Concretization of the Analysis of Contradictions Under Conditions of Developed Socialsim"), *Voprosy filosofii,* 1984, No. 2, pp. 130–140, especially p. 134.

24. A. P. Butenko, 'Protivorechiya razvitiya sotsializma kak obshchestvennogo stroya' ("The Contradictions of the Development of Socialism as a Social System") *Voprosy filosofii,* 1982, No. 10, pp. 16–29, especially p. 18.

25. *Ibid.* p. 18.

26. *Ibid.* pp. 22–23.

27. The *Novosibirsk Report* was published in *Survey* (London) No. 1, 1984, pp. 88–107. See especially p. 88.

28. D. D. Comey, 'Marxist-Leninist Ideology and Soviet Policy', *Studies in Soviet Thought* (Dordrecht and Boston), 1962, No. 4, pp. 315–316.

29. *Novosibirsk Report,* p. 92.

30. Yu.A. Vasil'chik, 'Sootvetstviya proizvodstvennykh otnoshenii kharakteru i urovnyu razvitiya proizvoditel'nykh sil zakon' ("Law of Correspondence of Production Relations to the Character and Level of Development of Productive Forces") in *Politicheskaya ekonomiya*, Moscow, 1979, Vol. 3., p. 589.

31. *Novosibirsk Report*, p. 97.

32. *Ibid.* p. 97 and *Filosofskii slovar'*, Moscow, 1980, p. 116.

33. *Ibid.* p. 97.

34. *Ibid.*

35. See also Karl Schlögel, *Der renitente Held: Arbeiterprotest in der Sowjetunion 1953–1983*, Hamburg, 1984, pp. 207–237.

36. Butenko, 'Eshche raz o protivorechiyakh . . .' pp. 124–129, especially p. 128.

37. *Ibid.* p. 129.

38. R. Kosolapov, 'Sotsializm i protivorechiya' ("Socialism and Contradiction"), *Pravda* 20 July 1984, pp. 2–3; V. Kuz'menko, 'Obshchestvoznanie: nekotorye aspekty diskussii, kritiki i samokritiki. Zametki na polyakh' ("Social Cognition: Some Aspects of Discussions. Criticism and Self-Criticism. Marginal Notes"). *Kommunist*, 1984, No. 11, pp. 112–117.

39. V. I. Kerimov, A. E. Razumov, G. I. Volkova, M. O. Mnatsakanyan, 'Sotsial' no-filosofskie problemy razvitogo sotsialisticheskogo obshchestava: diskussiya po aktual'noi probleme. Obzor otklikov' ("Social-Philosophical Problems of Developed Socialist Society: Discussion on a Topical Problem. Survey of Responses"), *Voprosy filosofii*, 1984, No. 2, pp. 116–123. Butenko, 'Eshche raz . . .' pp. 124–129. Semenov, 'K teoreticheskomu uglubleniyu . . .' pp. 130–140. A. D. Kosichev *et al.* in a review of P. N. Fedoseev, *Filosofiya i nauchnoe poznamie* (Philosophy and Scientific Knowledge), Moscow, 1983 in *Voprosy Filosofii*, 1984, No. 2, pp. 167–171, especially p. 171.

40. *Pravda*, 4 March 1983, pp. 2–3.

41. *Pravda*, 20 July 1984, pp. 2–3.

42. Kuz'menko. 'Obshchestvoznanie' pp. 112–117.

43. E. Bugaev, 'Strannaya pozitsiya' ("A Strange Position"), *Kommunist*, 1984, No. 14, pp. 119–126. Cf. also Bernd Knabe, 'Krisenbewusstsein und Krisenmanagement in den sozialistischen Landern— eine Stellungnahme aus Moskau', in: Bundesinstitut für ostwissenschaftliche und internationale Studien—*Gelesen, kommentiert . . .* (Cologne) 1984, No. 7. It seems to me that this thoroughgoing criticism by Kuz'menko (in July 1984) and by Bugaev (in September 1984) of the protagonists was the decisive impulse for the leadership of the CPSU finally to stifle this scandalous view and to cut short the debate

on contradictions in the main philosophy journal (see note 45 in particular).

44. *Voprosy filosofii*, 1984, Nos. 2–8; 'Obzor otklikov' *Voprosy filosofii*, 1984, No. 2, pp. 116–123.

45. 'Peredovaya: Marksistsko-leninskaya filosofiya—ideinoteoreti-cheskaya osnova sovershenstvovaniya razvitogo sotsializma' (Leading Article: "Marxist-Leninist Philosophy as the Theoretical Basis for the Perfecting of Developed Socialism"), *Voprosy filosofii*, 1984, No. 10, pp. 3–19. For a comment on this, see Elizabeth Teague, 'Philosophy Journal Under Fire for Unorthodox Views' in *Radio Liberty Research* 1984, No. 436, pp. 1–5.

46. M. S. Gorbachev, *Pravda*, 23 April 1984, pp. 1–3; K. U. Chernenko, *Kommunist*, No. 9, 1983, pp. 17–39; Yu. V. Andropov, *Kommunist*, No. 9, 1983, pp. 4–16.

47. 'Peredovaya: Ideologicheskuyu rabotu—na uroven' zadach sovershenstvovaniya razvitogo sotsializma' ("Ideological Work is to be Raised to the Level of the Tasks of Perfecting Developed Socialism") *Kommunist*, No. 10, 1983, pp. 3–14, especially p. 7.

48. Ts. A. Stepanyan, 'K voprosu o edinstve i protivorechivosti razvitiya sotsialisticheskogo obshchestva' ("On the Unity and Contradictoriness of the Development of Socialist Society") *Sotsiologicheskie issledovaniya*, No. 3, 1983, pp. 63–71.

49. K. Chernenko, 'Delo vsei partii, dolg kazhdogo kommunista', *Kommunist*, No. 15, 1983, pp. 18–34.

50. *"Alle Kollisionen der Geschichte haben also nach unserer Auffassung ihren Ursprung in dem Widerspruch zwischen den Produktivkräften und der Verkehrsform,"* den *Produktionsverhältnissen.*

"Dieser Widerspruch zwischen den Produktivkräften und der Verkehrsform, der, wie wir sahen, schon mehreremal in der bisherigen Geschichte vorkam, ohne jedoch die Grundlage derselben zu gefährden, musste jedesmal in einer Revolution eklatieren, wobei er zugleich verschiedene Nebengestalten annahm, als Totalität von Kollisionen, als Kollisionen verschiedener Klassen, als Widerspruch des Bewusstseins, Gedankenkampf etc., politischer Kampf etc." (K. Marx, F. Engels, *Werke* Berlin (East), 1959, Vol. 3: 'Die deutsche Ideologie', pp. 73–74).

51. *Novosibirsk Report*, p. 92. Cf. also Elizabeth Teague, 'Further Polemics over Economic Reform', *Radio Liberty Research*, No. 437, 1984, pp. 1–4.

52. F. V. Konstantinov, *Istoricheskii materializm*, 2nd edition, Moscow 1954.

53. A. F. Silov et al., *Vorposy filosofii*, No. 2, 1955, pp. 213–220. Makarov's statement is on p. 216. See also E. N. Loone, *Sovremennaya*

filosofiya istorii (Contemporary Philosophy of History) Tallin, 1980:
P. N. Fedoseev, *Filosofiya i nauchnoe poznanie* (Philosophy and Scientific
Knowledge) Moscow, 1983.

It is worth noting that Butenko took the opportunity of an interview
with the Bulgarian newspaper *Rabotnichesko delo* (Sofiya) 19 November
1984 in Moscow to disavow his previous notions on the reasons for
the manifestations of antagnostic contradictions under socialism. Such
causes are no longer produced by socialism itself, but are henceforth
declared to be only the legacy of the petty bourgeois past and of
peculiar relapses into its brand of political order and social thought.
Phenomena of this kind must be seen as immoral, criminal and
parasitic—completely inconsistent with a correct understanding of
social justice. This position conforms to that of Stepanyan and
Kosolapov and has nothing in common with Butenko's previous
stance.

3

The Place of Economic Policy Objectives on the List of Soviet Political Priorities

Hans-Hermann Höhmann

In all political systems economic policy objectives are by their nature intermediate objectives or instruments for socio-political purposes lying outside the field of the economy. All the same, pursuit of economic targets, and in particular growth targets, has varying urgency in different systems and countries, depending on the nature of the ultimate socio-political objectives, the level of development of the economy and the current economic situation. The Soviet system came into being as a mobilisation regime with the aim of overcoming the economic and social backwardness of Russia in the shortest possible time. The political and economic alternatives which the bolshevik leadership saw itself facing at the end of the First World War were dramatically summed up by Lenin: " . . . either perish or overtake and outstrip the advanced countries economically. . . . Perish or forge full steam ahead. That is the alternative put by history."[1]

High Priority for the Economy

Ever since that time comparison with the West has provided the standards for the pace and progress of the effort to catch up in industrialisation, for the rhythm of the "economics of virtuous haste" (G. Grossman), and the pressure of time under which the Soviet leadership felt itself also had a far-reaching influence on its ideas on economic systems, leading to a policy of constructing a system of hierarchical administrative economic planning on the basis of collective ownership, which was (thought to be) appropriate for industrialisation.

Stalin took up Lenin's slogan with increased urgency at the beginning of the 1930s: "We are fifty or a hundred years behind the advanced countries. We must make good this distance in ten years. Either we do it, or they crush us."[2]

Under Khrushchev too the programme of "catching up and overtaking" was of course of considerable importance. Yet now it appeared not so much as a simple striving for survival, but rather as a component of the plan for the staged construction of the "material-technical basis of communism" which was incorporated in the 1961 CPSU Party Programme. The reason for this, among other things, was the attempt to create a new legitimacy for Soviet policy after the suppression of the Stalin years and the losses of the Second World War. If the traditional principle of Soviet economic policy is no longer applied literally nowadays, this is because of the manifest impossibility of approaching this target at present.

The Soviet Union did not achieve its aim of catching up, its level of economic development has remained relatively low, and today this is exacerbated by the acute problems of a low rate of economic growth. It is not only the economists among Sovietologists who see the relatively and absolutely unsatisfactory economic situation as the greatest political problem facing the USSR at present. The urgent need for reorganisation and re-construction of the economy is reflected in the daily and the specialist press, the speeches of leading politicians, party and government resolutions, party work at all levels of organisation, the education system and so on. All these signs taken together indicate that economic policy objectives have a higher priority ranking than in Western countries.

Consolidation of the Soviet economy, still threatened by crisis, also occupies a high place on the list of policy priorities of the new General Secretary of the CPSU, Mikhail Gorbachev, who came to office in the middle of March 1985. In particular, in his "government statement", the speech to the Central Committee of the party on 23 April 1985, he again and again repeated variations on the principal theme of his policy: "The most important question at the present time is the following: how and by what means can the country succeed in accelerating its economic development? . . . The historical fate of the country and the position of socialism in the modern world depend to a great extent on how we pursue this matter."[3] The economic upswing is needed for many reasons. Those mentioned include above all the improvement of the population's standard of living, the strengthening of the defence capacity of the USSR and the comprehensive modernisation and intensification of the economy. Evidently all three points of the "major triangle" of Soviet economic policy—consumption, armaments and capital formation—have approximately equal priority for Gorbachev. This means that there can scarcely be any question of major restructuring of the utilisation of the social product as a means to economic progress and that the only way out of the general bottleneck situation is a substantial rise in the performance of the economy. Since continuation of the extensive growth policy is no longer possible owing to the increasing scarcity of all factors of production—labour, capital and natural resources— economic progress requires steady improvements in productivity. The term used for this as a rule by academics and the political leadership in the USSR is "intensification". According to Gorbachev the intensification of the economy today must "be accorded the same degree of political importance as the industrialisation of the country enjoyed in its time".[4]

The importance of the economy in Soviet policy has thus increased still further. Nevertheless, when assessing the "economic obsession" of the USSR in comparison with the place of economic objectives in Western industrial systems the differences in the character of the political processes, and above all the relationship between politics and public opinion, should not be overlooked.

Hierarchy of Economic Objectives

The growth targets already mentioned are not, however, the only economic objectives. As in all systems, there is a multitude of objectives in the Soviet system which are hierarchical in character and can conveniently, if imperfectly, be arranged in a pyramid of objectives. An example of this is given by diagram 3.1 in the appendix to this chapter. Beside (or rather below) the vague ultimate objective of "construction of the communist society" there are the socio-political objectives like power, prestige, privileges, legitimacy, welfare and participation which rank above economic policy and express the basic political conception of the ruling elite. Among the objectives of economic policy, as well as the growth targets already mentioned, we can distinguish structural, performance, stability or equilibrium targets and targets relating to the economic system. These targets are interdependent, they exhibit certain basic structures in their respective concrete forms, and their mutual interrelationships are marked by either harmony, neutrality or conflict.

The concrete constellation of economic policy targets, the objective system, depends on what higher socio-political purposes the economic policy targets are designed to serve. As ideal types two partly conflicting and partly interconnected constellations of objectives can be distinguished for the USSR, one of which can be assigned to the higher objective of power and the other to the higher objective of legitimacy. The power type implies growth and structural targets which are directed towards the expansion of the power, prestige and privileges of the party elite internally and of the influence of the Soviet Union as a world power externally. The legitimacy type, on the other hand, aims more at promoting consumption, consensus and participation, that is to say at internal and external credibility. Conflicts which arise between the two types are less disputes about the priority of economics or politics than conflicts between different political objectives and the economic policy strategies to be adopted for their implementation.

Hitherto the objective system of the USSR has been predominantly of the power type. Consequently, capital formation and expansion of the armanents sector play a comparatively important role among the objectives of economic policy. Yet the point of view of legitimacy could not and cannot be completely neglected, since the extension of power is not possible without an increase in consensus and participation by the broad mass of the people, and that in turn means without a steady improvement in consumption. The new General Secretary of the CPSU has been by no means the last to indicate repeatedly that he is aware of this connection.

The consequence of the USSR's basic conception of growth and structural policy was that the share of consumption in the final utilisation of the social product diminished steadily, although at a varying pace, over the longer term, whilst the share of investment grew and that of armaments at least remained the same. But at the end of the 1970s a change occurred in this respect: the fall in growth which started in 1979 forced the acceptance of approximately equal rates of growth for the three main fields of utilisation.[5] Yet even before this the principle had been followed that whilst any available scope for additional growth was to be used for accelerating investment, growth shortfalls were in turn to be absorbed on the accumulation side and not allowed to transmit their full impact onto the consumer. The sharp cutback in investment growth planned after 1976 could not be enforced. The actual growth of capital formation was clearly above the planned rate.

Past plans had repeatedly envisaged a faster improvement in the standard of living. The ninth five-year plan (1971–1975) had provided for a faster growth of Group B industry and a rise in the share of consumption, the tenth five-year plan (1976–1980) provided for a rise in the share of consumption, and the eleventh five-year plan (1981–1985) again envisaged a faster increase for Group B and a rise in the share of consumption. But as a general rule these targets were not achieved. The reasons for this include:

- Shifting of priorities during the currency of the plans because the growth of the economy was lagging behind the plan figures
- Dependence of improvements in consumption on the chronically disappointing results from agriculture, which recorded satisfactory development in only one of the last six five-year plan periods—the eighth, from 1966 to 1970
- Effects of the centralised administrative economic system, the organisational structure, constellations of interests and

mechanisms of functioning of which impede structural
changes and tend to perpetuate the expanded reproduction
of the established growth pattern

The low economic growth at present, caused by increasing
factor scarcity and declining productivity, is leading to shifts of
emphasis within the structure of economic policy goals. The
relative upgrading of consumption has already been indicated.
In order not to shatter the legitimacy of the Soviet system at
home and abroad completely and not to let the growth of the
standard of living drop below the productivity and stablility
threshold, stabilisation of consumption per head at the minimum
level necessary for this is essential. All annual plans since the
end of the 1970s have provided for faster growth of Group B,
and investment too shows a corresponding, even if modest, shift
of emphasis. Furthermore, the importance of equilibrium targets
is increased, both at the macro and microeconomic level. The
effects of repressed inflation, wrong assortment, imbalances and
sectoral and regional bottlenecks increase with low growth.
Above all, however, the fulfilment of performance targets like
increasing efficiency and productivity becomes more and more
urgent. If the overall economic growth rate of the USSR is not
to fall below 2–2.5 percent, with declining input growth, at the
very least a further deterioration in productivity must be avoided.

Effects on the Development of Theory

The arguments about the priorities of Soviet economic policy
and the shifts between them, in particular between more and
less consumption-oriented sectors, also play a significant role
in the development of Western theories of the political and
social system of the USSR. R. Amann has distinguished graphically between Group A theories and Group B theories.[6] In
both, economic objectives play an important role. Group A
theories start from the assumption that economic policy conceptions like forcing capital formation or strengthening the
military-industrial basis of the country represent intermediate
objectives or means for the internal and external expansion of

political power. Typical examples are the totalitarianism theory and the mobilisation theory.[7] Economic strength is mobilised for the purpose of increasing the power of the party, the USSR's domestic policy appears repressive and its external policy aggressive. Group A theories thus belong to the "power type" discussed previously. The improvement of the population's living standard, on the other hand, enjoys a low priority.

Group B theories also start from the assumption of the primacy of the communist party. But promotion of the welfare of broad strata of society, harking back to utopian communist ideas, plays a larger role in the party's aims. Group B theories thus belong rather to the "legitimacy type". Typical examples of such theories are G. Breslauer's concept of "welfare state authoritarianism"[8] and the different varieties of convergence theory.[9] An important implication of the convergence theory, for example in the version presented by J. Tinbergen, had been the increasing similarity of the structure of economic objectives in East and West, which was expected to lead to a corresponding assimilation of economic policy instruments too. Assimilation of objectives meant above all expansion of consumption in the socialist planned economies of Eastern Europe with a parallel development of market economy steering mechanisms, because only in this way was it thought possible for economic policy to accomplish the aim of improving consumption more rapidly.

Chronologically, Group A theories are older. They seek above all to explain early phases of Soviet industrialisation, phases when, in Stalin's words, it was a matter of overcoming the "Russian" backwardness of the USSR, making the country a "country of metal, a country of automobiles, a country of tractors", putting "the USSR on an automobile and the muzhik on a tractor", "increasing to the utmost the defence capacity of the country",[10] when targets for increasing consumption played a minor role. The fact that, with the change of economic structure which has taken place in recent years in the USSR and the upgrading of consumption objectives which we have mentioned, Group B theories began to play a larger role has not led to the disappearance of Group A theories. Today we can observe competition between the two explanations.

The theories we have outlined have nothing directly to do with the question of the primacy of economics or politics. the point is rather that they give prominence to particular political objectives of the Soviet leadership, to which particular economic priorities correspond. Conflicts which arise are not so much arguments about the priority of politics or economics as conflicts between different political objectives and the economic policy strategies to be adopted in order to attain them. Above all this is a question of the alternatives of expansion of power internally and externally or increasing the welfare of the people. It follows from what we have said that there need not be any competition between economic and political objectives. In the numerous cases in which economic objectives are intermediate objectives or instruments for political purposes, there can be complete harmony of objectives. The question of the primacy of politics or economics is bound to arise, however, when there are contradictions between the achievement of political and economic goals, so that political objectives can only be attained with economic losses and economic objectives can only be attained at the expense of political damage.

On the Priority of Politics or Economics

The question of the priority of politics or economics in the USSR is an old one. By his statement that "communism is Soviet power plus electrification of the whole country" Lenin indicated that the desired industrialisation had to be carried out on the basis of a specific political foundation, namely Soviet power.[11] Elsewhere he quite clearly postulates the priority of politics over economics: "politics must take precedence over economics. To argue otherwise is to forget the ABC of marxism".[12] And this thesis has been repeated to the present day.[13] All the same, Lenin characteristically commented on it that "we need more economics and less politics, but if we are to have this we must clearly be rid of political dangers *and political mistakes*" [emphasis in original].[14] This can also be seen as the origin of the traditional principle of Soviet policy that economics occupies a high place in the USSR's political priority system, but subject to the premise that the stability of the regime is ensured. Lenin himself of course showed considerable flexibility in the application of his own principle. The New Economic Policy (NEP) introduced a little later meant running substantial political risks, both in fact and in the light of Marxist theory. The partial return to capitalist production relations did indeed involve the danger of what the communist leadership regarded as a reactionary trend in the consciousness of the population, the structure of society and the political superstructure.

If there is to be a conflict between politics and economics, contradictions between political and economic objectives must exist and/or be assumed by the political decision makers. Such cases are hard to identify in practice. There is virtually no possibility of testing. The discussion must necessarily therefore be extremely hypothetical. In the following examination of the problem we shall cite two cases, one from the Soviet past and one from the contemporary USSR: the collectivisation of Soviet agriculture at the beginning of the 1930s and the arguments about reform of the Soviet economic system which are going on at the present time.

Where collectivisation is concerned, the assumption of the primacy of politics over economics in Stalinist policy depends on the existence of alternative possible economic decisions and on awareness of these alternatives. If one shares what has long been the predominant view, that in order to achieve the economic development objectives, that is to say industrialisation, the relationship between agriculture and industry had to be changed so as to tap reserves for accumulation and ensure the supply of food for the new urban industrial centres being established, then collectivisation makes sense as an economic instrument, economics and politics are in agreement and there is no primacy of politics at the expense of the economy. The conclusion must be different, however, if alternative courses would have been possible, if NEP offered opportunities for development, or if misjudgements contributed to its termination. Today reinterpretations along these lines are increasingly to be found in Western research.[15]

Economic and Political Views
of Economic Reforms

On the question of economic reforms in the USSR the view is frequently found in Western literature that far-reaching changes in the present planning system were avoided primarily on account of the political implications associated with them, while economic considerations, in particular the prospects of improved coordination and greater efficiency, would point to fundamental reforms. Thus the formulation is that far-reaching economic reforms founder on the rock of the primacy of politics. If, however, economics had priority, this would lead to fundamental changes in the institutional arrangements and the mechanism of functioning of Soviet planning. By fundamental reform is meant a reform in which, first, the centre aims to carry out its principal economic policies predominantly by means of indirect, parametric instruments; second, coordination of the current operation of the economy is no longer done through administrative hierarchies but through contracts on markets; third, market prices become major bearers of economic information and, fourth, enterprise performance is no longer measured by fulfilment of plans but by earning profits.

The fact that such a reform would have serious political and social consequences and therefore encounters strong opposition from politicians and society has been stressed again and again in the Western literature.[16] The principal obstacle to reform is the political risks for the leadership associated with a comprehensive reform: loss of domestic political control through giving up the administrative economic planning which is also conceived and used as an instrument of ruling, loss of control in foreign policy by abandoning the planning system employed for the purpose of hegemonial control in the CMEA area, and loss of control in the field of nationality policy owing to the abolition, or at least weakening, of the central administrative hierarchies directed from Moscow. In addition, the social interests at all levels of the hierarchy graphically described in T. Zaslavskaya's "Novosibirk Report" also operate to paralyse reform.[17]

Nevertheless, we could only speak of unequivocal primacy of politics vis-à-vis economics in the question of reform if an alternative to the present planning system could be seen which from the economic point of view would be better and was recognised as such by the Soviet leadership. In both respects, however, reservations are in order (on this see diagram 3.2 and the accompanying explanation in the appendix to this chapter).

Is Economic Reform a Solution to the Problem?

First, is there convincing reason to believe that under present Soviet conditions an alternative to the (modernised and partially reformed) administrative planning system can be found which promises unequivocal improvements in performance? In Western analyses it is often argued that a fundamentally reformed, market socialist system would function better than the existing planning system, the dysfunctions of which are at the same time assumed to be irremediable. Do these perceptions stand up in the light of reality? Beside the size and heterogeneity of the country, and the length of time it has developed as a planned economy, there are the particularly large adjustment risks in respect of the stability of growth, employment and prices which would be involved in a reform which changed the system. Yet even if the transitional problems associated with such a reform could be solved, is there reason to believe that in the longer term an efficient, fundamentally reformed economic system could evolve which exhibited a substantial measure of market economy features? A market-oriented system needs particular institutional and behaviourist or motivational prerequisites. These include legal independence and financial autonomy of enterprises, the organisation of competition, the willingness to assume uncertainty and risk, readiness for mobility at all levels of society and finally, a high level of economic morality, since with greater economic freedom and diminishing supervision the opportunities for perverse behaviour increase. Is there not a danger that a combination of continuing inclination to intervene on the part of the political leadership, uncertain institutional backing for the reformed system and inadequate response to reform policy by society might give rise to a chronically weak mixed system in which the dysfunctions of the present system were exchanged for other and perhaps no less serious ones?

Should the doubts expressed concerning a successful (fundamental) reform process in the USSR on the basis of an analysis of reality, the demands for reform and the possibilities of reform be justified, they are undoubtedly further reinforced in the view of the Soviet leadership by ideological considerations.

It is true that Soviet ideology has at no time exercised a decisive effect on the economic system in the sense that the totality of the institutional arrangements, the mechanism of functioning and the objectives of Soviet economic policy have been laid down in detail.[18] Where the influence of Marxist ideas could be observed, their effect was more negative, that is to say in restricting efficiency. Such influences were eliminated by a process of de-dogmatisation, which aimed to resolve the contradictions between the constructs of political economy and the demands of reality. What has remained important as an ideological factor in Soviet policy is an economic model marked by elements of Marxism-Leninism, Soviet reality and pre-revolutionary Russian traditions of thought, which leads to particular preferences and taboos relating to economic systems and processes and colours the perceptions of the Soviet leadership so as to generate an attachment to traditional economic institutions and instruments. An ideologically tinted economic view of the world of this kind would not be able to determine a system in detail, but within an existing system it proves to be an effective "system preservative". This view can be described as a collection of diverse economic and ideological postulates which, all together, boil down to a preference for administrative economic planning. It thus works in directly the opposite way to the conception of reforms in socialist planned economies which predominates in the West. Whereas the latter as a rule contrasts the imperfect reality of the planned economy with the vision of a perfect reform, the former downgrades reform and uprates the reality and thus inclines to a strategy of "improvement" instead of a strategy of system change. With an outlook of this kind, and despite Gorbachev's dynamism it is likely to remain characteristic of the Soviet leadership for the foreseeable future—conservation in matters of reform, that is to say relying on improving the system by means of more logical institutional arrangements, more consistent implementation of partial changes, better back-up with operational and structural policy measures and more "moral engineering" instead of transformation of the system, does not mean primacy of politics over economics but a preference for a traditional solution on political and economic grounds equally.

Notes

1. V. I. Lenin, "The Impending Catastrophe and How to Combat It", *Collected Works*, Vol. 25, Moscow and London, 1964, p. 364.

2. J. Stalin, "The Tasks of Business Executives", *Problems of Leninism,,* Moscow, 1945, p. 356.

3. *Pravda*, 24 April 1985.

4. *Pravda*, 10 December 1984.

5. See H.-H. Höhmann, "Die sowjetische Wirtschaft nach dem Wachstumstief: Stagnation, Zwischenhoch oder anhaltender Aufschwung?" in H.-H. Höhmann and H. Vogel, eds. *Osteuropas Wirtschaftsprobleme und die Ost-West-Beziehungen*, Baden-Baden, 1984.

6. R. Amann, "Searching for a New Concept of Soviet Politics: the Politics of Hesitant Modernisation?" Conference paper, Birmingham, 1984.

7. See the contributions in C. Johnson, ed., *Change in Communist Systems*, Stanford, 1970.

8. G. W. Breslauer, *Five Images of the Soviet Future, a Critical Review and Synthesis*, Berkeley, 1978.

9. On the convergence theory see the list of references in H.-H. Höhmann and G. Seidenstecher, "Sowjetische Politische Ökonomie und Konvergenztheorie", in W. Förster and D. Lorenz, eds., *Beiträge zur Theorie und Praxis von Wirtschaftsystemen. Festgabe für Karl C. Thalheim zum 70. Geburtstag*, Berlin, 1970, pp. 105 ff.

10. J. Stalin, "A Year of Great Change", *Problems of Leninism*, p. 300; "The Results of the First Five-Year Plan", p. 398.

11. See "Elektrifikatsiya", in *Bol'shaya Sovetskaya Entsiklopediya*, Vol. 30, Moscow, 1978, p. 32.

12. V. I. Lenin, "Once Again on the Trade Unions", *Collected Works*, Vol. 32, Moscow and London, 1965, p. 83.

13. P. Ignatovsky, "O politicheskom podkhode k ekonomike", *Kommunist*, 1983, No. 12, pp. 60 ff.

14. V. I. Lenin, "Once Again," p. 85.

15. See J. Millar, *The ABCs of Soviet Socialism*, Urbana, Chicago and London, 1981, pp. 7 ff.

16. See H.-H. Höhmann, "Grenzen der Wirtschaftseformen in der UdSSR: Welche Rolle spielt die Ideologie", *Berichte des Bundesinstituts für ostwissenschafteiche und internationale Studien,* 1982, No. 25.

17. Text with commentary by H.-H. Höhmann and K.-E. Wädekin, *Osteuropa,* 1984, No. 1, pp. A1 ff.

18. See H.-H. Höhmann, "Grenzen." pp. 14ff.

55

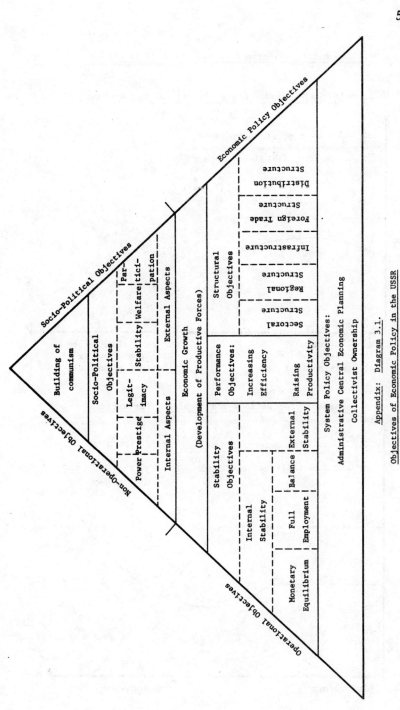

Appendix: Diagram 3.1.

Objectives of Economic Policy in the USSR

(with acknowledgement to G. Tuchtfeldt)

56

Appendix: Diagram 3.2. Perceptions of Reform

The Soviet Leadership's Traditional Perceptions

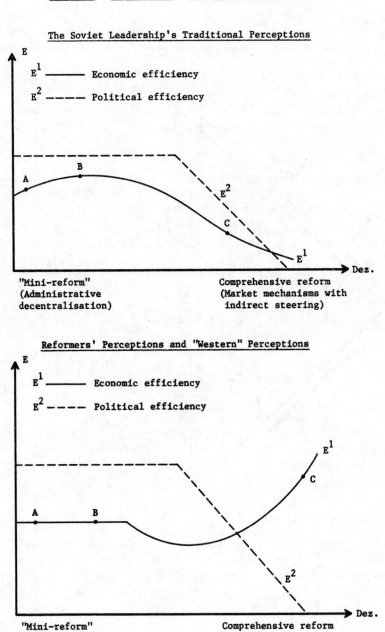

"Mini-reform"
(Administrative
decentralisation)

Comprehensive reform
(Market mechanisms with
indirect steering)

Reformers' Perceptions and "Western" Perceptions

"Mini-reform"

Comprehensive reform

Diagram 3.2 contrasts the Soviet leadership's traditional perceptions of reform with those prevailing in "Western" research and among advocates of a comprehensive reform in the USSR and Eastern Europe. E^1 and E^2 represent the trends in economic and political efficiency. By political efficiency we mean the degree of effectiveness of the traditional instruments of rule and the extent of political control which political bodies exercise over society. A, B and C are the selected variants of reform. We distinguish between "mini-reform" and "comprehensive reform". "Mini-reform" means processes of administrative decentralisation (or also recentralisation), improvement of planning methods, changes in the set of indicators, incentive mechanisms and prices, etc., while the basic institutions and mechanisms of administrative economic planning are retained. Comprehensive reform means a transition to market mechanisms, indirect steering, evaluation of enterprise performance by the earning of profits, etc.

In the traditional perception the "mini-reform" has both economic and political advantages. Position B is superior to position A without involving a deterioration in political efficiency. Point C, on the other hand, is an inefficient position from both economic and political points of view. There are no contraditions between economic and political effects on either the positive or the negative side, so one cannot speak of the primacy of politics in such a perception.

In the "Western" perception and the reformers' perception no improvements can be achieved by means of "mini-reforms". A comprehensive reform (position C), on the other hand, promises a considerable rise in economic efficiency - although at the price of losses in political control. With this view, if there is no decision in favour of position C it can be assumed that the leadership is guided by the primacy of politics.

4
Economic Institutions as Instruments of Political Rule

Georg Brunner

Introduction

The term "economic institutions" may be used in several ways. Instead of elaborating on the terminological problem it should suffice here to say that, in the following analysis, by "economic institutions" we mean Soviet political institutions dealing with the formulation and implementation of economic policy on the central level.

As a rule, the political process in the Soviet Union is organized in such a way that the party leadership takes the more important decisions, which are then executed by the government apparatus but under the supervision of the party apparatus. In the case of the economy this scheme is modified in favour of the more expert government, whose leading institutions are entitled to make important decisions. For analytical purposes it might be useful to divide the institutional setting dealing with economic policy into three levels: 1) institutions dealing with economic policy decision making, such as the Politbureau and the Central Committee Secretariat; 2) institutions of economic administration, such as the various government agencies with economic responsibilities; 3) institutions on the intermediate level, such as the Central Committee apparatus, the Council of Ministers, its Presidium and the different government agencies of functional competence (Gosplan, Gossnab, Gosstroi, Ministry of Finance, etc.), which are responsible, on the one hand, vis-à-vis the administrative institutions for coordinating and controlling their activities and, on the other hand, with regard to the institutions of policy decision making for initiating and preparing their decisions.

Despite the highly bureaucratized nature of the Soviet system an exclusively institutional analysis of our subject matter would not be sufficient. For, paradoxically, the present Soviet system still represents the type of personal power structure. Though in the course of Soviet history an enormous bureaucracy has taken over administration, the process of institutionalization has not yet reached the top of the power structure. At the highest level of policy decision making clear-cut responsibilities are still lacking and personal factors dominate the scene. For this reason, within the leading political institutions the current personnel situation must be taken into consideration. This, of course, renders an institutionally oriented analysis more difficult and hardly admits general conclusions valid for a longer time. The analyst's position is most complicated in times of succession crises, as in the first half of the 1980s when four General Secretaries followed each other at the top of the CPSU. Since Gorbachev took over in March 1985 a more stable future is in prospect but at present things are in a state of flux.

The Level of Policy Decision Making

It is generally assumed that economic matters play a great role in the Soviet policy-making process and this impression is reinforced by Soviet information policy. Nevertheless, a more thorough analysis of the activities and the composition of the policy-making bodies reminds us that, as in many other cases, more caution would be advisable. Of course, the analysis leading to caution must be handled with kid gloves itself because we simply do not know enough about the working of the highest policymaking institutions.

In any case, it is certain that the Politbureau is the "black box", the real cabinet of the Soviet system, even in economic matters. Exactly what are "the most important and urgent questions of internal and foreign policy", which are examined at the weekly meetings of the Politbureau, we do not know, because the agenda is shrouded in secrecy. For a long time, public references to the subjects dealt with most frequently concerned economic matters. The correctness of this impression has become questionable as a consequence of the practice started by Andropov in December 1982 of publishing communiqués on the meetings of the Politbureau. According to these communiqués, economic issues amount to about 37 percent of all the topics on the agenda of the Politbureau, thus ranking second, slightly behind foreign affairs.[1] It can be taken for granted that not all topics dealt with are mentioned in the communiqués and that economic issues are given most publicity. In fact, the real share of the economy in the business done by the Politbureau cannot be expected to exceed one third.

In view of the composition of the Politbureau, it is doubtful whether it is capable of considering economic problems in a substantial manner. It is true that at least half of its members are or were concerned with economic problems, either in their present position or at a former stage of their political career, but on the whole the number of Politbureau members with more profound economic expertise is quite small. Since the purge of the "Anti-Party-Group" by Khrushchev, in June 1957, economic expertise in the Politbureau has been reduced to some generalists whose full-time job involves—among other things—economic responsibilities, as is usually the case with the chairman of the Council of Ministers and one of his first deputies, one or two Central Committee secretaries and some regional party chiefs. The absence of economic specialists during the reigns of Khrushchev, Brezhnev and his successors contrasts sharply with the functional structure of Stalin's Politbureau, in which government officials were predominant. Until 1957, the Gosplan chairman and/or the equivalent chief planning official had a seat in the Politbureau *ex officio* (Kuibyshev 1927–1935, Voznesensky 1941–1949, Saburov 1952–1957, Pervukhin 1952–1957) and several branch ministries were represented as well.

At the final stage of the vanishing Chernenko Politbureau in March 1985, perhaps four of the eleven full members and one of the six candidates could be considered as occupying a position involving mainly economic responsibilities: Premier Tikhonov, First Vice Premier Aliev, Central Committee secretaries Gorbachev, Romanov and Dolgikh. Only Tikhonov (by no means an adequate substitute for Kosygin) and Dolgikh had substantial experience in economic management and administration, while Gorbachev and Romanov had risen as generalists through the party apparatus; Aliev's forty years of professional career were equally divided between the KGB and the party apparatus. In the wake of the Central Committee plenums of April and July 1985, where the new General Secretary Gorbachev succeeded in bringing about major personnel changes, raising, strengthening his position, and Politbureau membership to thirteen full and five candidate members, the situation has changed insofar as with Central Committee secretary Ryzhkov, responsible for supervising the economy, a politically influential expert has found his way into the Politbureau, while Romanov was ousted.

A comparable situation prevails in the Central Committee Secretariat, which is responsible for the preparation and execution of the decisions of the Politbureau and takes many important decisions on its own either at its weekly meetings or through the individual secretaries who have their own specific areas of responsibility. Unfortunately, these areas of responsibility are far from being delineated once and for all. Responsibilities shift to and fro between the ten or so secretaries as political and personnel circumstances may require. The situation is further complicated by the fact that—apart from the General Secretary whose jurisdiction is all-embracing—within the secretariat there is an informal hierarchy between "senior" and "junior" secretaries to which an overlapping subdivision of secretarial functions corresponds. So one may say that party affairs, ideology, cadres policy, the economy, internal security, international relations, etc., are the main fields of responsibility, but at the same time it must be added that these fields may be combined or divided and must be adapted to the prevailing hierarchy of secretaries. As a consequence, the functional structure of the Central Committee Secretariat is difficult to survey and the functional share of economic matters can hardly be measured. On the whole, I would guess that only 20–25 percent of the different responsibilities assigned to individual secretaries relate to economic affairs. In normal times overall supervision of the economy is the responsibility of a "senior" secretary and "junior" secretaries are responsible for industry and agriculture, respectively; a further subdivision of industry between heavy and light industry is not uncommon and the military industrial complex may be singled out for special supervision as well. With the shrinking gerontocracy of the 1980s, however, normal times in the Central Committee Secretariat have become a matter of memory in view of functional confusion. Restoring normality is one of the current tasks of General Secretary Gorbachev.

Chernenko's Secretariat comprised, apart from himself, only nine members whose spheres of competence shifted according to the current state of rivalries between Gorbachev and Romanov. Gorbachev, who had been responsible for agriculture since 1978, ultimately succeeded in gaining the post of de facto "second" secretary and in extending his responsibilities to the whole field of the economy. Under his supervision, newcomer Ryzhkov, who had left Gosplan for the Central Committee secretaryship in November 1982, managed to attain "junior" responsibility for economic matters. On the other hand, Romanov's economic jurisdiction was narrowed down to the military industrial complex and to supervising "junior" secretary Dolgikh, responsible for heavy industry. At the intersection of the two contenders' shadows, "junior" secretary Kapitonov was allegedly taking care of light industry. During the first months of Gorbachev's leadership Romanov and Dolgikh have been steadily declining in power whereas Ryzhkov's position as economic overlord has been strengthened. In April 1985, Nikonov was appointed Central Committee Secretary in charge of agriculture and subordinated to Ryzhkov. The redistribution of responsibilities after Romanov's dismissal and the appointment of two further secretaries on 1 July 1985 is not yet discernible.

Of course, policy decision making in the Politbureau and the Central Committee Secretariat is influenced by several secondary power-holders. An attempt to identify them or even to measure their influence exactly would be a fruitless undertaking. Nevertheless, a rough indicator may be used in order to get some impression of the respective weight of economic and noneconomic interests in the antechamber of political decision making. I refer to the functional or professional composition of the "leading party bodies", i.e. the Central Committee and the Central Commission. Though these bodies as such have, as a rule, nothing to say in political decision making, they are not at all meaningless. They perform, first of all, the important function of integrating the Soviet elites.[2] Membership in them conveys social prestige, privileges and political influence. On these grounds it may be assumed that representation of "interest groups" in the integrating party bodies is indicative of their official appreciation and political influence. Appendices I and II give figures on the representation of the party and government apparatuses with economic and non-economic responsibilities in the leading and integrating party bodies for the last fifteen years. A closer look at these figures reveals that the representation quota of non-economic agencies is higher than that of the economic ones. This is most evident from the qualitative point of view, which takes into consideration the differences in prestige between the five categories of full and alternate membership of the Politbureau, full and alternate membership of the Central Committee and membership of the CRC. If these differences are graded by giving the status-positions a certain number of points the result is that the scores of heads of economic agencies are about 70% of those of heads of non-economic agencies. A further device for getting an impression of the official appreciation of economic expertise may be found in a comparison of the representation of two segments of the intelligentsia in the CC and CRC, as shown in appendix III. The relationship between the technical-economic intelligentsia, consisting of industrial and agricultural managers, and the scientific-cultural intelligentsia, comprising top functionaries in the field of science and culture, roughly corresponds to the relationship between economic and ideological expertise. If the figures given in appendix III are interpreted in these terms they not only show that ideology has always been held in higher esteem than economic expertise, it also indicates a steady growth of this esteem since the early 1970s.

All this indicators taken together suggest that the standing of the economic factor in the process of policy decision making should not be overestimated.

The Level of Administration

In contrast to policy decision making administration of the economy by government agencies is firmly in the hand of professionals. Approximately 75 percent of the ministers and state committee chairmen sitting on the Council of Ministers have a professional background and rose through the administrative ranks to the top of their respective hierarchy.[3] Furthermore, most of the highest government agencies are concerned with economic tasks. At the time of Gorbachev's takeover seventy-four of the ninety heads of administrative agencies assembled in the Council of Ministers were responsible for a certain branch or function of the economy:

	Economic	Noneconomic	Total
All-Union Ministries	32	1	33
Union-Republican Ministries	24	7	31
All-Union State Committees	6	–	6
Union-Republican State Committees	9	7	16
Other Agencies	3	1	4
Total	74	16	90

The administrative branches are supplemented in each union republic by five to ten republican ministries, most of which are charged with special economic responsibilities according to the profile of the republic concerned.

Apart from the predominance of the economy in the overall state administration, the most striking feature of institutional development during the last two decades has been the growing number of government agencies. When the ministerial system following the branch principle was reestablished at the end of 1965, replacing the functional and territorially decentralized system of economic administration introduced by Khrushchev (state committees, sovnarkhozy), there were only sixty agencies represented on the Council of Ministers, of which fifty-two had economic responsibilities. Since then specialization and division of jurisdiction have reached such an extent that departmentalism has become the prevalent attitude on the highest administrative level. Struggle for greater shares in the state budget is one of the major activities in the Council of Ministers. The disintegrating effects of this development on the economic system are obvious and recognized even by Soviet observers. Recently, repeated criticism has been voiced concerning the excessive specialization and departmentalism of the ministerial structure.[4] It remains to be seen whether Gorbachev will muster the energy and power necessary to break down the resistance of vested bureaucratic interests blocking the way to worthwhile administrative reforms.

The Intermediate Level

Apart from the prospects for administrative reform, increasing departmentalism enhances the importance of the intermediate level coordinating the individual economic branches. For structural reasons, however, the intermediate institutions are extremely deficient in meeting the growing requirements of coordination and control as well as in performing functions of policy initiation. At the same time, it is the intermediate level where some institutional reforms have been started in order to improve efficiency since the early 1980s.

The Central Committee apparatus is the institutional complex most close to the decision-making party bodies. Nevertheless, it is supposed to play a rather passive role, more reacting than acting, both while influencing decisions of the party leadership and supervising their implementation by government agencies.[5] This is especially true of the departments with economic responsibilities, which have been established in growing numbers since the reintroduction of the branch principle in 1948. They account for nearly half of the overall department structure. Today there are eleven Central Committee departments that may be classified as economic, but ten of them are responsible for larger economic branches corresponding to the jurisdiction of several ministries. As a consequence, the attitude of departmentalism has taken possession of the party apparatus itself, endangering its integrative functions. Obviously, the shortcomings in the economic apparatus of the Central Committee have been realized by the party leadership recently. Since 1980, and on a larger scale after Andropov's accession to power, organizational and personnel changes were introduced in order to strengthen the party apparatus and to enhance its efficiency.

Organizational changes affected first of all agriculture and related areas, where a Department for Agricultural Machine-Building was created in 1980, the Agricultural Department obtained responsibility for the food industry in 1983, and, at the same time, the Light Industry Department's sphere of competence was expressly defined as covering the production of consumer goods. More important than the improvements claimed for these departmental frontier adjustments was the upgrading of the only department of a general-functional nature in the field of the economy: at the end of 1982 the Planning and Financial Department was transformed into an Economic Department. Though we do not know exactly what the substance underlying the change of name was, it seems that the Economic Department has been assigned the task of coordinating and supervising the activities of all other departments with economic responsibilities. This assumption is underlined by the fact that the new department was placed under the leadership of Ryzhkov, appointed a Central Committee Secretary at the same time. In April 1985 Ryzhkov was promoted to become a full member of the Politbureau, by-passing the candidate rung on the ladder. Ryzhkov is, as mentioned before, an experienced industrial manager, who has only worked in economic administration for ten years, first in the Ministry for Heavy and Transport Machine Building and then as First Vice Chairman of Gosplan. He may be considered as the economic overlord in Gorbachev's entourage, adding considerable new weight to the rather low representation of the economic departments in the leading and integrating party bodies (see appendix I). Further personnel changes in the Central Committee apparatus since 1982 testify to Andropov's and Gorbachev's willingness to rouse the party bureacracy into more action.

In the sphere of State organization the Constitution declares the *Council of Ministers* to be the Government of the USSR, the highest administrative and executive body, which is to ensure, among other things, the direction of the economic development of the country. In fact, the Council of Ministers is absolutely incapable of performing any functions apart from integration of chief government administrators assembled in it.[6] Since World War II it has grown too big to be a workable decision-making body.[7] With its present membership of 115 meeting four times a year in plenary session, the Council of Ministers has nothing in common with a cabinet. As well as the heads of the main administrative agencies of the Soviet Union it also includes the chairmen of the fifteen Union Republican Councils of Ministers. As a consequence, the departmentalism and quarrels between administrative branches referred to above are further complicated by regional interests.

Under these circumstances a smaller working body is needed, which could perform cabinet functions. In fact, this has been the case since the beginning of Soviet power. Until 1937 it was the Council for Labour and Defence *(Sovet Truda i Oborony)*, and subsequently the Economic Council *(Ekonomsovet)*. In 1949 the *Presidium of the Council of Ministers* was created and since then this body has been expected to counterbalance departmentalistic and disintegrating tendencies within the Council of Ministers. The Presidium consists of about fifteen members who meet weekly and are charged with the coordination of related economic branches, handling certain economic complexes considered as topical, or special economic functions (see appendix IV). More than half of the members not only hold economic offices but made their career in economic management and administration. In fact, the Presidium functions under the guidance of the CPSU leadership as the economic cabinet of the Soviet Union. Nevertheless, its present composition does not augur well for policy initiatives beyond more or less successful coordination of economic administration. There are three major reasons for this, partly personnel and partly organizational in nature.

First of all there is the age structure. At the end of Chernenko's reign the average age of the Presidium members was sixty-nine years—a period of life that is commonly not considered the most innovative. Of course, gerontocracy is a general burden of the Brezhnev legacy that does not need further elaboration.

Secondly, on the basis of its composition at the end of the Chernenko era the potential economic expertise concentrated in the Presidium does not bear much political weight. Its leading personalities are either not very influential at the highest level of policy decision making or lack sufficient economic expertise.

Only three of the fifteen members belong to the highest policy-making body, the Politbureau. Apart from the economically competent but eighty-year old Premier, Tikhonov, who is by his very nature an administrator and not a politician, these are two First Vice Premiers: Foreign Minister Gromyko, who is the only member of the Presidium without any involvement in economic affairs, and Aliev who is a KGB professional with the limited and general economic experience gained as Party Chief of Azerbaidzhan in the years 1969–1982. The third First Vice Premier, Arkhipov, is a specialist in foreign economic relations and politically not very important. From among the remaining eleven Vice Premiers six made their career in economic management and government administration, exclusively, and may be considered as economic experts (Antonov, Baibakov, Dymshits, Martynov, Smirnov, Talyzin). Four members of the Presidium may be classified as party apparatchiks with some economic experience (Bodyul, Nuriev, Ryabov, Shcherbina), while scientist Marchuk is a special case. All the Vice Premiers are full members of the Central Committee. Though the professional quality of the Presidium may be satisfactory, more political influence at the highest level would be needed to enable it to perform the intermediate functions of an economic cabinet.

The third and most important reason for the functional deficiencies of the Presidium concerns its mode of operation. In order to improve and support the work of the Presidium, several auxiliary bodies have been set up in the course of time. During Stalin's reign a committee system was organized on a branch basis in such a way that each committee coordinated the activities of central government agencies managing related branches of economic or other fields of administration. Later on the committees of the Economic Council were transformed into bureaux attached to the Council of Ministers, but the branch principle existed until 1955. From 1955 onwards, the branch committee system was replaced by several commissions not based on a comprehensive scheme but created for special tasks perceived as urgent by the government of the day. From among the earlier commissions established during the Khrushchev era those for consumer goods, foreign economic questions, Comecon affairs and the military-industrial complex are supposed to exist even today.[8] In accordance with Brezhnev's intention, announced at the Central Committee plenum in October 1980, of concentrating on complex economic projects, several new commissions were created recently: for the West Siberian petroleum and gas complex (1981), for the agroindustrial complex (1982) and for environmental protection and the rational use of natural resources (1983). All these commissions reflect current economic priorities of the political leadership. They are called upon to help to implement particular policy decisions by applying the technique of massed concentration. Shifting priorities and project campaigns, however, are not an appropriate substitute for comprehensive economic concepts and reforms whose institutional basis is still lacking. Furthermore, there is another factor causing some scepticism. This concerns the structure of the commissions. Apart from the Commission for Questions of the Agroindustrial Complex, established in June 1982,[9] whose statute has been published,[10] no further information about the composition, functioning etc. of the commissions is available. The Agroindustrial Commission, headed by Deputy Premier Nuriev, is entrusted with decision-making powers and is to meet twice a month. It consists of fourteen heads of different government agencies with economic responsibilities, i.e. contradictions between branch interests may be supposed to be a main feature of its deliberations. If the composition of the Agroindustrial Commission is to be considered as representative,[11] it is doubtful whether the commissions of the Presidium can escape the danger of departmentalism.

Finally, very important coordinating tasks on the intermediate level are performed by the *major state committees* with functional jurisdiction such as Gosplan, Gossnab, Gosstandart, *Goskom po tsenam, Goskom nauki i tekhniki*. In recent times, the political leadership seems to believe that the best method of countering departmentalism is to enhance Gosplan's powers. The various changes to this effect started around 1979–1980 and were summarized and further developed by the new Gosplan Statute of 17 June 1982:[12] strengthening of coordinating powers, establishing of "administrations for complex planning" *(upravleniya po kompleksnomu planirovaniyu)* under the direction of a Deputy Chairman of Gosplan with subordinate departments for related branches of the economy, appointment of Gosplan agents in the economic regions,[13] etc. Additionally, under the aegis of Gosplan, inter-branch commissions have been created that are expected to deal with general questions of managing the economy which surpass the boundaries of ordinary planning. One of the most hopeful bodies of this kind is the Interdepartmental Commission for the Application of New Methods of Planning and Economic Incentives, which ought to give an impulse to the improvement of the whole economic mechanism.[14] All these measures may be appropriate to assert the interests of the national economy as a whole and to keep departmentalism under some control. On the other hand, Gosplan least of all can be expected to promote economic reforms going beyond the limits of a rationalized system of central economic planning and bureaucratic administration.

Some Conclusions

The political constitution of Soviet economy in the spring of 1985 may be summarized as follows:

1. On the highest level of policy decision making the economic factor is rather underrepresented.
2. On the lower level of economic administration a high degree of fragmentation and bureaucratic pluralism are the most striking phenomena.
3. On the intermediate level the political leadership has initiated some institutional changes in order to improve the coordination of economic branch activities and to concentrate upon certain economic projects deemed vital.
4. The institutional preconditions for more far-reaching economic reforms of the system of central planning and bureaucratic administration are lacking.
5. The main purpose of the ruling oligarchy and of the executive bureaucracy alike is the preservation of power. Economic institutions are instruments of political rule and not of policy making.

All these circumstances are not too favourable to Gorbachev should he have any intention of bringing about basic changes. Nevertheless, we must not lose sight of the fact that, under the thick and petrified institutional crust of the Soviet system, the spirit of autocracy is alive.

Notes

1. Schneider analysed the communiques published between December 1982 and December 1983 and found out that 39.2 percent of the topics referred to concerned foreign policy, 37.2 percent economic policy and 5 percent foreign economic relations. Se E. Schneider and A. Rahr, *Biographien der sowjetischen Politbüro-Mitglieder*, Sonderveröffentlichung des Bundesinstituts für ostwissenschaftliche und internationale Studien, Cologne, April 1984, p. 31.

2. Though numerous studies have been written about particular aspects of the CC of the CPSU, a comprehensive analysis is still lacking. Parallel insights into the functioning of the CC of the SED in the GDR can be gained from the doctoral thesis by V. H. Alt, "Die Stellung des Zentralkomitees der SED im politischen System der DDR," Würzburg University, 1985.

3. J. F. Hough and M. Fainsod, *How the Soviet Union Is Governed*, Cambridge, Mass., 1979, p. 386. For the professional background of the newcomers since Brezhnev's death, see E. Schneider, "Der Ministerrat der UdSSR unter Andropow und Tschernenko," *Berichte des Bundesinstituts für ostwissenschaftliche und internationale Studien*, No. 16/1985, pp. 18f, 32f.

4. See for example, B. P. Kurashvili, "Gosudarstvennoe upravlenie narodnym khozyaistvom: perspektivy razvitiya", *Sovetskoe gosudarstvo i pravo*, No. 6, 1982, pp. 38–48 (45ff); I. O. Bisher, "Sovershenstvovanie otraslevogo upravleniza," *Sovetskoe gosudarstvo i pravo*, No. 4, 1984, pp. 27–34 (29ff).

5. Hough and Fainsold, *op. cit.*, pp. 423, 435.

6. For a comprehensive monograph on the Council of Ministers, see G. P. van den Berg, *Organisation und Arbeitsweise der sowjetischen Regierung*, Baden-Baden, 1984. See G. P. van den Berg, "The Council of Ministers of the Soviet Union", *Review of Socialist Law*, 1980, pp. 293–323; E. Tomson, *Der Ministerrat der UdSSR*, Berlin, 1980.

7. Figures on personnel growth are given by B. Meissner in M. Fincke (ed.), *Handbuch der Sowjetverfassung*, Berlin, 1983, p. 961f.

8. The commissions for prices (1958–1965), for questions of capital investments (1959–1967) and for the coordination of transport (1962–1967) were abolished. See Berg, *op. cit.*, pp. 305 and 302, respectively, where the sources are given.

9. Decree of the Council of Ministers of 10 June 1982 (*Sobranie Postanovlenii SSSR 1982*, Part I, No. 19, Art. 101).

10. Statute confirmed by decree of the Council of Ministers of 30 September 1982 (*Sobranie Postanovlenni SSSR 1982*, Part I, No. 28, Art. 146).

11. This impression is confirmed by the former Commission for Prices, whose composition along the same branch lines was made known by the publication of its statute confirmed by decree of the Council of Ministers of 13 October 1958 (*Sobranie Postanovlenii SSSR 1958*, No. 17, Art. 135).

12. *Sobranie Postanovlenii SSSR 1982*, Part I, No. 20, Art. 102.

13. Statute on USSR Gosplan-agents for the economic regions of the USSR, confirmed by decree of the Council of Ministers of 29 September 1982 (*Sobranie Postanovlenii SSSR 1982*, Part I, No. 28, Art. 145).

14. *Khozyaistvennoe pravo*, (ed. V. V. Laptev), Moscow 1983, p. 211 f.

APPENDIX I

Representation of the Central Committee Apparatus in the Leading and Integrating Party Bodies

At present, the Central Committee apparatus consists of at least 24 departments, 11 of which (45.8%) serve economic purposes. The others are in the fields of party organization (4), international relations (3), culture (2), propaganda (2), internal security (1), and defence (1).

Central Committee Department Heads in Leading and Integrating Party Bodies

	PB-M	PB-C	CC-M	CC-C	CAC-M	None	Total
April 1971							
Economic departments	1	-	1	3	3	2	10
Non-economic departments	-	-	7	2	-	2	11
Total	1	-	8	5	3	4	21
March 1976							
Economic departments	1	-	1	4	4	-	10
Non-economic departments	-	1	7	2	-	1	11
Total	1	1	8	6	4	1	21
April 1981							
Economic departments	-	-	4	6	-	1	11
Non-economic departments	1	1	9	1	1	-	13
Total	1	1	13	7	1	1	24
March 1985							
Economic departments	-	-	3	7	-	1	11
Non-economic departments	-	1	9	1	2	-	13
Total	-	1	12	8	2	1	24

Central Committee Department Functionaries in Leading and Integrating Party Bodies

	PB-M	PB-C	CC-M	CC-C	CAC-M	None	Total
April 1971							
Economic departments	1	-	1	4	5		11
Non-economic departments	-	-	7	3	5		15
Total	1	-	8	7	10		26
March 1976							
Economic departments	1	-	1	5	5		12
Non-economic departments	-	1	7	6	5		19
Total	1	1	8	11	10		31
April 1981							
Economic departments	-	-	5	7	-		12
Non-economic departments	1	1	14	5	2		23
Total	1	1	19	12	2		35
March 1985							
Economic departments	-	-	4	7	-		11
Non-economic departments	-	1	11	5	3		20
Total	-	1	15	12	3		31

PB-M = Politbureau Member
PB-C = Politbureau Candidate
CC-M = Central Committee Member
CC-C = Central Committee Candidate
CAC-M = Central Auditing Commission Member

APPENDIX II

Representation of the Government Apparatus
in the Leading and Integrating Party Bodies

At present, the Council of Ministers consists of 115 persons occupying 119
positions: 29 of these positions are of general jurisdiction, 90 involve
the direction of an administrative agency. Seventy-four agencies (82.2%)
serve economic purposes; the others are in the fields of culture (9),
internal security (3), international relations (1), defence (1),
labour (1), and government organization (1).

Members of the Council of Ministers
Directing an Administrative Agency
in the Leading and Integrating Party Bodies

	PB-M	PB-C	CC-M	CC-C	CAC-M	None	Total
April 1971							
Economic agencies	-	-	38	14	3	9	64
Non-economic agencies	-	1	9	2	2	-	14
Total	-	1	47	16	5	9	78
March 1976							
Economic agencies	-	-	47	16	2	2	67
Non-economic agencies	3	1	7	3	-	-	14
Total	3	1	54	19	2	2	81
April 1981							
Economic agencies	-	-	47	18	7	1	73
Non-economic agencies	3	1	8	3	-	-	15
Total	3	1	55	21	7	1	88
March 1985							
Economic agencies	-	-	39	12	6	17	74
Non-economic agencies	1	2	7	2	-	4	16
Total	1	2	46	14	6	21	90

APPENDIX III

Representation of the Intelligentsia
in the Integrating Party Bodies

	CC-M	CC-C	CAC-M	Total	Share %
October 1961					
Total membership	175	155	65	395	
Intelligentsia	9	11	5	25	6.4
Science and culture	5	7	4	16	4.1
Economic management	4	4	1	9	2.3
April 1966					
Total membership	195	165	79	439	
Intelligentsia	12	6	7	25	5.7
Science and culture	7	3	5	15	3.4
Economic management	5	3	2	10	2.3
April 1971					
Total membership	241	155	81	477	
Intelligentsia	12	8	7	27	5.7
Science and culture	7	7	4	18	3.8
Economic management	5	1	3	9	1.9
March 1976					
Total membership	287	139	85	511	
Intelligentsia	14	11	7	32	6.3
Science and culture	8	10	4	22	4.3
Economic management	6	1	3	10	2.0
March 1981					
Total membership	319	151	75	545	
Intelligentsia	14	11	3	28	5.2
Science and culture	9	9	2	20	3.7
Economic management	5	2	1	8	1.5

APPENDIX IV

Presidium of the USSR Council of Ministers
(March 1985)

Special Position Occupied in CM

Chairman

  N. A. Tikhonov   (1905)

First Deputy Chairmen

  G. A. Aliev   (1923)

  I. V. Arkhipov   (1907)

  A. A. Gromyko   (1909)   Minister of Foreign Affairs (relieved of office in July 1985)

Deputy Chairmen

  A. K. Antonov   (1912)

  N. K. Baibakov   (1911)   Chairman of State Planning Committee (Gosplan) dismissed in May 1985

  I. I. Bodyul   (1918)

  V. E. Dymshits   (1910)   Chairman of the Presidium Commission for the Development of the West-Siberian Petroleum and Gas Complex

  G. I. Marchuk   (1925)   Chairman of the State Committee for Science and Technology; Chairman of Main Committee for Exhibition of Achievements of the National Economy of the USSR (VDNKh)

  N. V. Martynov   (1910)   Chairman of State Committee for Material and Technical Supply

  Z. N. Nuriev   (1915)   Chairman of the Presidium Commission for Environmental Protection and the Rational Use of Natural Resources; Chairman of the Presidium Commission for Questions of the Agroindustrial Complex

  Ya. N. Ryabov   (1928)   Chairman of the Presidium Commission for Foreign Economic Questions (?)

  L. V. Smirnov   (1916)   Chairman of the Military-Industrial Commission of the Presidium

  B. E. Shcherbina   (1919)

  N. V. Talyzin   (1929)   USSR Permanent Representative in Comecon; Chairman of Presidium Commission for Comecon Affairs (?)

Further Members

  not known

5
Economic Activities and the Intermediate and Lower Levels of Party Organisation

Peter Frank

The organisational characteristics of political parties tend to be determined by the surrounding political environment. In a society where the route to governmental power is through the ballot box, parties are organised in such a way as to maximise the chances of their winning elections. The most obvious evidence of this is to be found in the practice of creating grassroots (or primary) organisations that are coextensive with electoral districts. In systems where political activity is proscribed and elections non-existent, any party that tries to organise itself is inevitably illegal and must therefore place a high premium upon its own security (which, in turn, requires secrecy). If, at the same time, this revolutionary, clandestine party is seeking to overthrow the regime, then, in an industrial society, it makes sense for it to exert pressure where it is likely to hurt most: at the point of production. This, of course, is a thumb-nail sketch of the factors which lay behind the organisational principles of the Bolshevik party in Russia. From the perspective of the party, the centralised, hierarchical, military-type structure with its primary organisations (cells) situated in the workplace was a rational, not to say inevitable, response to the conditions prevailing in Russia towards the end of the nineteenth century.

Whatever the logic of such a structure when the party was in its oppositional, revolutionary phase, reasons for persisting with it once the Bolsheviks became the party of government after 1917 are not so immediately obvious. Yet if the workplace cell was effective in exerting pressure at the point of production in a negative, disruptive, destructive sense, why should that capacity to exert pressure not also be deployed to achieve positive, productive ends?

Marxism-Leninism lays great stress upon struggle and conflict. The word 'crisis' occurs frequently in its vocabulary. For most of its history, the party has been involved in struggle and crisis; sometimes self-generated crisis, sometimes crisis from without. First there was the 'crisis' of the revolution, then civil war and foreign intervention. The NEP afforded a brief breathing space (although here, too, the party was riven by internecine struggle for power), followed by the virtual civil war in the countryside that accompanied the collectivisation of agriculture, which in turn was intended to generate the capital necessary to industralise the USSR. As if these 'crises' were not enough, there was the terror of the 1930s, precursor, as it turned out, of the horror and destruction of the 1941–1945 war. Not that the long-suffering Soviet citizens were allowed any respite after 1945: they were plunged immediately into the gigantic task of post-war reconstruction.

Now the point of this résumé of Soviet development is that these events have resulted in the perpetuation of a political form of organisation that, certainly up to the 1950s, had proved to be extraordinarily successful. It was successful in that it had shown itself to be extremely effective in terms of achieving specified 'grand' goals (revolution, modernisation, winning wars). At the same time, and for systemic reasons, it was a system that was exceedingly wasteful and inefficient in both human and material terms.

Since Stalin's death, Soviet development has become much more complex. What great goals are there left to achieve? Aside from the vague and fairly meaningless goal of 'communism', what, in the foreseeable future, are Soviet citizens being asked to strive towards? Now that military parity with the West has been attained, the answer to these questions, it would seem, is: produce more meat, milk and butter; raise the standard of living; maintain the defensive capacity of the state. There is nothing wrong with such objectives; they are to be found in

most modern societies. What is different, however, is that the
political structures which in the past have proved to be so
effective (albeit wasteful and inefficient) are turning out to be
less and less appropriate for the resolution of the apparently
less grandiose but in practice much more intractable problem
of meeting the Soviet consumer's rising level of expectation.
Put simply, it is much easier, in the context of the 1930s, to
build canals, factories and blast furnaces (or, indeed, BAM today),
than it is in the 1980s to ensure a regular, year-round supply
of meat and vegetables and the kinds of articles of everyday
consumption that are taken for granted in most other industrial
societies.

The problem is that there are two levels of rationality. One
level suggests that the USSR should undertake some form of
thorough-going economic reform, particularly with regard to
price setting, which involves decentralisation of decision making
down to the level of the enterprise. Whatever economic sense
such moves might make, they would, at a different level of
rationality (that of the party), be nonsensical: the consequence
would be pressures to extend the forum of decision making
into other realms, which in turn would undermine the principle
of democratic centralism, which in its turn would erode the
leading role of the party, and so on.

If this hypothesis is correct, then it raises the question: what
kind of role should one expect local party organs to play with
respect to the economy? The answer, it would seem, is one in
which the party does its utmost to encourage the maximisation
of production, while at the same time asserting and exercising
its 'right' to control *(rukovodit')*, yet without assuming direct
responsibility. Part of the contradiction inherent in such a role
is hinted at in paragraph 42, sub-section (a) of the CPSU *Ustav,*
which places upon republic, krai, oblast, okrug, city and district
party organisations responsibility for: "political and organisational work amongst the masses, mobilising them to accomplish
the tasks of communist construction, the greatest possible development of industrial and agricultural production, [and] the
fulfilment and overfulfilment of state plans. . . ."

The reference here to 'overfulfilment of state plans' is indicative
of the tension that exists between party and enterprise manager.

As Alec Nove correctly and tirelessly reminds us, a properly planned economy would have no place in it for over- or underfulfilment: actually to encourage overfulfilment is to make a nonsense of planning, particularly since other parts of the economy are, at any given time, experiencing shortfalls in output. Moreover, not only does the enterprise manager not operate within the framework of market forces, he has also to balance against the unjunction to overfulfil the consideration that this year's overfulfilment is likely to be next year's norm. On the other hand, if he fails to meet his target, he is putting his own job in jeopardy or, at least, creating problems for himself (in that inability to pay bonuses to his workforce may lead to problems of labour recruitment, absenteeism, falling productivity, and so on).

It is sometimes assumed that, given the opportunity, Soviet enterprise managers would opt for a more rational, market-oriented economic system. Such an assumption may be incorrect. Soviet managers are managers precisely because they satisfy the criteria necessary to fill that post; namely, that they have displayed the appropriate "partyness" in their attitudes and have shown themselves to be competent according to the criteria imposed by the actually existing economic set-up. Alexander Yanov describes an interview he had with a Leningrad enterprise manager who is obviously appalled by the incompetence of the *de facto* superior political authority:

> Total dependence on officials who have different degrees of responsibility but are equally incompetent, the necessity of constantly humbling himself before people to whom he, the director, is only a pawn in their own careerist game—that is what enraged my general director more than anything else.[1]

Yet, as Yanov pionts out, the director could not function within the system were it not for the very officials whom he despises. Further evidence of the functional symbiosis that exists between managers and the party apparatus is to be found in the answers five directors gave to Yanov's discreet enquiry as to what percentage of managers as a whole they believed were seeking to participate actively in a "reconstruction" (reform) of the Soviet economy. What is surprising about the responses is not so much that they thought that seventy to seventy-five percent were not anxious to do this, but, rather, that twenty-five to thirty percent were. Still, if these estimates are appproximately correct, they do suggest a high degree of support for present arrangements, notwithstanding their manifest wastefulness and inefficiency.

So, what is the party's role vis-à-vis the economy at the local level? The party does not have the technical capacity to run the economy directly, nor would it be prudent for it to do so. Under the present arrangements, the party can (and does) claim credit for economic performance when things go right, and is able to shift direct responsibility onto the industrial administrative apparatus when things go wrong. In other words, the party in effect rationally calculates the 'cost' of inefficiency against the 'cost' of relinquishing its monopoly over decision making. That being so, the party has to assume responsibility, at least tacitly, for coping with the negative consequences of a relationship which is rational in terms of power relations, but irrational in terms of economic efficiency. In other words, the party is the fixer, the facilitator, the gadfly that buzzes about the managers, sometimes smoothing the way and unstopping bottlenecks, sometimes hectoring and exhorting them to greater efforts.

Towards the end of 1983 and in the first two months of 1984, the party's regional committees met in plenary sessions to elect or re-elect their first secretaries and to receive obkom reports. Accounts of these gatherings, as printed in *Pravda*, afford an up-to-date opportunity to see what local party organisations' current economic concerns are, and to see what evidence they provide in support of the foregoing analysis.

E. Murav'ev, first secretary of Kuibyshev obkom, reported[2] the beneficial effects of the then current emphasis upon discipline: production in the period under review was up by a billion rubles (no base figure mentioned) and this was attributable entirely to increased productivity.

There had been a failure to reduce the number of enterprises not fulfilling plans or agreements; scientific-technical innovation had not in many enterprises resulted in a reduction in the size of the labour force, thus releasing workers to other plants in the Middle Volga region where demand for labour is considerable. Replacement of "physically and morally outdated" technology was proceeding too slowly. Party organisations must pay closer attention to publicising examples of good work, and the collective contract system must be extended, but not too hastily, as that would be counter-productive. The goal was (the slogan comes from an Andropov speech) an across-the-board increase in productivity of one percent, and a half percent reduction in costs. Large heavy-industry enterprises must be encouraged to produce more consumer goods. Finally, in order to strengthen discipline and improve organisation, enterprise management must become more involved in "ideological planning"; this, it had been shown, resulted in less absenteeism.

It is not difficult to see why enterprise managers are unlikely to relish the prospect of reducing their labour force in a system where end-of-month, end-of-quarter, end-of-year "storming" is the standard pattern. Nor will re-equipment of plant seem an attractive prospect if it interrupts the rhythm of production and requires re-training of a not especially enthusiastic labour force which stands to lose bonuses. Similarly, what is the incentive for the manager (and workers) of a heavy industrial enterprise to divert resources, human and material, to the manufacture of articles of everyday consumption? And is a manager really likely to welcome having "ideological" responsibility for improved labour relations thrust upon him?

The Kuibyshev first secretary's report illustrates nicely the local party's concerns vis-à-vis locally based industry. But the local party bodies also have a brokerage role to play with respect to the central party and governmental authorities. This is what an engine driver from Sverdlovsk passenger depot had to say at the Sverdlovsk oblast conference:

We have antiquated electric trains; every third station in our oblast is dilapidated. Sverdlovsk mainline station was built in 1928. How many decrees and orders have been issued by the Ministry of the Means of Communication, how many oral assurances and promises have there been about construction and repairs, and so on! Yet the situation remains the same. I know how people curse us, the railwaymen. And it serves us right: transport difficulties waste more than just time. . . .[3]

The implication is that the party obkom should intercede (with the ministry? the transport department of the Central Committee Secretariat?) to try to get something done.

Similarly, at the Chelyabinsk oblast party conference[4] much attention was devoted to the need to re-equip and reconstruct many ferrous metal enterprises, including the giant Magnitogorsk Combine ("Magnitka"), where breakdown of the production process was frequent: "fundamental renewal of enterprises and a transition to new technological processes" is what is needed. "Nevertheless, the USSR Ministry of Ferrous Metallury has so far not taken a clear decision on the timetable for reconstructing this enterprise". Again, the implication is that the obkom should chivvy the ministry into taking a favourable decision and putting the work in hand.

One could go on multiplying examples: the point is that the party's role is to facilitate, rather than to engage in production directly. To that extent, the party plays a functional role; yet it is functional only because the party itself has created a system that is inherently wasteful and inefficient. Former Soviet citizens go further than this and claim that the party treats the means of production as its own property. Yanov describes how an enterprise director goes about obtaining materials that are in short supply. The director telephones the obkom first secretary:

He is the only person who has the authority and power to order an all-Union dragnet, so to speak, for scarce raw materials. He alone can call . . . the Masters of other provinces and offer them a deal. He always has in reserve some raw material that is in short supply in another province, and there is always an opportunity to exchange it for what 'his enterprises' need at any given time. This makes it clearly evident who bears the final responsibility, so to speak, for the fate of industry in the province, for the life or death of any of its enterprises—in other words, who is their actual *owner*. It is the first secretary of the province committee. . . .[5]

The superiority of party functionary over enterprise manager derives, as we have seen, from the party's monopoly of the *rukovodstvo* function. In practical terms, the relationship is expressed in the nomenklatura mechanism. An authoritative party manual, taking Novosibirsk, a city with over a million inhabitants, as its example, describes the gorkom nomenklatura thus:

> Included [in the nomenklatura] are the secretaries and heads of departments of the bourgh raikoms, chairmen and deputy chairmen of the executive committees of borough soviets, *directors, chief engineers and secretaries of party committees of major industrial enterprises and construction sites,* heads of higher educational institutions, and other responsible officials (Emphasis added).[6]

The point here is that the gorkom first secretaryship and the directorship of a major enterprise are both nomenklatura appointments; but with two important differences. The gorkom first secretaryship is a party office that falls within the nomenklatura of a higher standing party organ, the obkom (whereas the directorship is a non-party post on a party nomenklatura); and, secondly, the gorkom first secretaryship is not only a nomenklatura appointment itself, it is also a post which carries with it power to appoint to other nomenklatura posts, both party and non-party. No such power attaches to the enterprise directorship.[7] This arrangement may be anomalous, in the sense that it does not follow necessarily that the "appointing" party official is technically and managerially more competent than the "appointed" enterprise director; yet the *de facto* political superiority of the former invites intrusion upon the rights of the latter. The following example may serve to illustrate this aspect of the relationship between party and enterprise.

The Lenin Metallurgical Combine in Magnitogorsk, "Magnitka", occupies first place in the USSR for the production of steel and second place for pig iron. With a labour force of sixty-three thousand (of whom nine thousand, 14.28 percent, are communists), it contains a primary party organisation more numerous and intrinsically more important than many district party organisations.[8]

The present director, L. V. Radyukevich, was appointed to that post in September 1979 at the age of forty-seven. Two years later, at the XXVI congress, he was named a candidate member of the CPSU Central Committee. A graduate of Magnitogorsk Mining and Metallurgical Institute, he began his professional career in 1955 at the combine and over the next fiteeen years he was successively a metal roller (*prokatchik*), foreman and workshop head. Party membership had come in 1959; in 1970 he was made chief metal roller and later deputy chief engineer for the entire combine. In 1977 Radyukevich was transferred to Moscow where for the next two years he headed a department in the all-Union Ministry of Ferrous Metallurgy; then it was back to Magnitogorsk as overall director of the combine.

The political standing of the directorship of Magnitka is high. D. P. Galkin, Radyukevich's predecessor from 1973 to 1979, was awarded full membership of the CPSU Central Committee at the XXV congress in 1976. However, following his appointment to the post of first deputy minister of ferrous metallurgy (in professional terms, ostensibly a promotion) in 1981 he lost his Central Committee status completely, being accorded only membership of the Central Review Commission.

Like Radyukevich, Galkin also had a long background of varied professional training. After graduation from Magnitogorsk Mining Institute in 1950, he returned to the Magnitogorsk Mining Concentrates Combine (which he had joined as a worker in 1943 at the age of seventeen) and was successively electrician, shift leader, workshop head, chief metal roller and chief engineer. Next came a spell as secretary of the combine's party committee before moving to Magnitka as its director. In other words, both men had had long professional careers which had given them experience of a variety of key production processes. How does this compare with their political superior, the "appointing" regional party first secretary?

From 1970 to January 1984 the Chelyabinsk obkom first secretary was M. G. Voropaev, a full member of the CPSU Central Committee since 1971. Apart from a two-year course at the Central Committee's higher party school in Moscow from 1958 to 1960, Voropaev's training consisted of attendance at the Rostov Railway Transport Institute, from which he had graduated at the age of twenty-two in 1941. Three years as an engine driver, five years as a Komsomol official, followed by another five years on the railways before embarking upon a full-time party career do not encourage one to think of his having professional skills superior to those of the two directors. What Voropaev did have, of course, was the political "clout" both to interfere in industrial matters whenever he felt it necessary and to use his influence to the advantage of the enterprise should problems arise. Once again, there are hints of the ambivalent relationship between party and the economy at local level.

Nowhere is party interference (*podmena*) more prevalent than in agriculture. Some indication of the party's domination of the agricultural sector is contained in a breakdown of the Kursk party obkom's nomenklatura. Since detailed references to nomenklatura are pretty infrequent, this passage, taken from a recent authoritative publication, is perhaps worth citing in full:

> Take, for example, the nomenklatura of Kursk CPSU obkom. Included in it are 1,840 posts, two thirds of which belong to the basic, and one third to the register-control nomenklatura. Twenty-six percent of the obkom nomenklatura are party officials. These are the apparat of the oblast committee, secretaries, heads and deputy heads of departments of party gorkoms and raikoms, and secretaries of major primary organisation party committees. A significant part of the nomenklatura (22 percent) consists of soviet cadres: leading officials of the oblast soviet executive committee, oblast boards and departments, and chairmen and deputy chairmen of city and district soviet executive committees. About four percent of nomenklatura offices are occupied by trade union and Komsomol cadres; twelve percent are cadres in industry, construction, transport and communications. The most numerous group of nomenklatura posts (36 percent) consists of officials in agriculture, including heads of oblast organisations, chairmen of *RAPO* [district agroindustrial organisations], directors of state farms, chairmen of collective farms, and so on.[9]

Any pretence that the collective-farm sector enjoys any real independence or autonomy is dropped whenever the all-Union party leadership decrees a major new policy for agriculture, whether that policy is sensible and potentially beneficial or not. The decision announced at the October 1984 Central Committee plenum to embark upon a long-term programme of irrigation and land drainage is a topical case in point.

Even before the programme is under way, the shortcomings are being exposed, most of them deriving from the producers' sense of not being "masters" (*khozyainy*) of their own affairs. Yet it is clear that the irrigation campaign will be just that, a campaign, under the direct and active *kontrol'* of the party, locally and from the centre; even though agriculture (still more than industry) is not amenable to external political and administrative inputs at the farm level.

General Secretary Chernenko's speech to the plenum made some general mention of present shortcomings; then prime minister Tikhonov, the other main speaker, revealed problems so disconcerting as to make the reader wonder what point there was in embarking upon new major initiatives without first having made present measures effective. This impression was reinforced three days later when *Pravda* published an article signed by a kolkhoz brigade leader in Krasnodar region, A. Babenko.[10] At the microcosmic level of the individual collective farm, it amounted to a virtual point-by-point critique of the macrocosmic programme formulated by the top party leadership.

Babenko's is a successful kolkhoz: "respectable harvests, no debts to the state, profitable". Lying as it does in a moisture-deficient, black-earth region where irrigation is necessary in dry years, the farm was long ago persuaded of the merits of irrigation. "However", says the brigadier, "let us evaluate what has been achieved from the perspective of the demands set out in comrade K. U. Chernenko's speech at the CC CPSU plenum."

Although yields have improved, they could be better. Thousands of hectares are under irrigation. Over the years much irrigation equipment has become obsolete "both morally [?] and physically". Some machines (the *Volzhanka*, for example) are difficult to use on long-stemmed crops such as maize, and since twenty-one of the farm's thirty-five sprinklers are *Volzhanki* there is an obvious problem (especially as, despite available funds to buy better equipment, "they won't let us" because of supply shortages). So inefficient is the *Volzhanka* that at best ten machines can irrigate at most about thirty hectares a day. In any case, as the article mentions later, there are no simple-to-manage, reliable, cheap machines to be had, for, despite the claims made for the new *Kuban* sprinkler, "it is no secret that the first batch have design faults".

Who does one turn to when things go wrong? Breakages in the irrigation system are frequent: pipes fracture, then pumps fail. Sprinklers are serviced by branches of Selkhoztekhnika, the irrigation network by a special section of the Kurgan irrigation board, while running repairs are done by the Krasnodar water system repair and construction board. The farm would like to make improvements, "but they tell us: 'There are no spare parts'".

"Another thing bothers us", complains Babenko. "For some reason the person who actually works the land [*zemledelets*] is 'excommunicated' from the design and construction of irrigation projects". Then Babenko goes on to cite the example of when Krasnodar water board came along and dug up a newly-laid piped water course that had cost tens of thousands of rubles and substituted different piping, the original materials having been of poor quality, badly laid, and with faulty joints. "It's underground, so on one will see it" had evidently been the response of the board's employees.

Such attitudes are apparently widespread and *beskontrol'nost'* is costing the state dear: "Mention waste and the answer you get is, why bother about kopeks: the kolkhoz isn't paying". An example of the consequences of this attitude is: "They build a pumping station by the Kuban river. Comes the time to test the irrigation network and . . . no water. A mistake, they say, has occurred. But someone did the research, made the calculations, drew up and approved the project. Yet the guilty person isn't found".

What does the kolkhoz brigade leader conclude from all this (assuming, that is, that Babenko did indeed absorb the General Secretary's speech, write a lengthy article, get it to Moscow to be read and approved by the editors, passed by the censorship, set up in print and published in *Pravda* just three days later!)? "Haste, failure to think things through, have led already to well-known undesirable consequences. To repeat mistakes is inept". Yet there appears to be very little scope for the kolkhozniki themselves to decide what is best in the light of local conditions. Hence, a consistent theme is the agricultural producers' seeming helplessness in the face of "them". Nor is the ameliorating "symbiosis" of party and producer so much in evidence in the agricultural sector as it is in the industrial. Material inputs, while important, are markedly less effective than human inputs. As Babenko points out, it is often the case that better results are obtained on unirrigated land, the decisive factor being the attitude of those working it. It is remarkable that more than half a century after collectivisation he finds it necessary to say that successful teams "in a peasant way" have a caring relationship with the land: *"po krest'yanski zabotlivo otnosyatsya zemledel'tsy k polyu"*.

It is the sheer complexity of the network of administrative relationships, formal and informal, that binds the production enterprise so tightly as to stifle initiative and militate against efficiency, as conventionally measured.

The factory stands at the base of a strictly centralised, hierarchical pyramid at the apex of which is the ministry. Naturally, the ministry is concerned primarily with maximising the output of its enterprises, for it is upon this that its own performance will be judged. On the other hand, the party at the local level must concern itself with political matters, although not, of course, to the exclusion of economic. It must, for example, involve itself in the ideological "upbringing" *(vospitanie)* of the labour force, maintain a watch over the moral climate in the factory (as well as morale), be responsible for "patriotic" activities, the induction of youth into the enterprise by arranging various forms of secular ritual, as well as controlling the cadres selection process and exercising *kontrol'* generally. And it may well be that these multifarious activities impede, rather than enhance, the actual production process itself.

If the involvement of the party organisations in the enterprise becomes too intrusive, then the director may decide to bypass the local party committee and appeal directly to the obkom, the regional party organ. Indeed, in the case of an enterprise of all-Union importance (such as, for example, the Kirov works in Leningrad), the director may well have access directly to the Department of Heavy Industry in the all-Union Central Committee Secretariat at the centre.

Many of the myriad linkages between enterprise, ministry, local soviet, and party could be dispensed with were market mechanisms substituted for administrative. But, as argued above, to do that would be to erode the party's leading role and its monopoly of political power; thus, any radical reform of the system is extremely unlikely. In that connection, it will be interesting to see how far the new General Secretary, Gorbachev, will be prepared to go. The early signs are that he will try to tackle the problem by attempting to make the present system work better (albeit accompanied by modest reform of the economic mechanism), notably by purging corrupt, inefficient and incompetent cadres and replacing them with more dynamic, technocratic appointees. Unless, however, he is prepared to permit a considerable degree of decision-making autonomy at the level of the individual enterprise it is likely that inertia will reassert itself.

The relationship between party and economy at the local level is determined by the nature of the salient characteristics of the Soviet political system. These include such features as democratic centralism, the leading role of the party, the nomenklatura system, and the division of the process of government into discrete elements with the party monopolising the *rukovodstvo* role. The party is neither capable nor willing to assume *directly* responsibility for the actual management of the economy, yet, for the reasons just given, it cannot afford to stand aside entirely from the production process. To that extent, its role is facilitating; but in the agricultural sector, under pressure of consumer demand, and lacking competent expertise, its interference in production is more harmful than useful. It is an economic system which traditionally has been effective but wasteful. That wastefulness, in the party's terms, is more than offset by the political advantages that derive from the arrangement. Whether that is so in the agricultural sector is increasingly doubtful. The party, where it comes face to face with the people—that is, at the points of production and consumption—is nowadays hard put to it to justify its preeminent position.

That it will continue to occupy that position there is little doubt: there are too many non-material supports for the regime in Soviet society for it to be otherwise.

Notes

1. Alexander Yanov, *Detente after Brezhnev* (Berkeley: University of California Institute of International Studies, 1977), p. 26.
2. *Pravda,* 27 January 1984
3. *Pravda,* 24 January 1984.
4. *Pravda,* 23 January 1984.
5. Ianov, *Detente after Brezhnev,* op. cit., p. 24. Emphasis is in the original.
6. *Lektsii po partiinomu stroitel'stvu* (Moscow: Politizdat, 1971), pp. 328–330.
7. This important and perceptive distinction was made by Dr. W. Brus in discussion at a seminar held at the London School of Economics on 23 October 1984. Responsibility for placing it in its present context is, of course, mine.
8. Information about the Lenin Metallurgical Combine, and the biographical data that follow, are drawn variously from: E. Z. Razumov, *Problemy kadrovoi politiki KPSS* (Moscow: Politizdat, 1983), p. 38 *passim; Ezhegodnik BSE 1981; Deputaty Verkhovnogo soveta SSR* (desyatzi sozyv) (Moscow, 1979), pp. 97, 102.
9. Razumov, *Problemy kadrovoi politiki KPSS,* p. 60. Razumov is a deputy head of the CC CPSU Secretariat's Department of Organisational Party Work. I am grateful to Mr. Martin Nicholson for drawing my attention to this important source of information on nomenklatura.
10. *Pravda,* 26 October 1984.

6
Economic and Political Aspects of the Military-Industrial Complex in the USSR

Christopher Davis

Introduction

Every nation in the world maintains state-financed armed forces for protection against external and internal threats. The military is supplied by national industries, which also have close links with the government. In consequence, virtually all societies possess a system of interconnected military, political and economic institutions that strives to promote national security. This system can be described as a military-industrial complex.[1]

Although military-industrial complexes are universal, there is considerable variation in their institutional features, scale, role in the economy, and political character as well as in the related national security decision-making process. In order to identify the unique features of a nation's military-industrial complex and to explain its behavioural pattern, a combined multidisciplinary institutional, theoretical and empirical analysis is required.

Western analysts have been writing about the Soviet "military-industrial complex" for the past fifteen years, and about the defense sector in the USSR for much longer.[2] Their research has overcome formidable obstacles imposed by Soviet secrecy and censorship and has provided much useful information. However, a review of the literature indicates that considerable uncertainty still exists about the role of the military-industrial complex in economic and political processes in the USSR.

Given the importance of the topic of the Soviet military-industrial complex and the magnitude of the past research effort in this area it is obvious that a short conference paper can at best make a limited contribution. Accordingly, this paper has four rather modest objectives. First, it outlines a simple model of the military-industrial complex in order to identify major institutions and their relationships. Second, an attempt is made to use this model to clarify the Soviet national security decision-making process. In particular, it is argued that an improvement in the national security of the USSR would not require increased defense spending. It could be made through arms control and economic reform. Third, an effort is made to sketch out the ideal characteristics of political and economic theories of the Soviet military-industrial complex. Fourth, a brief review is made of the empirical evidence about trends in Soviet national security and the defense sector during the past decade.

The Military-Industrial Complex in the USSR

The military-industrial complex in the USSR is made up of a variety of political and economic institutions which have as their overall, common objective the enhancement of the country's national security. These institutions have both hierarchical and horizontal linkages which influence their behaviour and national security decision making.[3]

The conventional political science approach to the description of the Soviet military-industrial complex concentrates on the vertical relationships between key institutions. At the top of the hierarchy is the Politbureau. It is assisted in decision making about defense and other related issues by the Central Committee Secretariat, which has a Department of Defense Industry and also links with the Main Political Administration of the Armed Forces.[4] The highest body devoted specifically to national security is the Defense Council, which is made up of a small number of top party, state and military officials.[5] It decides upon national security objectives, military doctrine and development plans for the military-industrial complex.

Most of the detailed planning and management of the military-industrial complex is carried out by state organisations subordinate to the Council of Ministers of the USSR, such as the

Ministry of Defense, the defense industries and military R & D institutions. A high-level inter-departmental Military Industrial Commission coordinates their activities.[6]

In order to describe the lower levels of the military-industrial complex and the national security decision-making process it is useful to consider the horizontal linkages between major institutions. Diagram 6.1 presents a simple model of these interconnections. It shows not only the institutions but also how they contribute to the production of national security.

The diagram shows that the final output of activities of the Soviet military-industrial complex, at least in theory, is the state of national security.[7] This is a rather difficult output to measure since it is non-material and surrounded by considerable uncertainty. Nevertheless, it can be assumed that the top Soviet leadership does attempt to make periodic objective and subjective assessments of trends in this output indicator.

National security (N) is a function of both the external threat environment (T) and Soviet military capabilities (M). So $N=f(T,M)$. Assume that N is a decreasing function of T and an increasing function of M. That is, if M is constant but the external environment becomes more (less) threatening then N deteriorates (improves). Conversely, if T remains constant but the capabilities of the armed forces improve (worsen) the national security is enhanced (undermined).

The external threat environment of the USSR is influenced primarily by military developments in other nations, but global political and economic trends are also important.[8] As a general rule, phenomena such as improvements in NATO's capabilities, increased US defense spending, the election of conservative governments and growth recovery in capitalist countries, effective reforms in the People's Republic of China and political instability in Eastern Europe would raise the threat level. On the other hand, unilateral Western disarmament, economic stagnation in the OECD region, and intra-NATO arguments would reduce the threat.[9]

Military capability is produced by the Soviet military, which is a branch of the service sector of the economy (or the "non-productive sphere" in Soviet theory).[10] The military is responsible

Diagram 6.1. The Soviet Military-Industrial Complex

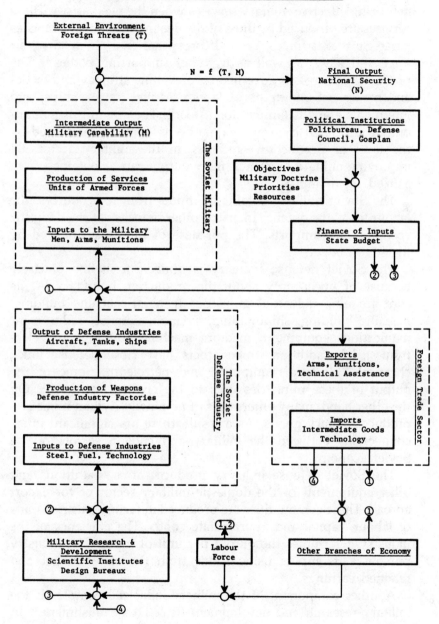

for maintaining planned levels of combat readiness and for delivering effective military services when the need arises. These services are produced by units of the five major military branches (strategic rocket forces, ground forces, national air defense, air force and navy) as well as by other supporting bodies.[11] The production process is governed by prevailing strategy and tactics and makes use of inputs of labour, capital (tanks, ships) and intermediate goods (ammunition, food). The amount of military output generated by a given quantity of input is influenced by the level of production efficiency in the military sector. By improving military efficiency, more output can be obtained from a fixed set of inputs.

The Soviet military obtains its inputs from four sources: the labour force, the defense industry, other branches of the domestic economy, and imports. The purchase of inputs is financed by the state budget.

The Soviet defense industry is difficult to define precisely because of uncertainty about the production boundary. At its core are nine industrial ministries (general machine building, machine building, shipbuilding, aviation, defense, radio, communications equipment, medium machine building, and electronics).[12] In addition, three others have close defense links: chemicals, electrical equipment and petroleum. Some of the output of these ministries goes to the civilian economy.[13] On the other hand, many enterprises of nominally civilian ministries produce military goods. As a result, there are significant interconnections between the military and civilian sectors of the Soviet economy.

The Soviet defense industry produces arms, munitions and other equipment for the domestic military sector or for export abroad. These commodities are produced in factories using inputs of labour, capital and intermediate goods. The efficiency of the industry determines the output per unit of input. The industry purchases its inputs using funds from the state budget and retained earnings.

Another component of the military-industrial complex is the military research and development (R & D) establishment.[14] In reality this is not an independent sector. Instead, the institutes and design bureaux are subordinate to diverse authorities including the military, defense industries, and the Academy of Sciences of the USSR. Nevertheless, it is useful to consolidate them for the purposes of this model.

The military R & D sector produces non-material services (such as designs) and commodity prototypes for the defense sector and carries out related theoretical and experimental scientific investigations and product testing. Production takes place within the sector's institutes, design bureaux and laboratories using inputs of labour, capital and intermediate goods. Here too, efficiency standards affect the output-input ratio. The state budget finances most purchases of the sector's supplies.

The Soviet military-industrial complex also has a foreign trade sector.[15] Exports of military equipment, munitions and technical military assistance services (not shown in the diagram) serve multiple functions. First, they strengthen socialist allies and the Warsaw Pact. Second, they support numerous revolutionary movements in the capitalist world which divert Western attention and resources. Third, arms sales are major sources of ruble and hard-currency export earnings.[16] Fourth, sales in foreign markets enable the defense industry to lengthen production runs, which in turn lowers unit costs, improves efficiency and increases enterprise profits. The Soviet Union imports military equipment and technology from its Warsaw Pact partners. This feeds into the military, defense industry, and the R & D sector. In addition, the USSR imports militarily-related goods and services from the West.[17] Legitimate transactions are carried out by the foreign trade organisations of the Ministry of Foreign Trade. However, CoCom and national restrictions by Western nations on technology transfer hinder legal trade.[18] To compensate for this interference, the Soviet Union employs the specialised import services of the KGB and GRU. These agencies ensure regular access by the Soviet military-industrial complex to the latest Western "secret" plans and technology.[19]

Having described the basic institutions of the military-industrial complex, it is now appropriate to reconsider the role of the top political leadership. In theory, the Politbureau, Defense Council and other organs are responsible for establishing the nation's long-term objectives and the military doctrine which will guide its actions in the event of war.[20] The leadership also sets out provisional short- and medium-term targets for national security as well as for the outputs of the various sectors of the military-industrial complex. However, at any given time the Soviet government has other non-military objectives and limited resources. During the formation of final plans it assesses the relative benefits of alternative patterns of resource allocation. Eventually a decision is taken on the final plan variant, which sets output targets and assigns labour inputs and material supplies to the various sectors of the economy.[21] An appropriate state budget is drawn up to finance planned activities and transactions.

Soviet National Security Decision Making

The production of national security in the USSR is a complex process that involves the interaction of numerous variables. Increases in the level of national security can be achieved through a variety of policies that influence either external threats or Soviet military capabilities. Given the nature of the production process shown in Diagram 1, the Soviet Union could adopt a strategy of enhancing national security without raising defense spending.

In order to understand how this could be accomplished, assume that the Soviet national security production process is functioning in a political and economic system which corresponds to a simple totalitarian model. That is, decision-making power is consolidated at the top and subordinate units follow orders without resistance. Assume further that the top leadership has a properly defined, measurable, national security output function. Leaders feed into this function their assessments of changes in the external threat environment and Soviet military capabilities. Finally, assume that there is imperfect information about threats, and a resulting bias toward worst-case thinking, but perfect information about the Soviet military.

Given these assumptions, suppose the Defense Council assesses the current state of national security (N_o), finds it inadequate, and recommends that it be increased to (N^*). This is accepted by the Politbureau and orders go out that by the end of the next plan period the national security indicator should

TABLE 6.1.   Soviet Policy Options to Enhance National Security

Objective: Improve National Security Without Increasing Defense Expenditure

Option 1:   Reduce External Threat

    1.   Make policy objectives less ambitious

    2.   Upgrade Warsaw Pact alliance

    3.   Undermine Western alliances and individual national defense efforts

    4.   Improve information gathering about the capabilities and intentions of potential opponents

    5.   Reach agreement on arms control

Option 2:   Improve Military Capabilities

    1.   Alter strategy and tactics

    2.   Raise efficiency of production of military services

    3.   Raise efficiency of defense industries

    4.   Raise efficiency of non-defense industries

    5.   Raise efficiency of domestic military R & D

    6.   Increase arms exports to achieve economies of scale in production

    7.   Improve R & D - related intelligence gathering

    8.   Increase imports of military-related commodities from socialist allies

be at N^*. That is $N^* = N_o + \Delta N$, $\Delta N > Q$. However, the stipulation is made that this should not entail higher defense spending.

On the assumption that the leadership is rational and moderately competent, it then realises that there are several ways in which the constrained objective can be attained. Basic option one is to hold military capabilities constant but reduce the external threat. Option two is to raise military capabilities while confronted by a constant threat (see Table 6.1).

If the option to reduce the threat level is selected, then several policies can be chosen. First, long-term strategic objectives could be modified to make them less ambitious and more easily attainable. Although Soviet strategic thinking is influenced by Marxist-Leninist ideology, there have been periodic revisions of military doctrine.[22] Even if the Soviet Union has a long-term expansionist strategy, it could decide that the current correlation of forces was unfavourable and revise downward its medium-term objectives. This would reduce the perceived external threats to the attainment of its more modest goals.[23]

A second type of threat reduction policy would be one which attempted to build up or undermine alliances. In the former case, efforts could be made to improve Warsaw Pact effectiveness by raising the military capabilities of East European allies through pressure on them to increase defense spending or production efficiency. In the latter case, the Soviet Union could encourage by various means conflict between and within capitalist countries in order to undermine NATO or national military capabilities. One tactic, discussed in recent articles by Hannes Adomeit and Gerhard Wettig, is to promote divisions between Western Europe and the US through propaganda campaigns capitalising on policy differences between western governments or public anxieties about peace.[24] A third policy could be to upgrade the intelligence-gathering effort in order to obtain better information about the intentions of potential opponents and alliances.[25] A final policy option would be to engage in serious arms control negotiations and reach agreement on measures to restrain the growth of weapons and military capabilities. This could reduce outside threats and the cost of military R & D and weapons procurement within the USSR.[26]

The second major option is to select policies which raise Soviet military capabilities without incurring additional expenses. In order to accomplish this, one possible policy would be to improve the efficiency of production of military services, keeping input costs constant.[27] This could be achieved by better management and rationalisation, military reorganisation, or substitution between inputs. Second, the USSR could raise the production efficiency of the defense industries so more output could be produced from a given allocation of resources.[28] This would enable the industry to supply the military sector with more weapons at lower cost. These efficiency improvements could come from reforms in planning, management, enterprise organisation or incentives. A third policy option related to the previous one is to improve the efficiency of military R & D and technological innovation. In various papers Ron Amann discusses appropriate R & D reform measures.[29] This would result in improvements in the quality of defense industry output, and subsequently in enhanced military capabilities, as well as in greater efficiency in industrial production processes. A fourth option, also reform-related, is to improve the efficiency of the civilian economy which provides inputs to the military-industrial complex. An effective civilian economy reform would enable the military-industrial complex to obtain more and higher quality inputs for a constant budget outlay, and would thereby contribute to an improved military capability.

Improvements in the foreign trade sector of the military-industrial complex could make a contribution to enhanced military capabilities. The Soviet Union could increase exports of weapons in order both to achieve economies of scale in production and to earn more foreign trade rubles and hard currency.[30] The extra earnings generated by these sales could be used to cover costs of two types of imports. First, the hard currency budgets of the KGB and GRU abroad could be raised in order to enhance their ability to purchase secret military R & D information and sub-systems (or complete copies) of new NATO weapons. Second, extra ruble earnings could offset the cost of additional imports of designs, components or weapons from CMEA countries.

This review of the Soviet military-industrial complex suggests that even if the USSR is run by a fairly rational, totalitarian government intent on raising its national security, this does not imply a commitment to increase the defense budget. Indeed, the model outlined in this paper suggests that such a government would be prepared to consider seriously policies of arms control and domestic economic reform.

Political and Economic Models of the Soviet Military-Industrial Complex

The simple totalitarian model of the Soviet political and economic system alluded to above does not now, and probably never did, correspond to reality in the USSR. This model has proved durable in spite of contradictory evidence because it is neat, comprehensible and ideologically convenient. However, even under Stalin the Soviet Union was less atomised and centrally controlled than has been suggested by Western analysts belonging to the totalitarian school. Instead, a situation existed of imperfect central control, bureaucratic rivalry (or interest-group conflict), and a fair degree of anarchy in production.[31] This general conclusion appears to be supported by available evidence from specific empirical studies of the Soviet military-industrial complex.[32]

Consider again Diagram 6.1 and the role of the political leadership in managing and planning the military-industrial complex. Although the Politbureau *et al.* are nominally in charge, the imperfect state of their knowledge about the world prevents them from making independent, rational decisions. The leaders are uncertain not only about the state of external threats, but also about real military capabilities and the level of national security. Given this, it is difficult for them to decide "how much is enough?"[33] In order to make such a decision, it is necessary for them to obtain assistance from the specialists in the different sectors of the military-industrial complex.

The first of these is the Soviet military. Evidence from the 1930s to 1984 suggests that there has been an uneasy relationship between senior military officers and the party leadership due to differing conceptions of the place of the military in society, military doctrine and strategy, and resource allocation patterns.[34] Among the episodes which illustrate this friction are the purges of the military in 1937–1938, Marshal Zhukov's demotions in 1945 and 1957, disputes between Khrushchev and the military in the early 1960s, conflicts between party and the military over arms control policies in the 1970s, and the recent re-assignment of Marshal Ogarkov.

The Soviet military is by no means unified. First of all, there have been conflicts between the professional military officers and the commissars of the Main Political Administration.[35] Second, some evidence exists about rivalries over strategy and resources between the five service arms of the military.[36] Over the past several decades there have been significant changes in the relative positions of the strategic rocket forces, ground forces and navy. Furthermore, it is well documented that considerable competition exists between military intelligence (the GRU) and the KGB. As a result of these intraservice disputes the leadership undoubtedly receives conflicting advice and distorted information.

The Soviet defense industry is neither homogeneous nor perfectly integrated into the military-industrial complex. It comprises numerous production ministries. As is the case throughout the Soviet economy, each ministry and enterprise attempts to maximise its assignments of labour, capital and other supplies and to obtain modest output targets.[37] No doubt the various defense industries compete with each other. Conflicts also can arise between industry and the military, which makes what the industrialists consider to be extravagant demands for product quality and technological innovation.

The third major sector of the military-industrial complex, military R & D, is administratively fragmented and its institutions have objectives and success criteria which are different from those of either the military or defense production enterprises.[38] The first factor is the result of the dispersion of R & D establishments among a large number of ministries, state committees and academic organisations. The second is due to the lack of integration of the Soviet research, development and technological innovation process. Institutes and laboratories function at different stages of the R & D cycle and it is difficult to coordinate their activities in order to move from discoveries in original scientific research to mass production of a new weapon. In a recent article, Hough provides historical evidence of conflicts in the R & D sector between the armaments administrations of the military, defense industries and the scientific-design community.[39] This must have further complicated top-level decision making about the total resource allocation to military research and subdivisions between major weapons development programmes.

Any political model of the Soviet military-industrial complex should incorporate its complex institutional structure, low-level bureaucratic conflict and the distortions in information sent upward. Furthermore, it should recognise that national security decision making at the top is hampered by uncertainty about external threats as well as the current state and future capabilities of the military, defense industry, and the R & D sector. The leadership's measurement of final output, national security, is difficult and can only be imprecise. Given this uncertainty the leaders cannot know in advance the outcome of a decision. Instead they are confronted by a variety of possible reactions, each with a different probability and pay-off. Since most Western studies suggest that Soviet decision makers are cautious, if not risk averse, the situation in the military-industrial complex is one which should produce behaviour which is careful, incremental and prone to over-insurance.[40]

Analysis of Soviet national security decision making based on a more realistic interest group model with internal and external uncertainty would undoubtedly indicate that even if Soviet leaders are dedicated to national security maximisation, they would consider arms control and economic reform policies. But given the inertia of the system and the imperfect control by the top, any new policies would have to be incremental and acceptable to the different constituencies of the military-industrial complex.

The simple model of the Soviet military-industrial complex which has been sketched out in this paper may have some use in illustrating the complexity of decision making and policy options at any given time. But such a static model is of less value in explaining the dynamics of defense sector development. This is a failing common to the more substantial studies by Western economists of the military-industrial complex in the USSR.

The cause of this chronic deficiency is inadequate theoretical work on the Soviet economy in general. To date, neither economists in the West nor those in the East have developed an original, coherent, macroeconomic theory of the imperfectly planned socialist economy. In the years 1965–1975 economists made use of optimal planning, material balance, or input-output models of the socialist economy. Although many of these exercises clarified aspects of Soviet economic behaviour, none was able to explain observable behaviour completely. In recent years it has become fashionable to employ econometrically-estimated production function models of the Soviet economy, such as SOVMOD and its offspring. But existing variants have weak theoretical foundations, a mechanical nature, and decreasing utility as Soviet and East European economic performance exhibits increasing unplanned variability.

In order to develop an appropriate model which could be applied to the defense sector, work must be done in three areas. First, a better theoretical description is needed of the objectives and priorities of top Soviet leaders and their interactions with planners. Second, an effort must be made to improve modelling of microeconomic behaviour in the economy. This should take into account the internal dynamics of Soviet institutions (output expansion, investment drive, hoarding) and features of retail and wholesale markets which give the economy an inertial, unplanned behaviour and generate widespread shortage phenomena.[41] Finally, the theory should explain the interactions between the leadership and planners and the economic institutions. Among the characteristics to be incorporated are the imperfect information of high level decision makers, political constraints on economic actions, and incomplete control by the top of subordinate economic processes.

An improved theory of the Soviet economy could assist the analysis of the military-industrial complex in several ways. First, it could be used to develop microeconomic models of military and R & D institutions and defense industry enterprises. The behaviour of the latter could then be compared with that of civilian enterprises to obtain a better understanding of relative efficiency and the effects of priority in a shortage economy.[42] Second, a proper theory could help to clarify the interactions between the different components of the military-industrial complex in the various markets for labour, capital, intermediate goods and services. Ideally, this microeconomic work should be coordinated with that of political scientists, since there is significant interdependence between economic and political phenomena in a planned society. Third, an adequate dynamic macroeconomic theory of the socialist economy would help to explain why the Soviet Union has developed a large military-industrial complex, its regulatory or destabilising role in the economy, and the extent to which the top politicians and planners can control its aggregate growth and performance.

**Recent Trends in the Soviet
Military-Industrial Complex**

This section presents a summary, subjective assessment of available evidence about recent trends in the Soviet military-industrial complex. As a prelude, a few comments are made about the three major sources of data. Then, an attempt is made to review separately recent developments in the Soviet Union's external threat environment and military capabilities. Then we examine the effect that their interaction has had on Soviet national security. We conclude with an evaluation of economic or political indicators to determine whether their trends suggest an enhancement of the role of the military-industrial complex in Soviet society.

Sources of Data

The Soviet Union maintains a policy of secrecy and strict censorship in the national security area. It publishes virtually nothing about the actual size and composition of the armed forces and little reliable data about defense spending. However, despite the censorship, information can be found on topics such as: military doctrine, strategy and tactics; operations and problems of the military services; the size, planning and performance of the defense industry and military R & D sector; foreign trade in military products; the institutions of the military-industrial complex; and national security decision making. In addition, published Soviet economic, social, political, and demographic data can be used to evaluate the scale of and trends in the defense sector.

The second major source of information is the US intelligence community. The American government, like many others in the world, gathers and analyzes data about the Soviet military-industrial complex. Unlike the rest, the US makes available to its citizens substantial amounts of material produced by intelligence analysts. Unclassified material on the Soviet military is provided in numerous publications by the CIA, Department of Defense and the US Congress.[43] As a result of the open nature of American society, some classified information about Soviet defense issues appears occasionally in the newspapers.

Although US intelligence reports on the Soviet military are valuable sources of data, they should be treated with caution by outside analysts because of the underlying uncertainty of intelligence estimates. In a recent book John Prados argues that US intelligence assessments of Soviet military strength since World War II have been plagued by inaccuracies, distortions and revisions.[44] He shows that there have been numerous cases of both overestimates of Soviet capabilities and underestimates. In the former case are the "bomber gap" (1955), the "ICBM gap" (1958–1960), ballistic missile defense in the USSR, MIRVing of Soviet missiles, first-strike capabilities, and the Backfire bomber. In the latter are the estimates of the pace of Soviet development of the atomic and hydrogen bombs, the ICBM build-up of 1966–1970, the level and rate of growth of defense spending in the early 1970s, Soviet SLBM development, and missile accuracy. Unfortunately, these problems have not stopped. For example, in 1983 the CIA revised downward its estimated annual growth rate of Soviet defense spending in constant rubles for the period 1977–1981 from 4–5 percent to 2 percent.[45]

The third source is the work of Western academic specialists. By now there is a substantial secondary literature on military, economic and political aspects of the Soviet military-industrial complex. Many of these researchers have made original findings of considerable value. This is particularly true of scholars who have carefully examined Soviet material on the defense sector.[46] Unfortunately, many others neglect Soviet information and accept uncritically US intelligence output. For example, in the period 1976–1982 most Western economists made use of the CIA estimates of Soviet defense spending annual growth rates of 4–5 percent in their analyses and models. Fortunately for them, Soviet studies is a compassionate discipline which rarely penalises its members for incorrect predictions about political succession, inaccurate economic forecasts, or faulty assessments of defense trends.

In preparing this paper only US government and academic sources were used. Original Soviet material was not examined due to time constraints. It is hoped that this deficiency will be remedied in future work.

The External Threat Environment,
Military Capabilities, and
National Security of the USSR

External Threat Environment. Over the past decade the external
threat environment of the USSR has changed considerably and,
from a Soviet perspective, probably has worsened. On the whole,
the Soviet position during the first half of the 1970s was relatively
favourable. This was the era of detente with the West. Arms
control agreements were signed, trade expanded with the support
of official government credits, and technology transfer controls
were liberalised. Due to developments in world markets, especially the oil price rise in 1973–1974, Soviet terms of trade with
the West improved dramatically. The prolonged recession in
OECD economies, accompanied by high inflation and unemployment, created domestic political difficulties and enabled the
Soviet Union to close the economic power gap. In the US, the
debacle in Vietnam combined with the Watergate crisis to reduce
defense spending, demoralize the military, and restrict foreign
policy initiatives.

The situation in the Third World was initially unfavourable
to the USSR, with a continuing risk of conflict with China, the
overthrow of Allende in Chile, and the defeat of the Arab armies
by Israel in 1973. But then there were improvements. Soviet
influence in the Middle East grew and close relations were
established with Libya, Syria and the PLO. In 1975 the North
Vietnamese army launched a successful invasion of South Vietnam and the Khmer Rouge triumphed in Kampuchea. The
Portugese colonial system collapsed and power in Mozambique
and Angola was taken by Marxist revolutionary parties. The
intervention in Angola by Cuban troops helped the MPLA to
consolidate its control in most of the country.

During the second half of the 1970s there were further positive
developments in the Third World. Military tension between the
USSR and China was reduced and Vietnam became more openly
pro-Soviet. A joint Soviet-Cuban military force helped the
revolutionary Ethiopian government to defeat the Somalians and
the Vietnamese were able to occupy Kampuchea. In Nicaragua,
the Somoza dictatorship was overthrown by the Sandinista

revolutionary movement. A threat to the Afghanistan Marxist revolution was eliminated by the invasion of that country by the Soviet army.

During the same period, however, relations with the West deteriorated and detente collapsed. The US government declined to ratify the SALT II treaty. Following the Soviet invasion of Afghanistan in 1979 and the imposition of martial law in Poland in 1981 the West imposed sanctions on the USSR. There was a growth in popular concern about the Soviet threat, which helped to elect conservative politicians such as Mrs. Thatcher in Great Britain, Mr. Reagan in the US, Mr. Kohl in the Federal Republic of Germany and Mr. Nakasone in Japan. Even the socialist government of Mr. Mitterand in France adopted a tough line toward the Soviet Union. Also, the drop in the world oil price after 1982 adversely affected Soviet terms of trade.

A further complication for the USSR was the growing instability in Eastern Europe. In 1976 there was unrest and rioting in Poland. Economic growth throughout the region declined. The Polish economy began to collapse in 1979, and the Solidarity movement emerged in 1980. In 1981–1982 several East European countries experienced debt repayment crises which damaged their credit ratings and access to Western markets.

The 1980s have not been a good period for the USSR in the Third World. Vietnam and Cuba continue to drain resources from the Soviet economy. Soviet-supported forces remained bogged down in civil wars in Ethiopia, Mozambique, Kampuchea and Angola. The Soviet military has not been able to secure a victory in Afghanistan. Soviet-Iranian relations have worsened. In 1982 Israeli forces expelled the PLO from Lebanon and inflicted a humiliating defeat on the Soviet-supplied Syrian airforce. The guerilla insurgency in Guatemala has been defeated. There has been some stabilisation of the situation in El Salvador and increased pressure by the US on Nicaragua.

Judged from the Soviet perspective, the military threat confronting the USSR has grown over the past decade. This is primarily due to improvements in American forces. Under President Carter US defense spending began to rise rapidly. The Department of Defense budget in current dollars increased from $96 billion in the financial year 1976 to $182 billion in the

TABLE 6.2. US and Soviet Strategic Nuclear Forces, 1976 and 1983

	USA		USSR	
	1976	1983	1976	1983
Total Delivery Systems	2,210	1,845	2,403	2,484
ICBM	1,054	1,045	1,507	1,398
SLBM	656	568	716	941
Strategic Bombers	430	241	180	145
Total Warheads	8,634	9,665	3,353	8,880
Total Megatonnage Deliverable		3,886		5,835

Source: SIPRI World Armaments and Disarmament Yearbooks, 1976 and 1984

financial year 1981.[47] Under President Reagan, defense budget growth accelerated. The administration obtained a defense budget authority of $297 billion for the financial year 1985. The greater spending raised the weapons quality and readiness of both nuclear and conventional forces.

Developments in strategic nuclear forces are shown in Table 6.2. The total number of US delivery systems declined from 2,210 in 1976 to 1,845 in 1983. On the other hand, the number of warheads rose from 8,634 to 9,665. Much of the warhead growth in the 1970s was due to the MIRV programme. There were qualitative improvements in all components of the triad as well as in the command and control system.[48] The accuracy of the Minuteman III missile was improved. In the submarine force Polaris missiles were replaced by Poseidon C3 and C4 missiles. In 1982 the first Trident submarine entered active service. The capabilities of the bomber force were upgraded by equipping B52Gs with ALCMs.

The US has also made major advances in its strategic nuclear R & D.[49] The MX missile was flight-tested in 1983 and the B-1 bomber is scheduled to enter active service in 1985. Progress is being made in the Midgetman, Trident II, and Stealth bomber programmes. The new Strategic Defense Initiative has raised the priority of ballistic missile defense.

The US intermediate nuclear forces have been upgraded through the addition of cruise missiles and the Pershing II. In addition, the US maintains a stockpile of about 9,000 land-based and naval tactical nuclear weapons.[50] Some of these also have been modernised.

Although the number of US conventional forces has remained relatively stable, their combat capabilities have been enhanced. All branches have been modernised during the past several years.[51] The naval fleet has grown from 479 ships in the financial year 1980 to 525 in the financial year 1984. The airforce, navy and marine corps have acquired several thousand advanced F14, F15, F16 and F18 aircraft. The army has added 500 M-1 Abrams tanks to its inventory as well as new anti-tank weapons, troop carriers and sophisticated helicopters. It also has developed the Rapid Deployment Force and new Airland Battle tactics.

There is some debate in the US about the effect increased spending and new weapons have had on military readiness. A 1984 report prepared for the House Appropriations Committee claimed that readiness has declined in recent years.[52] On the other hand, Secretary of Defense Weinberger asserts that force readiness has improved by 39 percent since 1980.[53] Mr. Weinberger's assessment has the support of his counterparts in the Soviet Ministry of Defense, who agree that US military capability has been enhanced.[54]

With respect to NATO, increased real defense expenditures by most countries since 1978 have contributed to improvements. According to US sources, the combat potential of NATO forces in the Central Region has grown by 40 percent since 1965.[55] The recent deployment of GLCMs and Pershing II in Western Europe has upgraded intermediate nuclear force capabilities. The present stockpile of about 6,000 tactical nuclear weapons in Western Europe is more than enough to cover all potential targets.

Soviet Military Capabilities. The Soviet armed forces are responsible for possessing or developing capabilities to deal effectively with present or future military contingencies. In any given period they always are expected to maintain their operational readiness and sometimes may be called on to provide concrete services (shoot down an aircraft, direct a counter-insurgency effort). The production of readiness and services involves a combination of men, weapons, supplies, strategy and tactics. All these factors should be considered in an assessment of Soviet military capability. Furthermore, examination should be made of trends in the major service branches.

The most important of these is the strategic nuclear force. Table 6.2 shows SIPRI estimates of Soviet strength in 1976 and 1983. The total number of delivery systems went up during this period because increases in SLBMs more than offset ICBM and bomber reductions. The Soviet MIRV programme, which started later than the US one, was responsible for the dramatic surge in war heads from 3,353 to 8,880. By 1983 Soviet strategic forces had the potential to deliver 5,835 megatons of destructive power versus 3,886 for the US.

The quality of strategic forces markedly improved.[56] By 1984 about 60 percent of ICBMs were recently deployed fourth-generation SS-17, SS-18 or SS-19. There were 308 of the big SS-18 which carry ten warheads. The number of ICBM warheads quadrupled from about 1,500 in 1974 to 6,000 in 1984. In addition, 818 of 1,398 missile silos have been re-built and hardened since 1972. The USSR increased its fleet of SSBN to 64. It began to deploy the new Typhoon-class SSBN with its SS-N-20 missiles; the Typhoon is larger than the US Trident SSBN. The number of SLBM warheads rose from 1,000 in 1976 to 2,500 in 1984. There is some dispute over trends in strategic bombers. SIPRI shows a decrease from 180 in 1976 to 145 in 1983 whereas the US Defense Department claims there has been an increase from 200 in 1979 to 300 in 1984. The difference appears to be due to the US inclusion of 130 Backfire bombers in the total.[57]

In the intermediate nuclear forces the Soviet Union has been replacing its SS-5 and SS-4 missiles with three-warhead SS-20. The deployment of the mobile SS-20 (range 5,000 km) began in 1977. By 1984 378 SS-20 were in the field; 162 in the Western USSR, 81 in Central Asia and 135 in the Far East.[58] Soviet tactical nuclear forces, which include 1,400 SSM and 900 long-range artillery pieces, are being upgraded as well.[59]

Overall, it appears that the number of Soviet nuclear warheads of all types has risen substantially. According to a recent US government report, the USSR passed the US level in 1978.[60]

By 1984 the Soviet Union had an estimated 34,000 warheads and the US 26,000.

The army is the most important branch of Soviet conventional forces. Over the past decade it appears to have improved the quality of most types of equipment.[61] By 1984 over one-third of the 52,000 Soviet main battle tanks were of the modern T-64/72/80 series. These are supposed to be much superior to older model T-62s, which have not fared well in competitions with Western tanks.[62] By 1984 1,100 T 80 tanks had been deployed in the Central European region. The quantity and quality of self-propelled artillery, SAMs, SSMs and helicopters have risen as well.

Recently Soviet military organisation has been changed to improve strategic and tactical effectiveness. Front-line units of all types are now grouped into integrated Theatres of Military Operations. Related to this has been the reorganisation and integration of tactical air and air defense forces. Several new fighter and bomber aircraft have been introduced since the mid-1970s.

The Soviet navy was the most neglected service until the mid-1960s. It then began to expand its capabilities in order to fulfill new missions in the areas of strategic nuclear deterrence (the SSBNs), lone-range interdiction of US aircraft carriers, and detection of US SSBNs.[63] The 1970s were a time of rapid growth of the navy, especially in the early part. In addition to modernising the SSBN force the Soviet navy introduced several new classes of attack submarines (MIKE, SIERRA, VICTOR III), and expanded its surface fleet and air arm. By 1984 it had 278 cruise missile and attack submarines, 3 VTOL aircraft carriers and 290 other principal combatant ships.[64]

As with NATO, the important issue is whether Soviet armed forces would be ready for and effective in combat. The Soviet Ministry of Defense claims that its forces are in a high state of vigilance and prepared to deliver a fitting rebuff to any aggressor. The US Department of Defense paints an even more positive picture of Soviet military capabilities and readiness. However, it is likely that Soviet forces look considerably better on paper than they would perform in the field. Soviet military units are plagued by numerous problems of bureaucratic interference, poor morale and resource constraints which adversely affect their performance.[65] Cockburn reports that Soviet fighter pilots are carefully controlled by ground staff and provided with only seven hours of flying time per month. In contrast, US pilots fly sixteen hours per month and Israeli pilots thirty hours. As a result of the various qualitative deficiencies, the capabilities of the armed forces of the USSR probably have not improved as much as the trends in quantitative indicators would suggest.

A review of the recent performance of the Soviet military provides some evidence in support of a sceptical assessment of its capabilities. In the case of Afghanistan, the initial invasion was carefully planned and effectively executed. However, during the subsequent five years a force of over 100,000 Soviet troops equipped with the latest weapons has proved unable to suppress a poorly-equipped and disorganised resistance movement.[66] During the recent Polish crisis several threats were made of intervention by Warsaw Pact forces. Related to this, in November 1980 an attempt was made to mobilise troops in the Carpathian, Baltic and Belorussian districts of the USSR. According to Cockburn, this exercise revealed a very low state of military readiness.[67] A third illustration is provided by the Korean airliner incident in 1983. In this case the Soviet air defense forces seemed to experience serious technical difficulties in tracking and intercepting a high-flying civilian plane which was neither taking evasive action nor using electronic counter-measures. As a result of this incompetence and the panicky decision by the Soviet military to shoot down the plane, 269 passengers and crew were killed. This action reflects poorly on several aspects of Soviet society, including the professional capabilities of the armed forces.

Soviet National Security. In the section of this paper discussing Soviet national security decision making the national security function, $N=f(T,M)$, was described. Trends in N would be unambiguous in two cases. First, if the threat (T) rose and military capabilities (M) declined then N would fall. Second, if T declined and M improved then N would rise. The ambiguous cases are when both T and M rise or fall during a period of observation. In these circumstances it becomes difficult to assess the combined effect on N of the contradictory influences of trends in T and M.

On the basis of available evidence it seems that the development of Soviet national security in the period 1974–1984 should be classified as an ambiguous case. We have argued above that the Soviet external threat environment changed character and worsened during the decade. On the other hand, our review of Soviet military capabilities suggested that there have been significant improvements in both nuclear and conventional forces. Although one should be sceptical about the military's claims concerning competence and efficiency (even when made about potential adversaries), there seems little doubt that the Soviet armed forces would be able to carry out any mission in a more destructive manner today than they could ten years ago.

If potential contingencies only involved conventional weapons then this increase in power probably would have enhanced the national security of the USSR. But in the nuclear age power equations become a bit more complex. This is because however many times over the military in one country can destroy another society using nuclear weapons, opposing forces only have to make a relatively modest effective response for the national security register to indicate zero. Although philosophical observations of this sort may not be heard frequently in the corridors of the Soviet Ministry of Defense, the military men do not completely control the military-industrial complex or the national security evaluation process.[68] Instead, decisions about the state of national security are made by the Communist Party leadership. It would not be surprising if the Soviet leaders, after careful assessment of negative external threat and positive military capability trends, reached the conclusion that national security of the USSR had declined over the past decade.

The Political and Economic Significance of the Soviet Military-Industrial Complex

During the past several years a number of Western specialists have argued forcefully that the Soviet military-industrial complex has been growing in political and economic significance. Evidence in support of this argument has been found in various developments in high-level party institutions as well as in the seemingly inexorable rise in the economic defense burden. Given the topic of this paper it seems appropriate to conclude with a re-evaluation of the important issue of trends in the influence of the military-industrial complex in the USSR.

In the political realm, one indicator of the rise of the military-industrial complex was supposed to be the membership in the Politbureau of Marshal Brezhnev, General Andropov, Marshal Ustinov and Mr. Gromyko. However, it should be kept in mind that although these men were closely associated with the national security establishment, none of them were professional military officers. After Brezhnev's death in 1982 the military supposedly supported Andropov in his contest with Chernenko. Naturally, after Andropov emerged as the winner it was assumed that this key constituency would be amply rewarded.

Although this argument may have had some attraction in the early 1980s this is not the case after February 1984. First of all, Chernenko became General Secretary. One can assume that like most politicians he was displeased with those who did not support him when it counted, like the military. Second, in December 1984, Ustinov died. His replacement, Marshal S. L. Sokolov, does not have the same stature and has been given only Candidate Membership in the Politbureau. Third, in March 1985 Chernenko died and Gorbachev was selected as the new General Secretary. He appears to have had minimal direct links with the national security complex, so his appointment cannot be interpreted as beneficial to the military.[69]

According to a February 1984 article in the *New York Times,* one indication of the enhanced political role of the military was Marshal Ogarkov's press conference following the destruction of the Korean airliner. In retrospect it appears that this was more punishment than reward. The demotion of Marshal Ogarkov in September 1984 is a further signal of the party's determination to keep the military in a subordinate position.[70]

If the military had acquired additional political influence during the past five years one would expect to see this reflected in the composition of the Supreme Soviet. Seats in this ceremonial body are distributed between various groups in society roughly in accordance with the importance attached to them by the leadership. In 1979 fifty-six of the elected deputies were members of the military, or 3.73 percent of the total. In the 4 March 1984 elections the number of military deputies chosen was unchanged.[71]

It is generally accepted that the military-industrial complex plays an important role in the Soviet economy and has a high-priority claim on scarce resources. But there is less certainty about the appropriate measure of and trends in the defense burden. During the early 1970s the CIA estimated the burden at 6-8 percent of Soviet GNP and the growth of annual real defense spending at 3 percent.[72] In 1976 the CIA revised upward the defense share to 11–13 percent of GNP and the growth rate to 4–5 percent. These revised numbers remained the authoritative estimates for the next seven years. Soviet GNP growth rate declined from 3.7 percent in 1971–1975, to 2.7 percent in 1976–1980, to about 2 percent in 1981–1983. Since the 4–5 percent defense rate of increase was higher than that of general growth it appeared that the defense burden was increasing. In turn this suggested that even in a time of economic stringency the Soviet military-industrial complex had the political power to maintain its high growth and to obtain an increasing share of the nation's resources.

Unfortunately for the adherents of this argument, the CIA again revised its estimates of Soviet defense spending. This time it retrospectively lowered its estimate of defense spending growth during the 1977–1981 period to about 2 percent per year. In consequence, defense growth was lower than general economic growth throughout this period, which suggested a slight decline in the defense burden. If CIA figures describe the actual situation, then they do not provide evidence in support of theories or assertions about the overriding economic priority of the military-industrial complex in the USSR.

Soviet policies of secrecy and censorship make it difficult to conduct a detailed study of the role and importance of the military-industrial complex in the USSR. Evaluation of the limited publicly-available evidence indicates that the military and its supporting defense industries do have privileged positions in the economy and their representatives exert a powerful influence on the political system. Although comparative measurements are difficult, it does appear that the military-industrial complex occupies a more prominent role in Soviet society than do its counterparts in the West. However, this paper has argued that there has been some exaggeration of the growth in the influence of the military-industrial complex in the USSR during the past decade.

Notes

I would like to express my appreciation for a Ford Foundation post-doctoral "dual-competence" fellowship that enabled me to study national security and arms control issues at the M.I.T. Center for International Studies between January and August 1984. The Birmingham Centre for Russian and East European Studies supported the preparation of this conference paper. My thanks to the Conference commentator, Dr. Hannes Adomeit, for his helpful criticisms and suggestions.

1. For a recent comparative study of defense industries see N. Ball and M. Leitenberg (eds.), *The Structure of the Defense Industry: An International Survey* (London: Croom Helm, 1983).

2. Among the basic references are: V. Asparturian, "The Soviet Military-industrial Complex—Does it exist", *Journal of International Affairs*, vol. 26 (1972), no. 1; M. Agursky and H. Adomeit, "Soviet Military Industrial Complex", *Survey*, vol. 24 (1979), no. 2; A. S. Becker, *The Burden of Soviet Defense* (Santa Monica: RAND R-2752-AF, 1981); D. Holloway, *The Soviet Union and the Arms Race* (London: Yale University Press, 1983); H. F. Scott and W. F. Scott, *The Armed Forces of the USSR* (Boulder: Westview Press, 1981); and J. Erickson and E. J. Feuchtwanger (eds.), *Soviet Military Power and Performance* (London: Macmillan, 1979).

3. Descriptions of the institutions in the Soviet military-industrial complex can be found in: Scott and Scott, *The Armed Forces*, R. E. Gottemoeller, "Decision-making for Arms Limitation in the Soviet Union" in H. G. Brauch and D. L. Clarke (eds.), *Decision-making for Arms Limitation* (Cambridge: Ballinger, 1983); J. McDonnell, "The Organization of Soviet Defense and Military Policy Making" in M. McGwire and J. McDonnell (eds.), *Soviet Naval Policy: Domestic and Foreign Dimensions* (New York: Praeger, 1977); and E. L. Warner, *The Military in Contemporary Soviet Politics* (London: Praeger, 1979).

4. T. W. Wolfe, *The SALT Experience* (Cambridge, Ballinger, 1979).

5. Gottemoeller, "Decision-making," and E. Jones, "Defense R & D Policymaking in the USSR", in J. Valenta and W. Potter, *Soviet Decisionmaking for National Security* (London: George Allen & Unwin, 1984).

6. Holloway, *The Soviet Union and the Arms Race,* p. 111.

7. This model is derived from the one I developed for analysis of the Soviet health sector. In that case the final output is the population's health status, the "threat" is the illness pattern, and the intermediate outputs are medical services. The services are produced in hospitals and polyclinics using a variety of inputs. The medical system is supplied by the Soviet medical industry and supported by the biomedical R & D establishment. The medical-industrial complex exports and imports pharmaceuticals and medical equipment. See C. Davis, "The Economics of the Soviet Health System" in US Congress Joint Economic Committee, *Soviet Economy in the 1970s: Problems and Prospects* (Washington, D. C., 1983), and C. Davis, "The Health and Pharmaceutical Sector in the Soviet Economy" (Washington, D.C.: Wharton Econometric Forecasting Associates *Special Report*, 1984).

8. It is recognised that additional work is needed in order to define fully the role of "external threats" in the national security production process. This paper suggests that the threats could be multivariate: military, economic, and political. The development of Soviet military capabilities may be primarily responsive to trends in the international balance of forces. Also, one function of the Soviet military may be to help maintain internal order. If so, then national security decision makers in the USSR will not consider only external factors.

9. In order to analyse the issue of threat assessment in the USSR fully one must examine carefully the important role of ideology in both Soviet strategic thinking and Western interpretations of Soviet international behaviour.

10. According to Soviet Marxist-Leninist economic theory, an economy is divided into the productive sphere (industry, agriculture, trade), which contributes to the formation of national income, and the non-productive sphere (health, education), which is supported by redistributed income. In this scheme the military and security services belong to the non-productive sphere. However, not all contemporary Soviet economic theory books make it clear that the military is producing 'non-productive services'.

11. Scott and Scott, *The Armed Forces*, op. cit., and Holloway, *The Soviet Union and the Arms Race.*

12. Holloway, *The Soviet Union and the Arms Race* and "The Soviet Union" in Ball and Leitenberg, *The Structure*, op. cit., and J. McDonnell, "The Soviet defense industry as a pressure group," in M. McGwire, K. Booth and J. McDonnell, *Soviet Naval Policy: Objectives and Constraints* (New York: Praeger, 1975).

13. J. Cooper, "The Civilian Production of the Soviet Defense Industry", Birmingham. Paper presented at Symposium on Soviet Science and Technology, 1984.

14. Jones, "Defence R & D," op. cit.; Holloway, *The Soviet Union and the Arms Race*, Chapter 7 and "Innovation in the Defence Sector," in R. Amann and J. M. Cooper, *Industrial Innovation in the Soviet Union* (London: Yale University Press, 1982).

15. J. Cooper, "Western Technology and the Soviet Defence Industry," Birmingham, CREES Discussion Paper, 1984; M. Checinski, "Poland's Military Burden," *Problems of Communism*, vol. 22 (1983), May–June; and R. Kanet, "Soviet and East European Arms Transfers to the Third World", in NATO Economics Directorate *External Economic Relations of CMEA Countries* (Brussels, 1983).

16. SIPRI, *The Arms Trade with the Third World* (Stockholm, 1974), and US Central Intelligence Agency, *Arms Flows to LDCs: U.S.-Soviet Comparisons* (Washington, D.C., 1978).

17. The US government argues that there has been a large-scale legal and covert transfer of technology from the West to the USSR which has assisted the development of the Soviet military-industrial complex. See US Department of Defense, *Soviet Military Power* (Washington, D.C., 1984). However, some scholars argue that the scale of and benefits from this transfer have been overstated. See J. Cooper, "Western Technology."

18. An excellent assessment of Western export controls is provided in D. Buchan, "Western Security and Economic Strategy Towards the East", IISS, *Adelphi Papers*, No. 192, 1984.

19. There can be little doubt that Soviet intelligence services have registered successes in their efforts to obtain Western militarily-related secrets. But is is unclear whether they have been efficient as well as effective. For a review of covert technology acquisition see Buchan, "Western Security."

20. For a comprehensive review of Soviet defense decision making see S. Meyer, "Soviet national security decisionmaking: What do we know and what do we understand?", in Valenta and Potter, *Soviet Decisionmaking*.

21. Evaluations of Soviet planning procedures can be found in M. Ellman, *Planning Problems in the USSR*, Cambridge, Cambridge Uni-

versity Press, 1973 and A. Nove, *The Soviet Economic System* (London: George Allen & Unwin, 1977).

22. Among the books which examine Soviet ideology and military doctrine are Holloway, *The Soviet Union and the Arms Race;* Warner, *The Military;* and H. Adomeit, *Soviet Risk-taking and Crisis Behavior* (London: George Allen & Unwin, 1982).

23. The assessment of whether modification of Soviet strategic objectives is feasible depends upon one's model of the USSR. For example, Luttwak would probably argue that the Soviet Union could not become less expansionist or its empire would collapse due to internal contradictions. See E. N. Luttwak, *The Grand Strategy of the Soviet Union* (London: Weidenfeld and Nicolson, 1983).

24. H. Adomeit, "Capitalist Contradictions and Soviet Policy," *Problems of Communism*, vol. 33 (1984), May–June, and Gerhard Wettig, "Security, Diplomacy and Propaganda in Soviet Foreign Policy: The INF Controversy", Washington, D.C., Paper presented at the Kennan Institute for Advanced Russian Studies, 25 April 1985.

25. For information about the Soviet intelligence apparatus see J. Richelson, *Sword and Shield: Soviet Intelligence and Security Service Operations* (Cambridge: Ballinger, 1985).

26. P. Hanson, "Soviet Economic Problems? An Opportunity for Progress in Arms Control", *Detente*, no. 1, October 1984.

27. For a good general presentation of the economics of defense see G. Kennedy, *Defense Economics* (London: Duckworth, 1983).

28. One reason the CIA revised upwards its estimate of Soviet defense spending in 1976 was that it discovered that the defense industry was less efficient than formerly believed. See US Central Intelligence Agency, *Estimated Soviet Defense Spending in Rubles, 1970–75* (Washington, D. C., 1976).

29. R. Amann, "Industrial Innovation in the Soviet Union: Methodological Perspectives and Conclusions," in Amann and Cooper, *Industrial Innovation*, and his contribution in this volume, Chapter 7, "The Political and Social Implications of Economic Reform in the USSR".

30. Kanet, "Soviet and East European Arms Transfers," op. cit.

31. For a discussion of the early rather chaotic economic history of the USSR see A. Nove, *An Economic History of the USSR* (Harmondsworth: Penguin, 1972), and E. Zaleski, *Stalinist Planning for Economic Growth* (London: Macmillan, 1980).

32. Holloway, *The Soviet Union and the Arms Race* and "The Soviet Union"; J. F. Hough, "The Historical Legacy in Soviet Weapons Development," in Valenta and Potter, *Soviet Decisionmaking*, and J.

Cooper, "Defence Production and the Soviet Economy, 1929–41" (Birmingham: CREES Discussion Paper, 1976), and A. Alexander, "Decision-Making in Soviet Weapons Procurement", IISS, *Adelphi Papers*, No. 147 and 148.

33. This refers to the well-known book about the US military sector by A. C. Enthoven and K. W. Smith, *How Much is Enough?: Shaping the Defense Program, 1961–69* (New York, 1971).

34. M. J. Dean, *Political Control at the Soviet Armed Forces* (London: Macdonald and Jane's, 1977).

35. *Ibid.*

36. Scott and Scott, *The Armed Forces . . .* and Holloway, *The Soviet Union and the Arms Race.*

37. See Nove, *The Soviet Economic System* for a discussion of ministerial and enterprise behaviour in the Soviet economy.

38. Holloway, "Innovation," op. cit.

39. Hough, "The Historical Legacy," op. cit.

40. Adomeit, *Soviet Risk-Taking*, and D. Ross, "Risk Aversion in Soviet Decision making," in Valenta and Potter, *Soviet Decisionmaking*, op. cit.

41. In my opinion the work of the Hungarian economist Janos Kornai contains some interesting concepts which could be used to analyse the Soviet economy. See J. Kornai, *The Economics of Shortage* (Oxford: North-Holland, 1980).

42. The issue of priority in the Soviet economy is discussed in Chapter 3 of this volume, H. -H. Höhmann, "The Place of Economic Policy Objectives on the List of Soviet Political Priorities".

43. Useful information can be found in the annual hearings of the US Congress Joint Economic Committee on Allocation of Resources in the Soviet Union and China. The Department of Defense publishes the Soviet Military Power booklets as well as more specialised literature. During the 1970s the CIA provided the tax-paying public with some useful reports. Unfortunately since 1981 the CIA has adopted a short-sighted restrictive publication policy.

44. J. Prados, *The Soviet Estimate: U.S. Intelligence Analysis and Russian Military Strength* (N.Y.: Dial Press, 1982).

45. US Central Intelligence Agency, *Estimated Soviet Defense Spending in Rubles, 1970-1975* (Washington, D.C., 1976), and R. F. Kaufman, "Causes of the Slowdown in Soviet Defense", *Soviet Economy*, Vol. 1 1985, No. 1, pp. 9–31.

46. Among Anglo-American scholars who make careful use of Soviet material in their research are John Erickson, Abraham Becker,

Arthur Alexander, Vladimir Treml, David Holloway, Julia Cooper, Steve Meyer, and Jerry Hough.

47. US Department of Defense, *Report of the Secretary of Defense Caspar W. Weinberger to the Congress* (Washington, D.C., 1984), and G. F. Seib, "Arms Build-up Ordered by Reagan Could Be Less than Meets the Eye", *Wall Street Journal*, 29 October 1984.

48. This section is based on US Department of Defense *Report*, op. cit. and USSR Ministry of Defense, *Whence the Threat of Peace (3rd edition)* (Moscow: Voenizdat, 1984).

49. *Ibid.*

50. Class notes from an M.I.T. course given by Professor W. Kaufmann on "General Purpose Forces".

51. US Department of Defense, *Report*, op. cit.

52. R. Halloran, "18–month Survey Finds U.S. Forces Lacking Readiness", *New York Times*, 22 July 1984.

53. US Department of Defense, *Report*, op. cit., p. 45.

54. USSR Ministry of Defense, *Whence*, op. cit.

55. US Department of Defense, *Report*, op. cit., p. 24.

56. This section is based on US Department of Defense, *Soviet Military Power*, and *Report*, op. cit. Statistics should be evaluated with caution because of the possibility of institutional bias. An alternative perspective on Soviet military capabilities is provided in Andrew Cockburn, *The Threat: Inside the Soviet Military Machine* (New York: Vintage, 1984).

57. IISS, *The Military Balance 1984–1985* (London, 1984), p. 17.

58. *Ibid.*

59. For an authoritative assessment of Soviet non-strategic nuclear forces see S. Meyer, "Soviet Theatre Nuclear Forces: Parts I and II", IISS, *Adelphi Paper:* Nos. 187 and 188, 1984.

60. R. Halloran, "Soviets Said to Lead U.S. by 8,000 Warheads", *New York Times*, 18 June 1984.

61. US Department of Defense, *Soviet Military Power*, op. cit.

62. Cockburn, *The Threat*, op. cit., Chapter 8.

63. J. E. Moore, "The Soviet Navy," in Erickson and Feuchtwanger, *Soviet Military*, op. cit.; Cockburn, *The Threat*, op. cit., Chapter 15; US Department of Defense, *Soviet Military Power*, op. cit.

64. IISS, *The Military*, op. cit., p. 19.

65. Cockburn, *The Threat*, op. cit.

66. IISS, *Strategic Survey: 1983–1984* (London, 1984), pp. 82–85.

67. Cockburn, *The Threat*, op. cit., pp. 178–180.

68. At least some Soviet military officers appear to appreciate the diminishing returns from the build-up of nuclear forces. For example,

in an interview in *Krasnaya Zvezda*, 9 May 1984, Marshal Ogarkov observed that: "As a result [of the build-up], a paradox is forming: On the one hand, it would seem that a process of steady increase in the nuclear powers' potential to destroy an enemy is taking place, while on the other hand, the potential of an aggressor to deliver a so-called 'disabling strike' against its main adversary is just as steadily—or, I would say, even more sharply—diminishing." See *Current Digest of the Soviet Press*, vol. 36, no. 36 (3 October 1984).

69. A. Rahr, "Mikhail Gorbachev: Current Heir Apparent in the Kremlin", *Radio Liberty Research Bulletin*, RL 151/84, 12 April 1984.

70. B. Murphy, "Chief of Soviet General Staff Removed", *Radio Liberty Research Bulletin*, RL 338/84, 7 September 1984.

71. P. Kruzhin, "Military Personnel in the Supreme Soviet of the USSR", *Radio Liberty Research Bulletin*, RL 149/84, 10 April 1984.

72. Kaufmann, "Causes," op. cit. and D. Ignatius, "U.S. Data Contradict Claims of Soviet Military Build-Up", *Wall Street Journal*, 1 November 1984.

7

The Political and Social Implications of Economic Reform in the USSR

Ronald Amann

The current state of political life in the USSR presents a contradictory and paradoxical picture to Western theorists, who try to grasp its essence in terms of general concepts. On the one hand we have a state that is still quite ruthless in dealing with the few persistent critics who dare to challenge its ideological precepts frontally; it is dominated by a functional elite (successors to or remnants of the 'service nobility' of Stalinist industrialisation) whose members exhibit a proprietorial attitude towards state assets and are tempted to supplement their institutionalised privileges with the fruits of widespread dishonesty. Yet equally, the regime displays a genuine concern for economic development (submitting the nation and the bureaucracy itself to a "treadmill of reform");[1] it has sought the advice of specialists, expanding in the process the parameters of permissible discussion, and has tried to achieve stability for future development through a tacit deal based on gradually improving levels of mass welfare.[2]

The theoretical view that seems to capture and reconcile these contradictory elements best is that of a state socialist society in transition. By this I do not mean the official version of the transition to communism, involving the eventual introduction of payment according to need and the withering away of the state. Following Andropov's lead, orthodox theorists now concede that this is an extremely prolonged process because 'developed socialism' is only at an initial stage: for all practical purposes, therefore, the transition to communism in these terms is a theory of permanent transition. Like the horizon, communism recedes as one approaches it. Nor is the possibility of a transition to a new revolutionary form of working-class power a very distinct possibility, firstly because the problem of how to harmonize large-scale production other than by traditional central planning or the market is unresolved on the theoretical plane and secondly, because there is in any case no evidence of such a trend. Nor is the restoration of capitalism likely except, perhaps, in very small doses. Joseph Berliner, paraphrasing Kenneth Boulding and turning him on his head, has argued that the return bus journey from socialism to capitalism leaves early in the morning and if you miss it you remain in the socialist state for ever.[3] Conceivably, Hungary may have "caught the bus back", at least part of the way, but it is extremely doubtful after all this time whether the USSR could (or would want to) make that unsettling journey. The form of transition which I have in mind is less spectacular than the above alternatives but one which is significant nevertheless. It concerns, rather, a society in which economic and institutional de-Stalinisation has not followed on the heels of the formal abandonment of mass terror in 1956, where the relations of production (economic management) act as a fetter on the promotion of advanced technology (the forces of production), and where extensive forms of economic development have not yet given way to intensive modes. It is, in short, a society "between two ages"[4] in which the cultural imprint of Stalinism vies for influence with the exigences of modern development. The leading political office-holders are *hesitant modernizers*, exposed to intensifying economic pressures but fearful of the practicality, and of the political consequences for society and themselves, of fundamental reforms—by which I mean measures that would change the character of the core influences on the economic system: centralised supplies, prices, absence of direct relations with customers and lack of real rewards for success and penalties for failure.

The Political Implications of Fundamental Reform

To my mind it is essential to try to analyse these dilemmas and hesitations further, because they represent the key to our understanding of the present political system in the USSR and the way in which it is likely to evolve in the future. I do not want to say very much in this paper about the economic pressures for reform, stemming from falling rates of growth and flagging technological progress, nor about the extent to which most of the major options, short of radical reform, have been tried and found wanting. These aspects have already been thoroughly explored in the existing literature.[5] In the face of these considerable economic pressures it is, rather, the roots of the leadership's obduracy and misgivings which may tell us most about the underlying character of the political system. Why is the Soviet leadership hesitant, largely confining itself to incrementalism, compromise or traditional solutions? What are the political obstacles to a really far-reaching economic reform?

First, it is clear that there are powerful vested interests opposed to a radical reform in the Soviet Union.[6] Reform of the traditional central planning mechanism would remove or dilute several of the most important sources of power of the party apparatus: principally the 'prefectorial'[7] control of regional party officials over the process of resource allocation and the substitution of the impersonal criterion of technical competence for nomenklatura placement. It is true that, in principle, the party could retain its inspirational or "guiding role" but in the long run, without effective power this could easily (but not inevitably) become an empty shell. Certainly, with such a change in the distribution of power, the party could no longer expect to prevail automatically in any conflict situation; it would have to earn its authority. Another powerful institution opposed to a radical reform would almost certainly be the military and its associated defence industrial complex, assured of priority in procuring scarce supplies by the operation of the traditional central planning system.[8] We may further surmise that these vested interests are by no means narrow or isolated but can draw upon popular cultural supports derived from deep-rooted fears of chaos, patriotism and (among some circles) nostalgia for a strong boss. But quite apart from vested interests, a market or quasi-market reform would transgress one of the most fundamental principles of Soviet-style socialism—the claim of a class-conscious elite to express the "real" social interest. This "solidarity conception", as Gregory Grossman has called it,[9] has been re-stated vigourously by P. Ignatovsky, the editor of the leading Soviet planning journal *Planovoe khozyaistvo,* in an article in the party theoretical journal *Kommunist.*[10] Ignatovsky contends that "commodity relations" in the Soviet economy have already gone too far and have to be reined in by selective party controls; only in this way can corrosive selfishness and the predominance of narrow departmental interests be avoided. From a theoretical point of view this is perhaps the crucial conservative argument against a radical approach to institutional reform in the USSR. As Hoffman and Laird have noted, "What is implied but never stated in contemporary Soviet writings is that the CPSU is the sole centripetal force in a society consisting of increasingly powerful centrifugal forces".[11] In more recent writings such misgivings are being openly stated.

Second, the introduction of a market element would produce economic distortions such as regional imbalances and unemployment, which could only be overcome by forms of indirect control which are unfamiliar (and, perhaps, culturally alien) to the Soviet leadership. It seems likely, for example, that given their narrow academic training and experience, many Soviet economists and economic planners would find almost inconceivable the prospect of applying market principles to such a huge and diverse land as the USSR. On the other hand, a more modest approach whereby the familiar planning mechanism might be retained while legalising the freedom of private enterprise to function at the margins of the economy (in the retail and servicing sectors, especially)[12] could run into the danger of sapping the long run vitality of major investment schemes in the state sector. This would come about because employees would find it more profitable to spend the greater proportion of their time and effort on private activities[13], diverting labour power and (pilfered) materials from the state sector. Thus, one might envisage a paradoxical outcome: the private consumer goods sector, ultimately restricted in scale by the absence of large-scale investment, could thrive at the same time as heavy industry, the major recipient of state investment and focal point of plans for technical development, could stagnate, with incalculable long term consequences for the performance of the economy as a whole. Soviet political theorists are, of course, familiar with the general notion that personal property and private property under socialism can "overflow" and erode what should be the dominant form.[14]

Third, a far-reaching economic reform could heighten social tension in a number of ways. Income differentials would increase, especially between unskilled industrial workers on the one hand and non-nomenklatura specialists on the other, who would be the main beneficiaries of reform and therefore the main social stratum pushing for its implementation. This would reverse the general trend towards the narrowing of differentials, which has been a feature of the post-Khrushchev period, at a time of growing working-class immobility and frustration. Also, to the extent that the reform succeeded in achieving a more efficient use of labour and thus in alleviating the problem of overall labour scarcity it would destroy the only real lever which workers presently have to bid up their wages.[15] Unlike a conservative Western government, the Soviet government could not withdraw from the fray and justify these developing inequalities in terms of "human nature" or "the objective order of things"; under state socialism, which lacks the benefit of commodity fetishism(!), economic inequalities are widely perceived as being political in origin and therefore squarely within the remit of the state. Under these circumstances, political leaders are inevitably drawn into a process of active mediation between the need for managerial incentives and the need to avoid the activation of latent class antagonisms.[16] An attempt is made in Figure 7.1 to represent these social relations schematically.

Fourth, it is likely that Soviet political leaders would only seriously contemplate a bold reform if they had confidence in the ability of officials at all levels of the system to carry such a reform out. According to evidence collected by Ron Hill[17] this confidence does not exist and there is, in any case, little objective basis for it. After decades of Stalinist central planning the economic system is not bursting with enthusiastic officials. No doubt there are some, perhaps growing in numbers, who long to be given a chance to take clear responsibility and to introduce new technologies but many of their colleagues have assimilated the existing rules of the game and prefer the "stable state".[18] Indeed, the most remarkable feature of the famous Zaslavskaya

130

Figure 7.1.   Attitudes of Different Social Strata Towards the Redistributive
Implications of Economic Reform

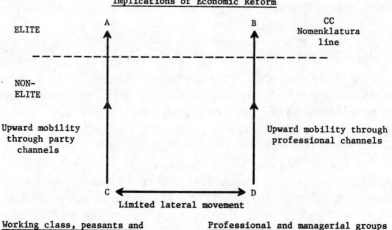

Working class, peasants and
lower white-collar employees

Professional and managerial groups

Notes to Figure 7.1

D The non-nomenklatura members of this group would be the main beneficiaries of an economic
reform. Lacking discreet privileges, they require systemic change in order to obtain higher
rewards for specialized skills and responsibilities. These aspirations are also coloured by resentment
at the narrowing of income differentials between themselves and non-professional groups,
especially at the overlap in income levels between the technical intelligentsia and skilled workers.
The group as a whole possesses a relatively high sense of political efficacy.

C Frustrated by the limited opportunities for social mobility compared with the Stalin years, this
group would be resentful at the widening of income differentials between themselves and group
D, especially since these would take the form of conspicuous consumption compared with under-
the-counter privileges. They would be opposed to a more demanding work regime and growing
managerial authority.

B These are the members of the technical intelligentsia who have "made it" into the elite. While
accepting the intellectual case for reform they no longer have a material interest in it (though
no doubt they are influenced by the expectations of their subordinates). In short, this group
has a commitment to reform but does not have the power or the ideological credentials to carry
it through on its own account.

A This is the professional party component of the elite, drawn originally from the lower orders
of society (though this may soon change). Their interest in reform is pragmatic rather than
intellectual or self-interested. Whilst an improvement in economic performance would be welcome,
their broader social experience and position of ultimate responsibility alert them to the dangers
of instability. They are a mediating force.

References for Figure 7.1

I found the following items particularly useful in thinking about these relationships:

Stephen White, "Contradiction and Change in State Socialism," *Soviet Studies*, vol. xxvi, No. 1
(January 1974), pp. 41–58.
Alex Pravda, "Is there a Soviet Working Class?" *Problems of Communism*, November–December
1982.
Marc Rakovsky, *Towards an East European Marxism*, 1978, especially Chapter 2.
Zigmund Bauman, "Systemic Crises in Soviet-type Societies," *Problems of Communism*, December
1971.
W. Brus and H. H. Ticktin, "Is Market Socialism Possible or Necessary?" *Critique 14*, 1981, pp.
13–39.
R. V. Burks, "The Political Implications of Economic Reform," in M. Bornstein, ed., *Plan and
Market: Economic Reform in Eastern Europe*, New Haven, 1973.
W. D. Connor, "Social Consequences of Economic Reforms in Eastern Europe," in Z. M. Fallenbuchl,
ed., *Economic Development in the Soviet Union and Eastern Europe*, Vol. I, New York, 1975, pp.
65–99.

paper is that whereas the author is utterly convincing when she analyses the major sources of opposition to reform within the government bureaucracy, she fails to identify any major institutional group which is in favour of reform.

It is not, however, just a matter of competence and enthusiasm but also a question of how far the political leadership could trust the moral qualities of economic officials and managers in the more institutionally autonomous environment of a major economic reform. Here, the omens are not good. Grossman reports a widespread view among Western observers that "grasping, hustling and wheeling-and-dealing have been gaining ground in recent years",[19] especially in official circles; to introduce an economic reform without having first imposed a strict code of moral restraint would be tantamount to opening the floodgates. Echoes of these fears found expression in Chernenko's speech to the Party Plenum in June 1983[20] and Andropov's speech to the special meeting of party veterans in August 1983.[21] In the latter case, members of the older generation of party members, tested by the trials of industrialisation and war, were depicted as the ultimate trustees of the nation's soul. In this context, the reluctance of the older generation in the politbureau to make way for a younger successor after the death of Andropov may not be insignificant. Thus, in contradistinction to the conventional view, one might argue that one of the main features of the 1970s and after has been "distrust in cadres", not trust. The low rates of turnover among officials which persisted up to the Andropov period reflected a mutual desire for tranquility after the turmoil of the Khrushchev era; but as a mark of positive satisfaction and trust on the part of the leadership, such stability was an optical illusion.

Finally, even if they decided to go ahead with reform, Soviet leaders would almost certainly recognize that the economic benefits could only be enjoyed, if they occurred at all, in the long term whereas the political costs summarized above would be experienced with certainty in the short run. This perspective would be bound to make them err on the side of caution.

My personal view, therefore, is that as far as one can see at present the process of political transition in the USSR is unlikely to culminate either in a redemption of the revolution by the working class or in the restoration of capitalism as a result of a fundamental change in organisational logic from plan to market. The process is perhaps best viewed in Weberian terms as a transition from a primitive bureaucracy to a modern bureaucracy. More specifically, this might involve a movement (a) from the rigid determination of priorities at the centre to broader con-sultation in the formulation of plans and (perhaps) a limited market element, (b) from stringent administrative controls over resource allocation to greater enterprise autonomy, a substantial diminution in the powers of branch ministries and flexible coordination of complex programmes, reinforced by effective legal contracts, (c) from maximisation of output to encouragement of creativity and novelty and (d) from traditional stress on discipline and obedience to greater reliance on material incentives and "output participation".[22] This would still be a far cry from Western parliamentary democracy or consumer sovereignty but the aggregate effect of such changes could be quite substantial both for the character of Soviet society and for the outlook of its new generation of political leaders.

The Political Implications
of Realistic Reform

Although the political and social obstacles to a truly fun-damental reform of the whole central planning system in the USSR seem overwhelming at first sight there is nevertheless an underlying sense of urgency and an evident willingness on the part of many leading officials and academics to contemplate the kind of substantial overhaul indicated at the end of the previous section. The frequent use of terms such as *"fundamental'naya"* or *"serez'naya perestroika"*, *"radikal'nye izmeneniya sistemy ru-kovodstva proizvodstvom"* or talk of the need for measures which have a *"kompleksnyi kharakter"* has not abated noticeably since the death of Andropov; these terms were constantly repeated during the Chernenko period and by Chernenko himself[23]. Western economists who regard an annual rate of growth of GNP of between 2 and 3 per cent as "tolerable" tend to underestimate the basic impulse for reform[24] because their evaluations of the situation are based on an implicit Western notion of "muddling through" from a position of relative affluence. Arguably, such a suggestion underplays certain sociopolitical aspects of the situation as they might be viewed by Soviet leaders themselves. First, and most obviously, the USSR is not in a favourable position in terms of relative levels of national wealth. Pressing claims on national resources (especially from the defence sector) in conditions of falling growth rates may intensify the "politics of stringency". Under these circumstances if reform is intended it is best to undertake it as soon as possible because the short and medium-term economic dislocations that a reform will inevitably bring become progressively more difficult to accept as resources become scarcer. The successful launching of the new Hungarian economic mechanism in 1968 would seem to illustrate the importance of introducing the reform at a time when the most favourable internal and external circumstances are present. To "tough it out", therefore, may not be a rational option if one foresees a slow but steady deterioration in future performance. Second, and more speculatively, there is a broader ideological dimension to the problem which stems from a basic difference between countries like the United States, which are trying to conserve a utopia based on universalistic values, and those like the Soviet Union, which are trying to achieve utopia through conscious historical progression. For the leaders of the latter, the transparent loss of *perspektiva*, and the growth of public cynicism could be profoundly disturbing. In these kinds of societies, where economic performance and political legitimation are so closely linked (especially within the concept of "developed socialism", "muddling through" may not be regarded as a satisfactory remedy. The few fragments of survey evidence that we have seem to confirm that up to a point there is quite widespread support for reform among Soviet officials and specialists; a survey carried out in Georgia in 1982, for example, indicated that the majority of respondents who expressed a preference were in favour of substantial reform and as many as 20 per cent of the total sample (including don't-knows) were in favour of "radical reform"—defined in terms of greater enterprise independence, enhanced role of the customer and the creation of a single ministry for industry. The authors of the study argue that this result, if anything, underestimates reformist sentiment and conclude with some confidence that "the reformist orientation is beginning to prevail over the conservative". More recently, a survey of enterprise directors reported in the Siberian economic journal *EKO* arrived at broadly similar conclusions.[25] In the light of these socio-political considerations, taken together with long recognized economic pressures, it is perhaps not surprising that during his short but interesting term in office, Andropov arrived at the conclusion (announced at the June 1983 Plenum of the Central Committee) that economic reform "was not simply a wish . . . but an objective necessity".[26]

The most ambitious published reform proposals to come out recently are to be found in the writings of B. P. Kurashvili, a Section Head at the Academy of Sciences' Institute of State and Law in Moscow.[27] It is worth concentrating on Kurashvili's ideas and trying to evaluate their socio-political implications, first because they are reasonably coherent and, secondly, because they probably represent the maximum programme of institutional reconstruction that would be acceptable to the central authorities under present political circumstances.

In common with several other writers,[28] Kurashvili considers that the present system of branch ministries lies at the heart of the Soviet Union's economic problem and, hence, must be the major target for reform. The endemic "departmentalism" of the ministries is regarded as inimical to technical progress, which places increasing demands on inter-branch cooperation. Their petty tutelage is an obstacle to greater enterprise independence, yet only greater enterprise independence can relieve the ministries of the necessity to intervene in detailed matters of day to day administration: these are rightly viewed as two aspects of the same problem, which can only be resolved by a complex systemic approach. In many cases, the steady march of ministerial autarky has led to a quite illogical situation in which branch ministries no longer even control all relevant enterprises producing a given type of product. The concept of "branch" has thus become a largely administrative one, lacking its original raison d'être.

In order to deal with this situation Kurashvili considers three variants of reform: minimal reform (*stabilizatsionnaya al'ternativa*), moderate reform (*umerennaya perestroika*) and radical reform (*radikal'naya perestroika*).

The guiding principle of a *minimal reform* would be that everything must improve but nothing should change. Branch ministries would remain in existence but renewed attempts would be made to develop inter-branch coordination either through the creation of a few "superministries" responsible for producing related families of products or through the strengthening of inter branch programmes. Emphasis would also be placed on the improvement of contractual relations between enterprises. Kurashvili doubts whether this approach would be nearly enough to make the ministries more flexible or outward-looking, given that "the command style [of management] is in their blood".[29] It is much more likely in his view that the economy would carry on in the same old way as before with no authority able effectively to uphold and impose the overall social interest in the face of each ministry's toleration (even cynical encouragement) of formalistic plan fulfilment on the part of its constituent enterprises, reflected in various kinds of output distortion. Micro rationality would continue to triumph over macro rationality.

A *moderate reform*, by contrast, would attempt to strengthen real central control by reducing the number of ministries from over fifty to about ten, each responsible for a broad area of economic activity (energy, metallurgy, engineering, transport, etc.). This would be less disruptive than a radical reform and would have the advantage of providing a relatively easy path of retreat to tougher and more directive forms of planning if the need arose (an ominous argument when we remember the fate of earlier reforms!). However, Kurashvili notes astutely that moderate reform is half-hearted and its likely outcomes would be undesirable. Without the much more radical measure of greater enterprise autonomy, either the newly enlarged ministries would become hopelessly overloaded with detail or the old ministries, in the guise of *glavki*, would reoccupy the power vacuum, thus restoring the essentials of the previous system. In any event, moderate reform along the lines described makes no provision for rational economic integration at the republican and regional level—surely a key objective of any institutional reform.

Radical reform, which derives its philosophy, though not its specific institutional details, from Hungarian experience, envisages the division of the whole of Soviet material production into four spheres: the economy, municipal services and communications, transport, and defence. The first sphere, which is Kurashvili's main concern, would be administered entirely by a Ministry for the National Economy *(Minnarkhoz)* with parallel organs at the republican and regional level *(sovnarkhozy)*. Gosplan would become responsible for planning the general social and economic development of the country (though its specific relationship to *Minnarkhoz* in this respect is unclear). In principle, the granting of substantial autonomy to enterprises would allow all the central agencies to confine themselves to long-term strategic decisions and not become drawn into day to day management. In short, a radical reform based on territorial areas rather than on increasingly artificial branches could offer all the benefits of the 1957 *sovnarkhoz* reform yet avoid its major weakness—the lack of central control. The planning process envisaged by Kurashvili would have the following specific features:

- Long, medium and short-term plans for national development, based on forecasts and research into prevailing national economic needs and conditions, would be handed down by *Minnarkhoz* to *sovnarkhozy*, but not directly to enterprises.
- Industrial enterprises would pass up plans to *sovnarkhozy* based on a portfolio of orders freely negotiated with other enterprises and cemented by contract.
- National plans and enterprise plans would (in theory) be reconciled by a process of adjustment in the light of "recommendations" made by *Minnarkhoz* and its subordinate organs. *Minnarkhoz* would indicate to enterprises the areas in which investment funds, credits and tax advantages would be available. It would also lay down aggregate performance requirements based on value-added criteria and very general constraints on product assortment.

- Freed of the need to involve itself in detailed management, *Minnarkhoz* could concentrate on the realisation of selective major objectives by means of programme planning, both nationally and regionally; the orders arising from such programmes would supplement those which enterprises had initiated themselves in forming their plans. Furthermore, *Minnarkhoz* would retain in this connection a number of strategic powers: (a) the sole right to create new enterprises (in order to prevent monopoly, among other things) and (b) direct control over the whole industrial R & D network.
- Minimum wages would be laid down by the state together with the appropriate salary increments for increased academic qualifications. But beyond this minimum level, salaries would depend on actual performance and significant income differentials could be expected between individuals and institutions in the same line of work.
- *Minnarkhoz* would retain the right to confirm the appointment of enterprise directors, who might eventually be elected by their labour collectives.
- The above system of economic planning would involve a change in the law in order to facilitate the legal transfer of productive assets to enterprises, who would pay interest to the state for land and deposits of raw materials as well as for capital equipment.

The general hope would be that a fairly radical reform of this type would finally deliver the economic planning system from "the plague of departmentalism".[30] It would remove the barriers to cooperation between organisations currently locked into ministerial compartments, thus promoting sensible integration both nationally and regionally. With the abolition of the administrative framework which had given rise to formalistic plan fulfilment, the reform would give a better deal to the consumer by balancing real demand (transmitted through orders) against carefully formulated national needs. Finally, instead of being swamped with detail the centre would now possess a real capability to make and implement decisions of long-term significance.

Before we consider the socio-political implications of these ambitious (but realistic?) proposals it is worth noting how cleverly the case is argued, presumably in order to disarm opposition from the most obvious quarters. The defence sector is preserved as a separate entity in the proposed scheme. The danger of the black economy getting out of control as a result of inadequate legal regulation of enterprise activity is also anticipated;[31] according to the reformers, greater enterprise autonomy should in no sense be seen as a concession to anarchosyndicalistic tendencies, a distinction which Andropov was at pains to make in his key article in *Kommunist* which gave initial encouragement to the reform debate in the USSR.[32] The major ideological justification for institutional reform is to be found, rather, in the search for an optimal balance between authority and autonomy. As Engels pointed out in his classic article "On Authority", "Authority and autonomy are relative things and the way in which they are applied varies with different phases of social development. . . . Future social organisation will tolerate authority [interpreted as socialist state power by Kurashvili] only within those limits which are made unavoidable by the conditions of production".[33] Thus, the main thrust of the reformist argument is that an optimal balance between state power and enterprise autonomy will actually increase the real capacity of the centre to determine essential priorities and to protect the overall social interest: central political power will therefore be enhanced. It is a formulation which in principle protects the flank of the reformers against the vested interests of the military-industrial complex and charges of ideological heresy from conservatives such as Ignatovsky.[34] Whether it does so in practice, of course, is another matter.

Turning to the broader political implications of these reform proposals, one needs to make the obvious point that the potential sources of opposition which would inhibit the introduction of a fundamental reform, summarized in the previous section of the paper, are not entirely circumvented by the somewhat more "realistic" approach outlined in this section. The latter approach, on the surface at least, avoids the most controversial features of the former: the free movement of prices and the specific commitment to dismember the mechanism of centralised supplies. It would therefore be less threatening to the party's leading role or to the traditional expectations of the defence sector. On the other hand, such a scaled-down reform would still raise the spectre of social tensions arising from widening income differentials and would place new and unwelcome demands on many officials and managers who had learned to live with the traditional planning system. In addition to these general considerations, the Kurashvili-type reform proposals raise a number of specific political and administrative issues.

First, it is not at all certain that the social groups whose position would be enhanced by reform, in terms of either income or power, would succeed in getting it introduced. It is plausible to suppose that the younger and more dynamic managers and technocrats would be in favour of reform. Although they may not yet constitute an overwhelming majority of their profession, the Georgian survey cited earlier hints that their numbers may nevertheless be substantial. Recent writings in *Pravda*, which extol the virtues of regional development programmes (successes in the Ukraine seem to be referred to most frequently) also indicate that many regional party officials could be expected to favour a reform based on a new territorial form of organisation. These individuals would be powerful supporters for this variant of reform, which unlike a more radical market reform would provide them with an opportunity to play a crucial coordinating role, as Romanov apparently did during his time as the Leningrad party boss.[35] On the other hand, there is no disguising the fact that the creation of a new Ministry for the National Economy (*Minnarkhoz*) would come as a crushing blow to the industrial ministries and to the status of their officials, only some of whom could be absorbed into the new administrative apparatus if the intention of the reformers is to be realised. The side-effects of this reform in terms of status anxiety and job insecurity would go far beyond the conversion of ministries to state committees in 1957 or the bifurcation of the party in 1962. A related issue is the position of Gosplan itself. Beyond verbal re-assurances about the continuation of its major role it is not clear specifically whether the existing branch departments (*otdely*) of Gosplan and Gosstroi and their officials would form the basis of *Minnarkhoz*[36] or whether *Minnarkhoz* would be formed as a separate institution, usurping some of these powers in the course of time. This is, to put it mildly, a controversial matter. But whatever decision might finally be taken on this score, the pragmatic argument against having only one central organisation ultimately responsible for running the whole national economy is that the administrative burden would be too large. Bisher, for example, who is generally sympathetic to reform, believes that the proposal is impractical on these grounds alone.[37]

Second, Kurashvili's reform proposals contain a potential contradiction. This stems from those very aspects of his proposals which may help them to gain political acceptability: the central contradiction is between enterprise autonomy and substantial remnants of direct central control. On the one hand, enterprises enter into contracts with other enterprises for supplies and deliveries, yet superimposed upon this arrangement is the defence section, which comes under a different chain of command, and centrally or regionally administered development programmes. In theory there is no inevitable contradiction here because state or territorial organisations might be regarded as customers, just like any other. In practice, however, there are strong historical grounds for thinking that in the USSR priority sectors could begin to encroach on the others. General economic guidelines could quickly become detailed instructions if the machinery existed to facilitate it and the circumstances were deemed to warrant it. External military pressures which lead to a greater emphasis on defence (a distinct possibility) or intractable bot- tlenecks in key areas of the economy which threatened major development programmes would provide such grounds. More- over, within the reform proposals potential instruments are available for much more detailed influence over the day to day activities of enterprises: the application of stronger direct controls to enterprises whose plans are consistently out of line with central guidelines, the right to choose (and, presumably, dismiss) directors, the prohibition of "unjustifiably" large wage differ- entials (enjoyed by firms pursuing their own interests) and the regulation of contract prices. All these powers, taken together, could represent the thin end of the wedge and thus demonstrate the difficulty in practice of reconciling the political logic of central planning with the economic logic of greater enterprise autonomy. This difficulty is appreciated by leading Soviet economists such as Aganbegyan, who summed up a recent round table discussion sponsored by the journal *EKO* in the following way:

> The hardest thing to do will be to combine national-economic centralisation organically with expanded independence for primary economic units, the all-round democratisation of management and the enlistment of broad masses of the working people in it.[38]

Finally, reform proposals of the type advanced by Kurashvili by no means guarantee the removal of administrative barriers. The separation of the R & D network from production would be perpetuated and perhaps even intensified because the two sides would no longer be brought together even within the confines of industrial ministries: this could be a recipe for encouragement of ivory tower attitudes among research personnel, though it would avoid the danger of subordinating technical policy to narrow departmental interests. It is also not clear how the danger of *mestnichestvo* would be avoided in circumstances where the real locus of power would be bound to lie at the republican and regional level. Conservatives like Ignatovsky may have a point when they assert in the context of giving greater powers to republics and regions that localism as much as departmentalism conflicts with the Leninist principle of control and runs counter to the objective "integrity" *(tselostnost')* of the socialist economy.[39]

Conclusions

The *sovnarkhoz* reform of 1957 decentralised the levels of economic decision making but retained the traditional system of detailed success indicators. The 1965 reform recentralised the administrative structure but simplified the enterprise's success indicators, giving greater emphasis to sales and profitability. Neither of these reforms succeeded, partly because they did not go far enough and the logic of centralised directive planning reasserted itself. The same fate awaited the incremental reforms of the later Brezhnev period, which rested upon the false assumptions (a) that organisational arrangements that had been successful in the defence sector could be successfully transplanted on a much less resource-selective basis in the civilian sector and (b) that in some sense, streamlining the process of decison making could be a substitute for raw dynamism. Compared with these attempts at reform, the proposed reform we considered above goes much further because it addresses itself both to administrative decentalisation and to greater enterprise autonomy. In the light of our previous analysis it is probably the very most that would be politically acceptable in the USSR today. However, even though such a scheme avoids the most radical features of a full-blooded market reform it still presents potential political, social and administrative problems. Whether such a reform is adopted and whether it can be sustained depends a great deal on the political determination and adventurous spirit of the next post-Stalin generation of political leaders. Have they the nerve to relax control?

Notes

1. Gertrude E. Schroeder, "The Soviet Economy on a Treadmill of Reforms", in *Soviet Economy in a Time of Change* (Washington, D.C.: Joint Economic Committee of the US Congress, 1979), pp. 65–88.

2. See the interesting articles by Valerie Bunce, in D. R. Kelley, ed., *Soviet Politics in the Brezhnev Era* (New York, 1980), and "The Political Economy of the Brezhnev Era: The Rise and Fall of Corporatism", *British Journal of Political Science*, Vol. 13, 1983, pp. 129–158.

3. Joseph Berliner, "Managing the Soviet Economy: Alternative Models", *Problems of Communism*, January–February 1983.

4. Fedor Burlatsky, "Mezhdutsarstvie", *Novyi Mir*, 1982, No. 4, pp. 205–228, contains a fascinating discussion of the general issues of reform in an oblique form. The so-called Novosibirsk Report, written by Professor Tatyana Zaslavskaya and first reported in *The Washington Post*, 3 August 1983, is the leaked version. The most outspoken published versions are: B. P. Kurashvili, "Gosudarstvennoe upravlenie narodnym khozyaistvom: perspecktivy razvitiya", *Sovetskoe gosudarstvo i pravo*, 1982, No. 6., pp. 38–48 and "Sud'by ostraslevogo upravleniya", *EKO*, 1983, No. 10, pp. 34–55.

5. Seweryn Bialer, *Stalin's Successors: Leadership. Stability and Change in the Soviet Union* (Cambridge, 1980), Part V; Philip Hanson, "Economic Constraints on Soviet Policies in the 1980s", *International Affairs*, Winter 1980/81, pp. 21–43; R. Amann, "Technical Progress and Political Change in the Soviet Union", in A. Schuller *et al.*, eds., *Innovatsionsprobleme in Ost und West* (Stuttgart and New York, 1983), pp. 197–212; Gregory Grossman, "Some Implications of Low Growth for Soviet Economy and Society", unpublished discussion paper, 1984; E. A. Hewett, "Soviet Economic Reform: Lessons from Eastern Europe", paper presented to NASEES Conference, Cambridge, March, 1984; R. W. Campbell, "The Economy", in R. F. Byrnes, ed. *After Brezhnev*, London, 1983, pp. 68–124; J. P. Hardt and Donna L. Gold, "The Soviet Economy: Can the Economic Programme of the Post-Brezhnev Leadership Make a Difference?" paper delivered at conference organised by the CSIS of Georgetown University and the Konrad-Adenauer-Stiftung, Bonn, April, 1984.

6. A tentative attempt to quantify this, though this was not its explicit purpose, is T. M. Dzhafarli *et al.* "Nekotorye aspekty uskoreniya nauchno-tekhnicheskogo progressa", *Sotsiologicheskie issledovaniya*, 1983, No. 2, pp. 58–63.

7. This term comes from Gerry Hough, *The Soviet Prefects* (Cambridge, Mass., 1969).

8. The procedure by which the military producers "plunder" the economic system for supplies is described by Alexander Yanov, *Detente After Brezhnev* (Berkeley, 1977) Chapter 2. This picture is, of course, very much opposed to one which assumes that no military industrial complex exists in the USSR and that the economy is equally at home producing guns or butter (see, for example, Zhores Medvedev, *New Left Review*, No. 130, December 1981, pp. 5–22).

9. Quoted by R. V. Burks, "The Political Implications of Economic Reform", in M. Borstein, ed. *Plan and Market: Economic Reform in Eastern Europe* (New Haven, 1973), p. 381.

10. P. Ignatovsky, "O politicheskom podkhode k ekonomike", *Kommunist*, 1983, No. 12, pp. 60–72. See also E. Rubik, "Antimarksistskie kontseptsii upravleniya sotsialisticheskim proizvodstvom", *Voprosy ekonomiki*, 1983, No. 7, p. 142. I am grateful to Bob Davies for pointing out to me that these kinds of arguments are not in the least new (see, R. W. Davies, "The Socialist Market: A Debate in Soviet Industry 1932–33", *CREES Discussion Paper*, SIPS No. 23, 1982).

11. E. P. Hoffman and R. F. Laird, *The Politics of Economic Modernization in the Soviet Union* (Ithaca, NY, 1982), p. 70.

12. Berliner, "Managing the Soviet Economy," op. cit. sees this as one of the most realistic reform options.

13. I. R. Gabor, "The Second (Secondary) Economy: Earning Activity and Regrouping of Income Outside the Socially Organised Production and Distribution", *Acta Oeconomica*, Vol. 22, 1979, pp. 291–311. (I am grateful to Judy Batt for drawing my attention to this interesting article.)

14. A. Eremin, "Formy sobstvennosti pri sotsializme", *Voprosy ekonomiki*, 1983, No. 9, pp. 3–13.

15. Viktor Zaslavsky, *The Neo-Stalinist State* (London, 1982), Chapter 3, pp. 44–65.

16. M. Rakovski, *Towards an East European Marxism* (London, 1978), Chapter 2, pp. 18–38; Zigmund Bauman, "Systemic Crises in Soviet-type Societies", *Problems of Communism*, December 1971, pp. 45–53.

17. R. J. Hill, *Soviet Politics, Political Science and Reform* (Oxford, 1980), Concluding Chapter.

18. Donald Schon, *Beyond the Stable State* (New York, 1971) shows how all large bureaucracies will desperately hang on to an established pattern of relationships in the face of change.

19. Grossman, "Some Implications," op. cit., p. 8.

20. Konstantin Chernenko, address to the plenary session of the Central Committee, *Pravda*, 15 June, 1983.

21. Yu. V. Andropov, speech to party veterans in *Pravda*, 16 August 1983.

22. The concept is elaborated by T. H. Friedgut, *Political Participation in the Soviet Union* (Princeton, NJ, 1979), pp. 13–20 to distinguish it from a narrrow concern with input articulation, which is the more characteristic form of political participation in Western systems.

23. I. O. Bisher, "Sovershenstvovanie otraslevogo upravleniya", *Sovetskoe gosudarstvo i pravo*, 1984, No. 4, p. 27. See, also, the address of M. Gorbachev to the All-Union Conference on ideology, *Pravda*, 11 December, 1984, and the major editorial article in *Pravda*, 17 January 1985.

24. See for example, Hewett, "Soviet economic reform," p. 36; David Dyker, "Soviet Planning Reforms: Andropov and After", paper given to Symposium on Soviet Science and Industry, University of Birmingham, September 1984, pp. 20–21.

25. Dzhafarli et al., "Nekotorye aspekty," p. 62; E. Kolosova, "Pyat' voprosov direktoru", *EKO*, 1984, No. 12, pp. 72–76.

26. Quoted by Kurashvili, "Sud'by otraslevogo upravleniya", p. 35.

27. *Ibid.*, pp. 34–55; "Gosudarstvennoe upravlenie," pp. 38–48. Kurashvili was also co-author of the article by Dzhafarli *et al.*, "Nekotorye aspekty."

28. Bisher, "Sovershenstvovanie," p. 29; R. G. Karagedov, "Ob organizatsionnoi strukture upravleniya promyshlennost'yu", *EKO*, 1983, No. 8, pp. 50–69; G. Popov, "The Development of Branch Industrial Management", *CDSP*, Vol. XXXV, No. 23, 1982, p. 2 (translated from *Kommunist*), 1982, No. 18.

29. Kurashvili, "Sud'by otraslevogo upravleniya", p. 38.

30. M. Mikhailov, "Po povodu vedomstvennosti", *Kommunist*, 1981, No. 8, p. 105.

31. T. I. Zaslavskaya, "Ekonomicheskoe povedenie i ekonomicheskoe razvitie", *EKO*, 1980, No. 3, quoted by Kurashvili, "Sudby otraslevogo upravleniya", p. 41.

32. Yu. V. Andropov, "Uchenie Karla Marksa i nekotorye voprosy kommunisticheskogo stroitel'stva v SSSR", *Kommunist*, 1983, No. 3, p. 19.

33. Kurashvili, "Sud'by otraslevogo upravleniya", op. cit., p. 42.

34. Ignatovsky, "O politicheskom podkhode," op. cit., pp. 60–72.

35. Blair Ruble, "Romanov's Leningrad", *Problems of Communism*, November–December 1983, pp. 36–49; Terry McNeill, "Grigorii Vasil'evich Romanov—The Other Heir Presumptive", *Radio Liberty Research*, 25 January, 1985.

36. In his 1982 article, "Gosudarstvennoe upravlenie," op. cit. (p. 146) Kurashvili hints at this, but the suggestion is not repeated in the later 1983 article, "Sud'by otraslevogo upravleniya".

37. Bisher, "Sovershenstvovanie," op. cit., p. 31.

38. A. G. Aganbegyan, round table discussion in *EKO*, 1983, No. 8 (abstracted in *CDSP*, Vol XXXV, No. 48, 1983, p. 10). A recent article by an emigre Soviet planner, F. I. Kushnirsky, "The Limits of Soviet Economic Reform", *Problems of Communism*, July–August 1984, p. 39 suggests that since the real aim of reformers is to obtain enterprise autonomy and their apparent commitment to central control is merely political rhetoric, the contradiction is only superficial.

39. Ignatovsky, "O politicheskom podkhode," op. cit., p. 71.

8
The Political Economy of Soviet Nationalities and Regions

Hans-Jürgen Wagener

Introduction

To begin with, let me say a few words about those aspects of the political economy of Soviet nationalities which I actually do not want to discuss in this chapter. Simon has claimed that "the Soviet Union is the last colonial empire of European history."[1] Personally, I do not like this approach to the nationalities question or the regional problem of the Soviet Union, which I consider to be inappropriate. Colonialism may be impressive, but is nevertheless a reasonably well defined historical concept. Economic exploitation is certainly a necessary, although perhaps not sufficient, condition for colonialism. As I have shown earlier,[2] and as has been corroborated by other studies,[3] a huge transfer of resources from the more developed to the less developed regions of the USSR has been taking place at least for the last three decades. In terms of colonialism the former Central Asian colonies should be the "exploiters" while the Ukraine and the Baltic republics are the "exploited". Obviously, this is not a very meaningful approach.

It could perhaps be more pertinent to ask whether the formula with which Soviet historians describe Tsarist imperialism could not be applied to the present state of affairs: "Tsarism was a prison of peoples—this formula is fundamentally true. In this prison also the elder brother of our peoples was starving, the great Russian people".[4] This description reflects at least two important features of Soviet nationality policy: 1) the totalitarian rule and 2) the elevated position of the Russian people. Certainly, there is "voice" to be heard about this situation inside the Soviet Union. But it is methodologically a very delicate problem to find out whether there are peoples who actually would take the exit option if their formal constitutional right to secede from the Union were valid in practice. Anyhow, the verdict of "imperialism" seems to me to be a meaningful hypothesis only within the confines of Schumpeter's definition of imperialism as "objectless disposition of a state to forceful expansion without specifiable limit".[5] This idea has been formulated more accurately by Eisenstadt in his definition: "The term 'empire' has normally been used to designate a political system . . . *in which the center*, as embodied both in the person of the emperor and in the central political institutions, *constituted an autonomous entity*. Further, although empires have usually been based on traditional legitimation, they have often embraced some wider, potentially universal political and cultural orientation *that went beyond that of any of their component parts*"[6] (emphasis added).

To discover the social groups and ideologies which support this disposition or orientation is a problem of political sociology, not of political economy. Of course, building an empire has economic prerequisites and consequences and thus it will have implications for national economic policy. But the verdict of imperialism, even if it is sustained, does not generate fruitful hypotheses or insights into the economic relations of Soviet nationalities and regions. So, we will not pursue this question any further.

Dilemmas of Economic Policy

By now it is high time to spell out what I do want to discuss here. The starting point of the analysis is two major dilemmas of Soviet economic policy during the 1980s and 1990s: 1) the declining and eventually stagnating increment to labour supply while Soviet economic growth is still rather dependent on increasing factor inputs, and 2) the regional disparity in future labour supply: it will continue to grow in the less industrialized non-Russian south and decline in the highly industrialized western and Russian regions. Both dilemmas are caused by demographic factors and by the history of Soviet industrialization and development which will be assumed to be known. The problem has been stated quite appropriately by H. Carrère d'Encause.[7] We shall look at how Soviet regional economic policy has reacted to that challenge and what difficulties it has encountered or will encounter in the near future. The economic policy options will be considered in the light of recent developments in agriculture and industry. Our working hypothesis is that the Soviet economic system in its present form and with its present policy objectives is ill equipped to cope with the challenge.

First we must say a few words about the units we are dealing with, the Soviet union republics, and the data situation. Nationalities are not economic, but ethnic and cultural units. Their economic life can only be analyzed if they inhabit a political community which happens to be a unit of economic policy and of statistical data gathering. Soviet regionalization has followed two principles: 1) political units, autonomous republics and union republics, which, to a certain degree, reflect national units, and 2) economic regions which suit planning purposes and are more homogeneous from the economic point of view. In view of the vast size of the country, Khrushchev's 105 planning regions (sovnarkhozy) probably constituted a reasonable breakdown economically. They have disappeared, as did the nineteen large economic regions for which scanty data were last given in the 1975 statistical yearbook. At the same time, some detailed structural data disappeared from *Narkhoz* too (for instance the break-down of the industrial labour force). To add to our data problems, the publication of information from the 1979 census[8] has been rather restricted. The age composition of republican populations, for instance, is conspicuously missing. We are inclined to conclude that *TsSU* has been drawing a veil over certain regional and structural developments.

In fact, we have no option but to analyze our problem with union republican data. In general this is not the optimal choice from the point of view of economic regionalization. However, in our context demographic data and trends play a major role and they are nation-specific. With union republics we cover most of the major Soviet nationalities (except the Tatars, Germans,

TABLE 8.1. Estimated Increments to Potential Labour Force, 1970-2000
(average annual increase in 000s)

Period	Total	High Supply Regions	Low Supply Regions
1971 - 1975	2,545	956	1,589
1976 - 1980	2,081	929	1,153
1981 - 1995	636	756	-110
1996 - 2000	1,802	1,216	586

Source: Feshbach and Rapawy, 'Soviet Population', p. 129.

Jews, Chuvash), as they inhabit preferentially their titular republic and form the majority of its population (except for Kazakhstan, where the Russians are more numerous than the Kazakhs).

The increment to working-age population has been estimated by Feshbach and Rapawy.[9] Dividing the Soviet Union into two parts (north/north-west and south) yields roughly a division into high fertility/high labour supply regions and low fertility/low labour supply regions: 1) south (high labour supply): Central Asia, Transcaucasia and Kazakhstan, and 2) north/north-west (low labour supply): the RSFSR and the other European republics. It has been stressed that Table 8.1 is an estimate based upon the 1970 census and certain assumptions about reproductive behaviour. But even if the concrete figures should not be treated as precise, the general trend of demographic and manpower development is certainly realistic. Table 8.1 needs little further explanation. It clearly reflects the two dilemmas mentioned, a marked slow-down of additional labour supply and its concentration in the republics of the southern belt of the USSR.

Policy Options

In an economy where stagnating labour supply is one of the major constraints to economic growth, optimal utilization of existing capacities becomes of paramount importance for economic policy. Roughly speaking there are two options in the context of the supply situation we have described: 1) Bring industry to the labour reserves, i.e. accelerate economic growth in the high supply regions. This implies an intensification of the transfer of capital and material resources to those regions, or 2) bring the labour reserves to industry, i.e. intensify migration to labour deficit regions so that economic growth and development in these regions can be kept up.

We shall now examine which of these options Soviet planning has preferred and what are the instruments available and chosen in order to implement the policy. On a very general level we may state that it is easier for a socialist planner to move capital and material resources than to move labour resources. For there is free choice of working place while production decisions are taken centrally and the financial surpluses of firms are centralized and redistributed from the center. A policy maker in a market economy, on the other hand, has much greater difficulty in redirecting capital flows whereas the forces of the market make labour move quickly from surplus to deficit regions (the well-known *Mezzogiorno* problem). However, labour supply is not the only concern of Soviet planners. A major field of interest is Siberia. To settle and develop this vast part of the country is seen as a kind of historical obligation of Soviet policy. Apart from this general attitude, the Siberian reserves of national resources attract economic attention, especially since the two oil price shocks. The enormous investment requirements of this programme pose the choice of Siberia vs. the South as far as economic development is concerned.

Since the times of the first industrialization under Count Sergei Witte Russian and Soviet structural policy had a preference for raw material intensive heavy industries. This is also reflected in the Soviet export structure which is heavily dominated by raw materials, for a considerable part of Siberian origin. So, if a choice has to be made between a labour oriented strategy and a raw material oriented strategy, it should not be too difficult to guess which will prevail. Besides, it is rather tempting to look for a solution of the conflict in labour migration from the south to the north.

Table 8.1 has shown the projected development of the potential labour force. If we now turn to actual employment growth, we would expect it to decline sharply in the low supply regions after 1975, less sharply in the high supply regions, and to be considerably higher in the latter than the former. Table 8.A1 (in the Appendix) confirms this expectation. It is reasonable to assume that this trend will continue from 1983 onwards. Since Soviet economic growth is still rather of the extensive pattern, we would further expect the development of employment to be reflected in the growth of output (national income produced). This is true on the whole (see again Table 8.A1). But some remarkable exceptions have to be mentioned: In the first period (1971–1975) the low supply regions achieved an output growth slightly above average, which implies that their labour productivity was clearly above average. Out of the high supply regions— which at that time included also Moldavia—Central Asia, Kazakhstan and Moldavia could not fully exploit their labour resources or, in other words, their labour productivity was below average. During the second period (1976–1982) the low labour productivity of Central Asia and Kazakhstan becomes even more pronounced. Transcaucasia, on the other hand, now seems to exploit its supply optimally, even achieving above average labour productivity.

We see that among the high supply regions we have to distinguish between economically progressive Transcaucasia and Central Asia plus Kazakhstan where productivity growth is lagging behind. Since the first group of republics contains Azerbaijan one should be very careful about conclusions as to ethnic differences. We shall have to pursue this phenomenon further.

The general decline of labour productivity can certainly be partly ascribed to the slower growth of capital supply; newly installed fixed assets grew during the first period by 6.7 per cent on an annual average, but during the second period only by 3.7 per cent. If we look at the relative capital accumulation position of the different regions with respect to the RSFSR (table 8.A2), we find that all other republics lost some weight. This reflects the concentration of capital investment in the RSFSR and there, it is fairly safe to assume, in Siberia and the Far East. This concentration happened mainly at the expense of the relative position of Central Asia, Kazakhstan and Moldavia. The latter shows that such a decline need not necessarily result in a decline in labour productivity. Although Transcaucasia fell back with respect to the RSFSR, it was just able to maintain its share in total newly installed capital.

The absolute level of regional capital intensity is a matter of economic structure. Nevertheless it is remarkable that the share of Central Asia and Kazakhstan in total newly installed fixed assets fell from 13.13 per cent in 1970 to 11.85 per cent in 1982, whereas their share in total employment rose from 10.49 to 12.52 per cent.[10] The slowdown of labour productivity growth may be taken as an indication that this development was not accompanied by appropriate structural changes, but rather testifies to a deliberate neglect of available and potential labour supply.

Analysis of investment yields the same result. So we may conclude that accumulation policy does not show any reaction to the fact that during the coming decade potential labour supply will grow annually by about 1 per cent in Transcaucasia, 2 per cent in Kazakhstan and 3 per cent in Central Asia. On the contrary, the treatment of the RSFSR seems to indicate that Siberia and the natural resources of that region enjoy a higher preference with Soviet planners than the human resources of the south. The share of the RSFSR in newly installed fixed assets rose from 58.76 per cent in 1970 to 62.88 per cent twelve years later, while its share in employment declined from 56.76 to 55.69 per cent[11] and can be expected to decline more rapidly in the near future.

Regional Economic Development

Before jumping to conclusions I should prefer to take a closer look at regional economic development. Table 8.A3 gives data on agricultural and industrial growth; it tells a fairly simple story:

1. Agriculture:
   - the south (including Moldavia) has a considerably higher growth performance than the west and the north;
   - in the period 1976–1982 growth declined sharply in all regions except the Transcaucasus.

2. Industry:
- in the period 1971–1975 growth performance is fairly equal over all republics, the south being only slightly above average;
- sector A (means of production, i.e. mainly heavy industry and machine building) enjoys more rapid growth than sector B (consumer goods, i.e. mainly light and food industries) in all republics except Transcaucasia and Uzbekistan where both sectors are more or less on the same growth level;[12]
- during the period 1976–1982 growth declined sharply in all regions except the Transcaucasus;
- sector A is still predominant on average; however, in the south the situation is reversed (except for Kirghizia) and sector B grows more rapidly than sector A or, more correctly, growth in sector B declined less markedly than in sector A.

It is remarkable how this picture corresponds to the employment situation: an average decline in the second period and a sharp north/north-west vs. south differentiation. It seems reasonable to test the employment elasticity of output on the basis of cross-sectional data. Furthermore, agriculture is the main supplier of inputs for sector B industries. In 1966, for instance, 72 per cent of material inputs from other sectors into the textile industry came from agriculture.[13] Obviously, in the food industry this share is even higher. So a high growth of agricultural output induces a high growth of sector B industry, or otherwise the agricultural output has to be exported as is the case with Kazakh grain.

A cross sectional correlation test yielded the following results:

1971–1975

$$x_L = -.018 + 1.554e$$
$$(-.03) \quad (6.91) \qquad R^2 = .79$$

$$x_B = 5.757 + .310x_L$$
$$(8.44) \quad (1.79) \qquad R^2 = .20$$

1976–1982

$$x_L = -.209 + 1.304e$$
$$(-.27)   (3.60)   R^2 = .50$$

$$x_B = 3.244 + .823x_L$$
$$(6.98)   (5.15)   R^2 = .67$$

where,

x_L = average annual growth rate of gross agriculture production;

x_B = average annual growth rate of gross production in sector B industry;

e = average annual growth rate of total employment; the figures in brackets are t-ratios. The data are taken from tables 8.A1 and 8.A3.

The results are quite good for cross section analysis. It should be noticed that the employment elasticity of agricultural output is greater than unity and that there is no autonomous growth in this sector. The direct regression of industrial output growth on employment did not yield significant results. Labour supply seems not to be the directly effective constraint for industrial output. This confirms the findings of an earlier time series approach.[14] Especially in the second period the dependence of sector B industries upon agricultural supplies becomes quite evident.

The results of the statistical exercise and of table 8.A3 can now be interpreted in two ways:

View 1. Agricultural and sector B industry are labour intensive activities (the labour intensity of light industry and food industry was 29 per cent and 85 per cent above the industry average, respectively in 1975).[15] Higher growth of these sectors means a higher absorption of additional labour supply. Regional factor endowments require this type of regional specialization.[16]

View 2. The extremely high employment elasticity of argicultural growth reveals that the favourable development in the south is not so much the result of investment and economic policy, but simply the consequences of higher labour inputs into this sector. The favourable development of sector B industries in this region, then, must be considered a kind of spill-over effect. Economic growth which makes extensive use of material inputs and labour must entail a slow down of labour productivity development (see table 8.A1).

Moreover, the cross-section results imply an awkward time series corollary: if labour supply can explain the fall in agricultural output growth and indirectly also the fall in output of sector B industries, future prospects for all-union agriculture and consumer oriented industrial output are rather gloomy. For labour supply will decrease even further, as we saw. The development strategy for different regions should be reflected by inter-regional trade flows. If a region specializes, say, in textiles at the expense of machine building, its exports will consist mainly of textiles and its imports mainly of machinery. When specialization increases, the trade flows should increase as well.

View 1 is at least partially corroborated by the fact that the RSFSR specializes in capital intensive producer goods whereas the rest of the union republics specialize in labour intensive consumer goods. And this trend has increased during recent years.[17] According to the 1972 input-output tables, 70 per cent of the exports of the RSFSR consisted of means of production; for imports this percentage was only 60 per cent, the remaining 40 per cent being consumer goods.

The fact that interrepublican trade intensity declined during the 1970s for Central Asia (with the exception of Turkmenia) and for Kazakhstan while it grew on average[18] rather confirms view 2 and makes clear that the two views are not contradictory. At the beginning of the 1970s the intra-Soviet north-south relationship was characterized by a typically center-periphery pattern. This can be read from the following figures: 91 per cent of cotton cloth, 93 per cent of woollen cloth and 85 per cent of silk fabric were produced in the north/north-west regions while most of the cotton, wool and silk, quite naturally, were produced in the south.[19]

The above average growth of sector B industries in the south has, in the first instance, a negative effect on interregional trade: the south makes more use of local raw materials and it depends less on final products from the north. This is, of course, a positive development. The very few data which we have on regional production patterns (and which, most certainly, reflect

TABLE 8.2. Regional Shares in Overall Output of Light Industry Commodity
Groups 1960 - 1983 (in percent)

Commodity Group	Year	North/North- West	Transcaucasia and Moldavia	Central Asia and Kazakhstan
Socks and	1960	85.2	9.0	5.8
Stockings	1970	82.4	8.3	9.3
	1983	79.9	10.5	9.6
	1960	82.2	10.0	7.8
Underwear	1970	77.4	12.9	9.7
	1983	75.1	13.9	11.0
	1960	87.0	6.4	6.6
Knitwear	1970	80.5	9.4	11.1
	1983	72.6	14.4	13.0
Leather	1960	85.7	6.8	7.5
Shoes	1970	83.4	7.2	9.4
	1983	79.2	9.2	11.6

more favourable developments) show that the share of the south
did increase as expected (see Table 8.2). But it did not increase
very rapidly despite the considerable overall output growth of
the four commodity groups (1983 (1960 = 100): socks and
stockings 189, underwear 248, knitwear 423, leather shoes 178).
And it certainly did not increase enough to reverse the trade
flow of final products for Central Asia and Kazakhstan. One
should keep in mind that the share of Central Asia and Kazakhstan in total population is 16.3 per cent and that of
Transcaucasia plus Moldavia 7.0 per cent. A structural policy
which actively makes use of the labour reserves in the south
should not be solely import-substituting but should also be
export-promoting. It should transfer labour intensive activities
to the south, increasing the dependence of the rest of the country
on the south. In that case the interregional trade intensity will
increase, too. The difference between Transcaucasia and Central
Asia is quite obvious.

The question why the share of the south is so small in the
production of goods for which it should have considerable
comparative advantages cannot be answered solely by referring
to the planners' neglect of this region. We have already seen
that Transcaucasia performed significantly better than Central
Asia. This suggests the hypothesis that there are specific im-
pediments to larger scale industrialization in Central Asia.

Before coming to this problem, I should like to draw attention to Kazakhstan, which seems to be a special case. Table 8.A2 has shown that investment in Kazakhstan has always been well above average. This has been so since the 1950s and only recently was the preferential treatment somewhat reduced. All Granberg's figures on interrepublican trade show that there must be huge capital transfers to Kazakhstan, even compared with the other Central Asian republics. Its exports amount to 25 per cent of GSP produced, its imports are not less than 47 per cent of GSP consumed (these figures seem to pertain to 1972).[20] GSP consumed will certainly be higher in Kazakhstan than GSP produced.

Kazakhstan can be taken as an example for the raw-material oriented structural policy. The region's natural resources were the main reason for its economic development. Thus the republic has a net export position only in agricultural products (grain) and fuels. These surpluses seem to be produced at enormous cost. Compared with its high capital and labour inputs the Kazakh growth performance is extremely low. It is certainly not far-fetched to call Kazakhstan one of the sinks of the Soviet economy. And we may wonder whether the same is true of other raw-material intensive areas.

Problems in Central Asia

Now we come to the question whether there are factors that impede the implementation of a labour-oriented industrialization policy in Central Asia. A certain indication in this direction is given by the fact that only 48 per cent of the total labour force in Tajik industry in 1977 consisted of indigenous nationalities. In the food industry the corresponding percentage was 63, in light industry 51 and in machine-building and metal-working not more than 28.[21] According to the 1970 census more than 80 per cent of the Tajik population are of Central Asian origin.[22] The situation in other Central Asian republics is said to be similar. Two things are important here: the high share of non-Asian labour in Central Asian industry and the marked difference between sector A and sector B industries. From this we may conclude that even in Central Asia the retardation of sector A growth was due to labour shortages, major immigration of non-Asian labour now being out of the question. It is only sector B industries that to a certain degree could benefit from the high labour supply (see table 8.A3). Rapid industrialization of Central Asia along traditional Soviet lines, planned in order to absorb additional labour supply, thus could probably have a counter-productive effect.

It is well known, for instance, that new textile plants in Central Asian towns could not be manned sufficiently with local labour and thus have attracted workers from northern regions. One of the major reasons given for this situation is that job opportunities do not correspond to the behavioural pattern of the region: "The human factor of production in its qualitative aspects, including ethnic labour skills and experience, is ignored".[23]

For a long time, Soviet perceptions of national development were guided by the politically favoured idea of the Soviet melting pot (sblizhenie and sliyanie). Economic planners, concentrated in a far-away Moscow, worked under the assumption of common behavioural patterns. Bromlei and Shkaratan make quite clear that this has been an illusion leading to misallocations of resources.

One of the more obvious instances of behavioural differences is migration. The 1979 census has produced some interesting data (see Table 8.A7). On the whole the rural population in the south is extremely immobile. While for highly developed regions like the Baltic republics the urban-rural difference in migration behaviour is very small and the degree of urbanization very high, the opposite is true for the south: during the 1960s and 1970s urbanization hardly increased in the Asian republics and the rural populations preferred to stay where they were born. The high urban-rural difference in behaviour has partly to be ascribed to the concentration of the non-Asian population in the cities. A very superficial explanation would suggest that life in the village permits the continuation of traditional ways of life. Urban housing, on the other hand, is badly adapted to large family units.

Given the demographic development described, this is bound to lead to rural overpopulation. And indeed, table 8.A4 shows that on the same area of arable land on which one person is living and working in the RSFSR, 6–12 persons have to live and work in Central Asia and Transcaucasia. Soil productivity is considerably higher in these regions than on average, which is obviously to a certain degree due to extensive irrigation. But the limited soil cannot absorb additional labour indefinitely without adverse consequences for labour productivity and general welfare.

Corresponding to the policy options described above, the solution to the problem of rural overpopulation can be either to bring to the countryside economic activities that can absorb redundant labour and that are suitable for and accepted by the local population, or to induce underemployed workers to move to regions where they are needed urgently. We shall discuss both alternatives.[24]

It seems to me that the first alternative requires a different type of industrialization from the traditional Soviet one. To indicate what I mean in West European terms, instead of a "Ruhr-type" a "Black Forest-type" of industrialization is needed. This implies widely dispersed small and medium-sized firms, no extensive urban agglomerations, the possibility of keeping secondary agricultural activities. Of course, we know that the "Black Forest–type" of industrialization—which in Germany was also to be found in Saxony—was favoured by a long tradition in home industries that produced a highly skilled labour force. Such traditions are more or less absent in Soviet Central Asia.

But this is not the main impediment to a small scale type of industrialization. The major constraint must be seen in the Soviet system of central planning. Quite logically, it favours large economic units working according to standardized rules, which can be guided and controlled more easily from the center than can a multitude of small enterprises. The preference for big units is also reflected in the design of Soviet machinery. So a change in the industrialization strategy to "make it possible to include the population in modern production through the 'adaptation' of the latter to the particulars of labor resources"[25] would require a fundamental reform of the economic system and of Soviet product design.

When Bromlei and Shkaratan conclude by stressing that mature socialism demands also the "counteradaptation" of the population to labour activities "on the basis of internationalistic labor processes" by means of "controlled social education in childhood",[26] we can be pretty sure that this is not their own opinion, but the official party line. Of course, "counteradaptation" is a fact in the process of modernization. But this does not imply behavioural standardization. The Ruhr and the Black-Forest were one example of differentiation; Italy and Seden could be another and probably many more could be cited.

Thus we come to the second alternative which seems to be preferred by the party and the planners but which is likewise difficult to implement.[27] The party has long been talking about the necessity of a rational redistribution of labour resources, mainly from rural surplus areas to sparsely settled development regions in Siberia and the Far East.[28] However, in 1981 the Central Committee reported with a certain disappointment to the XXVI Party Congress that "people still often prefer to move from north to south and from east to west, even though the rational siting of the productive forces requires movements in the opposite direction".[29] It is not hard to guess why people prefer to go west and south: life is easier in those areas, at least if one has an opportunity to earn one's living. The same reason should *a fortiori* cause the native people to stay where they are if they are not forced to move by dire necessity. To see whether there are any economic motives for a voluntary redistribution of labour, we need to analyse regional income differentials.

Regional Income Differentiation

We do not have official data on per capita incomes, though there are some diligently worked out Western estimates.[30] Furthermore, retail trade turnover can be used as a proxy for money incomes, although these data exclude the kolkhoz market and the rest of the second economy. Tables 8.A5 and 8.A6 give the relevant data.

It should be noted that the ranking of the union republics according to McAuley's estimate for total per capita income and according to per capita retail trade turnover corresponds almost perfectly (Spearman's coefficient of rank order correlation $\rho = .99$). However, the variation of personal income per capita (CV=23.2 per cent) is lower than the variation of per capita retail trade turnover (CV=29.81 per cent; the coefficients of variation are unweighted). Income in kind seems to play an important role in the less developed but more rural and more fertile south. Undoubtedly, it is difficult to estimate income from the second economy and income in kind correctly. But even if the situation in the south is perhaps somewhat better than it appears, per capita income in the regions with mainly Asian population is around 60 per cent of the level of the RSFSR. McAuley concludes: "In all these areas, then, deprivation must be widespread".[31] This surely is exactly the situation which Soviet planners need in order to make voluntary migration an attractive option.

A certain modification of this conclusion is suggested by the fact that per capita incomes treat all persons equally, whereas per capita expenditures will be different for a five-year old child in a four-person family or for a single male adult. The appropriate correction can be made by calculation in consumer units or adult equivalents. They contain a certain degree of arbitrariness unless they are based on sound budget surveys. McAuley's scale[32] is based on Soviet data and allows for very little difference in expenditures. It is, then, perhaps not so surprising that "it has very little effect on interrepublican differentiation".[33]

If we apply a Western measure of consumer units which is far more differentiated, the impact will be rather sizable. This measure gives the age group 0–9 years a weight of 0.3 and the age group 10–15 years a weight of 0.45; the rest of the measure cannot be applied in our case because of a lack of appropriate Soviet data.[34] Table 8.A5 shows that for personal income the Asian republics gain more than 10 percentage points with respect to the RSFSR. The unweighted coefficient of variation for total personal income drops from CV=23.2 to CV=16.3 per cent.

It is even more difficult to estimate personal income in rural areas. However, it is mainly overpopulation in rural areas which interests us here. Data on personal income in urban and rural areas are not available. Retail trade figures are not a reliable proxy in this case because of differences in shopping behaviour and the second economy. So we have to accept the income of the social group of cooperative farmers as an indication of the situation in the countryside. It should be kept in mind, however, that the organizational structure of agriculture varies considerably. In Turkmenia in 1975 there were more than twelve kolkhozniki per sovkhoz worker, in Kazakhstan the relationship was reversed with more than four sovkhoz workers per kolkhoznik.[35]

Table 8.A5 gives McAuley's estimate of per capita personal income in kolkhozy. Again, figures per consumer unit may be more pertinent for comparative purposes. Figures per consumer unit in table 8.A5 are computed with average demographic data of the republics. It seems plausible to assume that the demographic composition of the kolkhoz population differs even more between north and south. In any case, the story of table 8.A5 is quite clear. We are not so much interested in the greater variation of kolkhoz income, which is due to the high income in the western regions, as in the difference between the south and the RSFSR. Here, it is important to note that with two exceptions (Azerbaijan and Armenia) the relative position of the south is more favourable for cooperative farmers than for the population as a whole.

Since absolute per capita income of cooperative farmers is on average about one quarter lower than total per capita income, it is evident that McAuley comes again to the conclusion "that there is widespread rural poverty in the Soviet Union",[36] and very much so in the south with the exception of Georgia. Again, we are rather reluctant to follow this conclusion. The poverty line which McAuley draws (50 rubles per person per month, which is a norm from an official Soviet source for the year 1965) does not take account of the family situation, nor does it seem plausible to me to apply the same amount of money as the poverty criterion for an Uzbek kolkhoznik and for an Irkutsk worker.

Data on retail trade turnover cannot be used as a proxy for the income situation in the countryside. However, they may serve as an indicator for the supply of consumer goods. Closer inspection of trade statistics (see table 8.A6) reveals: 1) In urban settlements the per capita or per consumer unit supply of non-foods is far below average for the RSFSR. The southern republics have a lower supply of foods through the network of state and cooperative trade, and 2) In rural areas differences in supply are more extreme. The lowest ranked republic (Azerbaijan) has only 30 per cent of the supply level of the highest (RSFSR). With respect to foods the differences are even more extreme. However, we should be careful with rash conclusions. In the south state and cooperative trade will suffer more from competition from the kolkhoz market. Furthermore, rural food supply in these regions will preferentially come from the second economy. The urban/rural differences in supply with non-foods should not be overestimated. For in less extensive regions central places have a supply function for the countryside. This hypothesis is backed by the correlation of rural trade turnover per capita and the population density of the republics. Spearman's coefficient of rank correlation is $\rho=0.61$.

It may be safe to conclude that money incomes in Asian rural areas are considerably lower than those obtainable from employment in the country's new territories where extra labour is needed. The situation is much less obvious where individual welfare levels are concerned. Here, natural, social and cultural factors will be arguments beside the pure economic factors. "Nevertheless, it is clear that rural living standards are generally below those of urban levels".[37] But even if we take this for granted, the size of the gap is of the utmost importance. The Anatolian villager working in Cologne certainly does not feel better there than at home. Alienation could not be worse. But the huge difference in income opportunities is a compelling reason for voluntary migration. An Uzbek villager certainly can support his family at home. The material standard of living which he could obtain from work in Siberia, unqualified as he is, can hardly be 50 per cent higher than what he has at home— and this we consider flattering for Siberia. Neither the absolute standard of living nor the expected difference seem to me convincing motives to accept alienation and to migrate north voluntarily. Exactly the same conclusion has been reached by

Feshbach: "Thus, it appears that differences in levels of living will not cause large-scale migration from the region".[38]

A policy which would deliberately depress the absolute standard of living in the south and increase the difference in income opportunities runs counter to all established values of Soviet social and regional policy. This does not exclude the possibility that both may result from a continuation of present trends: overpopulation of rural areas and a passive industrialization strategy in the southern regions. Yet, the most probable reaction of the rural population, apart from raising their voice, would be to search for work in national cities rather than to move north. It should be clear that we consider forced ways of labour redistribution not to be a feasible option for Soviet policy. Not that it has never been done, but it cannot be done any more.

Conclusions

Let us now try to summarize our findings. In a time when Soviet economic growth is still rather factor intensive, labour supply will be stagnating with the exception of the south where it is least needed, at present. The most obvious consequence for economic policy, namely to intensify the development of the south where returns on capital investment should be rather high, is impeded by several dilemmas.

First, there is the predilection for a raw material oriented structural policy which, by the way, cannot be wholly separated from the elevated position of Russians in the family of Soviet nationalities. For a raw material oriented structural policy implies a Siberia and Kazakhstan oriented regional policy. And these are regions mainly inhabited by Russians. As far as the enormous concentration of capital in these two regions has been motivated by world market prices, mainly for oil and gas, these investments must be considered extremely risky. If they ever have paid, which is a difficult question of production cost, opportunity cost and terms of trade, they may not pay any more in case of price reductions.

The politically favoured complement to the raw material oriented development policy is a redistribution of labour resources from south to north. But this is hardly feasible because of the second dilemma: the very success of egalitarian socialist welfare policy seems to make voluntary migration from the Central Asian village to any Siberian town a rather unattractive choice. The development of Siberia is hampered by serious labour shortages and will require even higher capital inputs.

The relatively immobile labour surpluses of Central Asia or the south in general, then, suggest a probably less risky labour force oriented growth policy. This, however, entails the third dilemma: available labour resources in Central Asia and to a lesser degree elsewhere in the south are not immediately utilizable under the prevailing Soviet mode of production. Urbanization, large scale enterprises, multiple shift work do not seem to correspond to the behavioural patterns of the Asian population. Recent economic achievements in Transcaucasia, however, suggest that this problem can be solved.

Although there are indications of rural overpopulation in the south, agricultural output growth is still very sensitive to employment growth. This causes the final dilemma: under present production conditions a reduction of rural overpopulation may threaten agricultural growth. Less agricultural supplies make more imports necessary, hence more oil and gas exports, hence more investment in Siberia—a *circulus vitiosus*. But let me add, just in order to avoid a completely inaccurate impression: the Soviet south is a comparatively prosperous region. However, it could be much more prosperous under different economic conditions.

Notes

1. G. Simon, 'Nationalitätenprobleme und die Regierbarkeit der Sowjetunion,' *Berichte des BIOst*, 1984, No. 21, p. 1.

2. H.-J. Wagener, *Wirtschaftswachstum in unterentwickelten Gebieten: Ansätze zu einer Regionalanalyse der Sowjetunion* (Berlin, 1972).

3. See J. W. Gillula, 'The Economic Interdependence of Soviet Republics,' in US Congress, Joint Economic Committee, *Soviet Economy in a Time of Change* (Washington, D.C., 1979), vol. 1, pp. 618–655; M. S. Spechler, 'Regional Developments in the USSR 1958–1978,' in

Joint Economic Committee, *Soviet Economy in a Time of Change*, Vol. I, pp. 141–163.

4. M. V. Nechkina, letter to the editors, *Voprosy istorii*, 1951, no. 4, cited in D. Morison, 'Kolonialherrschaft,' in C. D. Kernig ed. *Marxismus im Systemvergleich. Geschichte 2* (Frankfurt, 1974), pp. 243–266 on p. 258.

5. J. A. Schumpeter, 'Zur Soziologie der Imperialismen,' *Archiv fur Sozialwissenschaft und Sozialpolitik*, Vol. 46, pp. 1–39 and 275–310 on p. 7.

6. S. N. Eisenstadt, 'Empires,' in *International Encyclopedia of the Social Sciences* (New York, 1968), Vol. V, pp. 41–49 on p. 41.

7. H. Carrére d'Encausse, *L'Empire éclate. La Revolte des Nations en U.R.S.S.* (Paris, 1978), Ch. III.

8. *Chislennost' i sostav naseleniya SSSR* (Moscow, 1984).

9. H. Feshbach and S. Rapawy, 'Soviet Population and Manpower Trends and Policies,' in US Congress, Joint Economic Committee, *Soviet Economy in a New Perspective* (Washington, D.C., 1976), pp. 113–154.

10. *Narkhoz 1975*, pp. 441, 496; *1982*, pp. 262, 328, 367.

11. *Ibid.*

12. For further details on sector A and sector B see H.-J. Wagener, 'Über den Vorrang der Produktionsmittelerzeugung in der sowjetischen Strukturpolitik,' *Berichte des Bundesinstitut für ostwissenschaftliche und internationale Studien*, 1978, No. 16.

13. V. G. Treml *et al.*, *The Structure of the Soviet Economy. Analysis and Reconstruction of the 1966 Input-Output Table* (New York, 1972), pp. 458–459.

14. H.-J. Wagener and J. Muysken, 'Zur Verlangsamung der dynamischen Effizienz in kapitalistischen und sozialistischen Ländern,' in A. Schuller ed. *Wachstumsverlangsamung und Konjunkturzyklen in unterschiedlichen Wirtschaftssystemen* (Berlin, 1984), pp. 117–151.

15. *Narkhoz 1975*, p. 211; *1982*, p. 134.

16. See also H.-J. Wagener, 'Rules of Location and the Concept of Rationality: the Case of the USSR,' in V. N. Bandera and Z. L. Melnyk eds. *The Soviet Economy in Regional Perspective* (New York, 1973), pp. 63–103 and Gillula, 'The Economic Interdependence,' op. cit.

17. A. G. Granberg, 'Ekonomicheskie vzaimodeistviya sovetskikh respublik,' *EKO*, 1982, No. 12, pp. 3–37, translated in *Problems of Economics*, Vol. 26, No. 9 (1984), pp. 3–25 on pp. 21–22.

18. *Ibid.* p. 12.

19. *Narkhoz 1922–1972*.

20. Granberg, 'Ekonomicheskie,' op. cit., p. 20.

21. Yu. Bromlei and O. Shkaratan, 'Natsional'nye traditsii v sotsialisticheskoi ekonomike,' *Voprosy ekonomiki*, 1983, No. 4, pp. 38–47, translated in *Problems of Economics*, Vol. 26, No. 7 (1983), pp. 24–39 on p. 27.

22. *Narkhoz 1922–1972*, p. 644.

23. Bromlei and Shkaratan, 'Natsional'nye traditsii;' op. cit., p. 34.

24. See also Carrere d'Encausse, *L'Empire*, op. cit., pp. 109–116.

25. Bromlei and Shkaratan, 'Natsional'nye traditsii,' op. cit., p. 37.

26. *Ibid*.

27. The best survey of the literature and the problems involved is by M. Feshbach, 'Prospects for Outmigration from Central Asia and Kazakhstan in the Next Decade,' in Joint Economic Committee, *Soviet Economy in a Time of Change*, Vol. I, pp. 656–709.

28. A. V. Topilin, *Territorial'noe pere raspredelenie trudovykh resursov v SSSR* (Moscow, 1975).

29. Quoted by Granberg, 'Ekonomicheskie,' op. cit., pp. 8–9.

30. A. McAuley, *Economic Welfare in the Soviet Union. Poverty, Living Standards and Inequality* (Madison, Wisconsin, 1979), and 'Personal Income in the USSR. Republican Variations in 1974,' in NATO Economics Directorate, *Regional Development in the USSR* (Brussels, 1979), pp. 41–57.

31. McAuley, 'Personal Income,' op. cit., p. 44.

32. McAuley, *Economic Welfare*, op. cit., pp. 112–113.

33. *Ibid*. p. 113.

34. A. Lindbeck, 'Interpreting Income Distribution in a Welfare State,' *European Economic Review*, Vol. 21, pp. 227–256.

35. *Narkhoz 1975*, pp. 436, 441.

36. McAuley, 'Personal Income,' p. 45.

37. H. Vogel, 'Regional Differences in Living Standards: Efficiency of the Distribution Network,' in NATO Economics Directorate, *Regional Development in the USSR*, pp. 59–74 on p. 66.

38. Feshbach, 'Prospects,' op. cit., p. 660.

APPENDIX

TABLE 8.A1. Regional Employment, Output and Labour Productivity 1971 - 1982
(average annual growth in percent)

Republic	1971-1975			1976-1982		
	Employ-ment	Output	Produc-tivity	Employ-ment	Output	Produc-tivity
USSR	1.9	5.7	3.8	1.3	4.1	2.8
RSFSR	1.7	5.9	4.2	1.1	4.0	2.9
Ukraine	1.5	4.6	3.1	.7	3.3	2.6
Belorussia	1.9	8.3	6.4	1.2	5.2	4.0
Lithuania	1.6	5.6	4.0	1.2	3.1	1.9
Latvia	1.2	5.9	4.7	.7	3.5	2.8
Estonia	1.1	5.6	4.5	.9	3.8	2.9
Moldavia	2.5	4.9	2.4	1.0	4.9	3.9
Kazakhstan	2.6	4.1	1.5	2.1	2.7	.6
Georgia	2.1	5.6	3.5	1.8	6.9	5.1
Armenia	2.8	7.9	5.1	3.1	7.0	3.9
Azerbaijan	3.0	6.8	3.8	3.0	7.5	4.5
Uzbekistan	3.6	6.8	3.1	3.5	5.2	1.7
Kirghizia	2.7	4.7	2.0	2.4	3.8	1.4
Tajikistan	3.5	5.9	2.4	2.9	4.1	1.2
Turkmenia	3.7	5.6	1.9	3.1	1.7	-1.4

Sources: Narkhoz 1975, p. 441

Narkhoz 1982, pp. 262, 367, 379

TABLE 8.A2. Capital Accumulation Per Employed Person 1971 - 1982
(RSFSR = 100)

Region	Investment		Newly Installed Capital	
	1971-1975	1981-1982	1971-1975	1981-1982
RSFSR	100	100	100	100
Ukraine	74.1	63.3	76.8	65.7
Belorussia	80.7	75.1	84.1	76.6
Baltic Republics	93.9	84.9	99.8	87.4
Moldavia	77.6	65.5	80.5	64.4
Kazakhstan	126.3	103.1	131.6	100.4
Transcaucasia	79.8	75.1	76.8	70.5
Central Asia	103.1	81.4	104.6	78.3

Sources: Narkhoz 1975, p. 441

Narkhoz 1982, pp. 262, 328, 345, 367

TABLE 8.A3. Agricultural and Industrial Growth 1971 - 1982
(average annual growth in percent)

| Republic | Agriculture | | Industry | | | | | |
| | 1971–75 over 1966–70 | 1976–82 over 1971–75 | 1971–1975 | | | 1976–1982 | | |
			Total	A	B	Total	A	B
USSR	2.5	1.1	7.4	7.9	6.5	4.2	4.2	3.7
RSFSR	1.7	.6	7.3	7.7	6.2	3.8	3.9	3.1
Ukraine	2.9	.7	7.1	7.7	6.0	3.6	3.7	3.4
Belorussia	2.6	.7	10.4	11.6	8.3	6.5	7.0	5.7
Lithuania	2.5	.2	8.3	9.2	7.1	4.5	4.9	3.9
Latvia	1.7	1.1	6.3	7.6	5.0	3.6	3.7	3.4
Estonia	2.5	1.5	7.1	7.9	5.9	3.6	3.6	3.7
Moldavia	4.1	1.5	9.2	11.6	6.3	5.6	6.7	4.1
Kazakhstan	2.7	1.8	7.3	7.6	6.7	3.2	3.0	3.7
Georgia	3.5	4.5	6.8	6.8	6.7	6.3	6.3	6.4
Armenia	4.1	3.5	7.7	7.6	7.9	7.2	6.6	8.5
Azerbaijan	6.0	7.1	8.5	8.3	8.7	7.3	7.0	8.2
Uzbekistan	5.1	3.9	8.5	8.6	8.3	4.8	4.0	7.6
Kirghizia	3.5	1.5	8.7	9.3	7.3	4.6	5.0	3.8
Tajikistan	6.0	2.9	6.8	7.1	6.0	5.0	4.5	6.4
Turkmenia	6.0	2.8	9.0	9.6	7.0	2.1	1.5	5.0

Sources: Narkhoz 1975, p. 315

Narkhoz 1982, pp. 119–120, 194

TABLE 8.A4. Agricultural Land Per Capita of Rural Population 1982
(in hectares)

| Republic | Agricultural Land | | Arable Land | |
	Hectare Per Capita	RSFSR = 100	Hectare Per Capita	RSFSR = 100
USSR	5.76		2.35	
RSFSR	5.50	100	3.36	100
Ukraine	2.31	42.0	1.88	56.0
Belorussia	2.43	44.2	1.57	46.7
Lithuania	2.87	52.2	2.00	59.5
Latvia	3.25	59.1	2.21	65.8
Estonia	3.45	62.7	2.30	68.5
Moldavia	1.12	20.4	.77	22.9
Kazakhstan	28.86	524.7	5.24	156.0
Georgia	1.33	24.2	.29	8.6
Armenia	1.22	22.2	.47	14.0
Azerbaijan	1.38	25.1	.47	14.0
Uzbekistan	2.66	48.4	.41	12.2
Kirghizia	4.36	79.3	.56	16.7
Tajikistan	1.50	27.3	.29	8.6
Turkmenia	19.01	345.6	.62	18.5

Source: Narkhoz 1982, pp. 9, 209

TABLE 8.A5. Personal Incomes Per Capita and Per Consumer Unit 1974
(RSFSR = 100)

Republic	Total Population		Kolkhozniki	
	Per Capita	Per Consumer Unit	Per Capita	Per Consumer Unit
RSFSR	100	100	100	100
Ukraine	85.3	84.3	95.4	94.3
Belorussia	89.5	91.7	107.0	109.6
Lithuania	102.1	103.3	142.9	144.6
Latvia	107.6	103.9	158.6	153.1
Estonia	113.4	109.4	194.1	187.3
Moldavia	76.8	80.7	84.7	89.0
Kazakhstan	81.8	87.0	87.1	92.4
Georgia	76.8	79.7	98.4	102.1
Armenia	73.8	81.7	62.5	69.2
Azerbaijan	55.1	64.3	52.2	61.0
Uzbekistan	62.9	74.6	67.6	80.1
Kirghizia	63.0	72.6	69.3	79.9
Tajikistan	54.2	65.2	61.3	73.7
Turkmenia	69.4	81.1	84.6	98.9

Sources: Personal incomes: McAuley, 'Personal Income', pp. 43-44.
Consumer units: Lindbeck, 'Interpreting Income', p. 230.
A. Krasha and Yu. Kalinyak, 'O dolgosrochnykh tendentsiyakh vosproizvodstva naseleniya', Ekonomicheskie nauki, 1982, No. 8, pp. 63-70, translated in Problems of Economics, Vol. 26, No. 2 (1983) pp. 78-92, on p. 89.

TABLE 8.A6. Retail Trade Turnover Per Capita and Per Consumer Unit 1975 and 1982
(RSFSR = 100)

Republic	Total			Urban Settlement	Rural Areas
	Per Capita		Per c.u.	Per c.u.	Per c.u.
	1975	1982	1975	1975	1975
RSFSR	100	100	100	100	100
Ukraine	82.7	82.3	81.8	94.2	62.6
Belorussia	87.2	89.9	89.4	113.8	67.2
Lithuania	101.3	104.1	102.6	130.7	56.5
Latvia	128.2	125.9	123.7	137.6	81.1
Estonia	128.4	133.3	123.9	132.6	89.6
Moldavia	73.7	78.3	77.3	124.3	59.2
Kazakhstan	78.2	76.9	83.0	88.3	94.0
Georgia	71.3	76.3	74.0	102.3	43.7
Armenia	71.8	72.8	79.0	89.8	54.9
Azerbaijan	53.5	52.8	62.4	84.8	36.8
Uzbekistan	57.2	60.0	67.1	88.8	70.5
Kirghizia	65.2	63.1	74.7	98.8	77.9
Tajikistan	53.4	51.0	63.6	98.8	52.4
Turkmenia	63.5	62.9	73.1	93.2	64.0

Sources: Narkhoz 1975, pp. 619-620

Narkhoz 1982, pp. 430-431

Consumer units: see Table 8.A5

TABLE 8.A7. Share of Population Living in Its Present Place Since
Birth in 1979 and Share of Urban Population in 1959
and 1979 (percent)

Republic	Population in Place of Birth			Urbanization		
	Urban	Rural	Difference	1959	1979	Difference
USSR	43.5	68.2	24.7	48	62	14
RSFSR	40.8	58.1	17.3	52	69	17
Ukraine	44.6	74.4	29.8	46	61	15
Belorussia	40.1	73.9	33.8	31	55	24
Lithuania	36.5	56.6	20.1	39	61	22
Latvia	37.1	44.7	7.6	56	68	12
Estonia	36.5	40.5	4.0	56	70	14
Moldavia	42.0	83.1	41.1	22	39	17
Kazakhstan	40.2	59.0	18.8	44	54	10
Georgia	58.4	75.3	16.9	42	52	10
Armenia	64.3	82.4	18.1	50	66	16
Azerbaijan	64.1	90.9	26.8	48	53	5
Uzbekistan	62.6	88.2	25.6	34	41	7
Kirghizia	43.8	76.7	32.9	34	39	5
Tajikistan	54.4	80.7	26.3	33	35	2
Turkmenia	59.2	86.2	27.0	46	48	2

Sources: Narkhoz 1983, p. 8; Chislennost', pp. 8, 360-363

9
Inflationary, Political, and Social Implications of the Current Economic Slowdown

Gregory Grossman

In future chronologies of Soviet history the year 1979 deserves a modest place as a watershed of sorts, the year in which the Soviet economy began its present period of low growth and associated difficulties, now in its seventh year. There is little need to expand here on the well-known economic facts. In a few words: the six years, 1979 through 1984, have been characterized by (historically) low growth, overall and in a number of sectors, which promises to persist until at least the end of the decade; by relatively lower rates of capital formation; by six bad or mediocre grain crops in a row, causing unprecedentedly large imports of food and fodder; by levelling-off of energy production; and by growing difficulties in earning hard currency. These and other "real" developments have received ample attention in the West. Also noted in the West has been the plight of the Soviet consumer: unusually widespread shortages of goods, especially food; longer queues; informal and local formal rationing of certain major staple goods and other articles; higher prices in the open (kolkhoz) and black markets; spread of under-the-counter payments and of outright bribes; and growing corruption and slackening discipline all round, at least until Andropov's harsh campaign against them in early 1983.

The standard explanations for empty shelves and high free-market prices offered in the Western press and by unofficial as well as official Soviet sources point to shortfalls in supply. The

Soviet press has been conveniently playing up criminal diversion of supplies into the black market by "greedy" trade personnel, which may well have been the case under the circumstances, but is hardly the root cause of the shortages. On the other hand, official Soviet production and foreign-trade data provide no strong support for the popular impression of a serious decline in the availability of foodstuffs—not to say all consumer goods— in the recent period, though official data do show modest declines in per capita consumption of specific foods in certain recent years.[1] Of course, one must not take Soviet statistics at face value, particularly in a period such as the one under review. But could there be other factors at work to help bring about the observed phenomena?

Belaboring the obvious, let us remind ourselves, first, that physical shortages and their concomitant phenomena cannot arise and persist unless prices are fixed, which is indeed the Soviet case, and second, that a rise in effective demand, with prices fixed and supply unchanged (or, more generally, a change in the supply-demand balance in the appropriate direction), will also bring about empty store shelves, etc. But the ordinary consumer and the casual observer, faced with empty shelves and rising free-market prices, naturally, blames the shortage on shortage, i.e., on insufficiency of supply or production and not on an excess of money in the pockets of his/her fellow shoppers nor on unduly low (official) prices.

In this chapter we argue (1) that, since 1979, the Soviet Union has experienced not only low growth rates of a number of real indicators but also an acceleration in the rise in the money supply, and particularly in currency in circulation; (2) that this monetary development is at least in part a systemic consequence of the unanticipated slowdown in real growth; (3) that it has further worsened the economy's performance in real terms; (4) that certain important social and political consequences have stemmed therefrom, including a signficiant redistribution of private income and wealth; and (5) that these developments have aggravated the task of managing the economy and ruling the country, and have seriously complicated the prospect of a meaningful economic reform. Needless to say, to focus on the monetary nexus of social and political consequences of low growth is not to deny or ignore the other ways in which low growth may translate into socio-political problems, some of which indeed are discussed in other contributions to this volume.

The Mechanics of Currency Issue

First, a few elementary observations about money in the USSR (and other Soviet-type economies) as they relate to our thesis. Currency is almost the only means of payment by households for purchases of goods and services in official outlets and among themselves. State firms and institutions are permitted to use currency only for very small payments—other than for wages—and to hold only minimally necessary amounts on hand. (However, anecdotal evidence suggests that they may hold substantial concealed amounts for illegal purposes.) An important exception is the collective farms, which seem to possess considerably greater latitude to use and hold currency. Yet another important exception, of course, is the underground economy, which—as in other countries—relies almost exclusively on currency, for obvious reasons. The other major means of payment in the USSR is bank money, which is used solely within the socialist sector and consists of the clearing deposits of enterprises (*raschetnye scheta*, "settlement accounts"), other enterprise deposits, and the current accounts (*tekushchie scheta)* of kolkhozy and so-called social organizations. Soviet bank money functions somewhat like the checking or gyro accounts in the West, but its payment circuit is deliberately separated and to a considerable extent insulated from the currency circuit.

As already noted, there is almost universal price control, for both producer and consumer goods. In the household sphere the only lawful exceptions to price control are (1) most everyday transactions between individuals,[2] and (2) transactions in the kolkhoz market, but even here sporadic though mostly unsuccessful attempts at price control take place. The kolkhoz market deals mostly in foodstuffs, produced mostly by peasants and state-farm workers on their private account. Finally, there is a large black market, where, by definition, prices are free.

Any increase in the stock of currency in circulation must be created. In the USSR, as elsewhere, money is created by the banking system in the process of net lending. Since Soviet banks lend almost exclusively to the socialist sector rather than to households, nearly all newly-created money initially has the form of bank money *(supra)*. However, the bulk of firms' payments is ultimately for labor, which must be in currency; hence, most newly-created bank money is soon converted into currency and enters the household sector. In sum, an increase in bank loans outstanding is soon largely transformed into an increase in currency in the public's hands, unless offset in some manner (e.g., by an increase in the budget's cash receipts).

What, then, determines the aggregate volume of net bank lending to enterprises in a given period? According to Soviet textbooks, it is the "credit plan", part of a comprehensive national financial plan for the period, which in turn is supposedly drawn up in coordination with the national economic plan. The credit plan is disaggregated to set the limits of lending to each bank branch, and, hence, for the set of firms attached to a given bank branch. Yet, more careful reading of the relevant Soviet literature and interviews with knowledgeable persons in emigration lead to a somewhat different conclusion; namely, that the bank will typically lend to a firm to the extent of its needs to pay wages, settle with suppliers, and, in general, to stay solvent so as to keep operating.[3] In sum, the banking system lends to ensure that production is not interrupted and workers retain their jobs, credit plan or no. In this sense it acts as an active custodian of some of the most important values of the Soviet order—unhampered production growth, full employment, and the individual's job security—though at the risk of excessive credit, and money, expansion. At the same time, thanks to the bank's accommodating stance, the state firm faces a "soft budget constraint" (Kornai). For this, it does not need, nor is in fact allowed, to hold large money balances, as either currency or bank money; the bank's lending window is generally open to it for any lawful (or pseudo-lawful) need.

Finally, a budget surplus (deficit), in a cash sense, increases (decreases) the treasury's deposits with the banking system, and should to a comparable though probably smaller amount reduce (increase) currency in circulation.

A Hypothesis: The Effect of Supply Shocks on Bank Lending

In the event of significant and unanticipated supply shocks, the financial and monetary arrangements just described may virtually automatically turn into a mechanism for additional and presumably undesired money creation. In a price-controlled, resource-constrained economy, such as the Soviet, supply shocks tend to translate themselves into specific shortages and production bottlenecks. Production slows down in a number of industries and firms. For example, the major shock to the Soviet economy from the malfunctioning of the railways in 1979 had almost immediate negative effects on production in such industries as heavy chemicals, forest products, construction materials, and iron and steel, with further repercussions on the whole economy. Moreover, under Soviet conditions, setbacks to the production of finished goods cause neither a decline of overall labor employment (job guarantee), nor of the acquistiion by firms of material inputs other than those in diminished supply at the given moment. Instead, the shortages cause imbalances in inventory composition on the micro-level as between different materials, as between material supplies and finished goods, and as between labor employment and rate of production. Indeed, the inventories of materials which, at the moment and place, do not limit production may well accumulate enough to compensate for the decline of those of "deficit" materials, especially since hoarding of all materials now becomes more attractive to the firm. Yet, as noted, the bank virtually automatically furnishes currency to pay labor and bank-money to pay for those supplies that keep arriving, extending additional credit where necessary. And the additional credit may indeed be necessary should a firm's sales decline owing to supply shortages.

We submit, therefore, that unanticipated supply shocks under Soviet conditions tend to increase (rather than decrease, as might be expected in a demand-constrained economy) the amount of bank loans outstanding, with corresponding upward effect on currency in circulation. ("Unanticipated", because anticipated supply shocks can presumably elicit timely corrective action to forestall, or at least restrain, the surge in bank credit by redirecting supplies to minimize bottlenecks and scaling down production targets.) Moreover, as already mentioned, the structure of bank loans by purpose would tend to change: the proportion of loans extended to finance the holding of inventories of materials and goods-in-process, and for general liquidity purposes, would tend to rise; that of finished goods (at each stage of production) would tend to diminish.

We have so far spoken of supply shocks. But shocks can also come from sudden changes in the leaders' priorities. A war in Afghanistan, an emergency operation to support the Polish economy, a response to American re-armament—such demand shocks may also generate additional bank credit, not only to the positively affected industries but also to those whose supplies are interrupted by the shift in priorities and, of course, to the treasury.

Credit Expansion, 1979–1983

We now turn to the statistical evidence. Table 9.1 summarizes the evolution of loan balances in the domestic economy (excluding any loans to the treasury) and of goods inventories at enterprises against the background of real GNP growth (CIA series). All data are in current prices.

From 1966–1970 through 1979 the pattern is clear: almost steady decline in growth rates of all four series (lines 2., 4., and 5.), though in any period the rate of growth is invariably highest for loans, second for inventories, and lowest for GNP. However, the difference ("excess") between the rates of growth for loans, particularly short-term loans, on the one hand, and of the real rate of growth of GNP or inventories, on the other (lines 8a. and 8b.), steadily widens, bearing a hint of excessive currency issue (in relation to the first economy) in the years 1966–1979. That this should have been the case need not intuitively surprise anyone familiar with the Soviet economy, but we owe it to Igor Birman to have attempted numerical estimates of currency issue in those years, using a method different from ours, and to Wiles for carefully proofing them.[4]

TABLE 9.1. USSR: Basic Data on Bank Loans, Inventories, and GNP, 1970–1983 (billions of rubles, end of year, and percent increase for period[b])

	1970	1975	1978	1979	1980	1981	1982	1983[p]
1. Long- and short-term loans to socialist enterprises and to households[a]	132.2	222.9	302.6	329.8	376.5	455.2	487.4	515.8
2. Percent increase[b]	11.3[c]	11.0	10.7	9.0	14.1	20.9	7.5 (8.8)[f]	5.4
3. Short-term loans to socialist enterprises and to households[a]	110.6	179.4	233.7	254.4	295.4	369.0	398.8	423.5
4. Percent increase	9.4[c]	10.2	9.2	8.9	16.1	24.9	8.1 (9.7)[f]	6.2
5. Goods inventories[d]	163.4	234.3	286.5	302.6	321.9	360.4	390.2[e]	417.1
6. Percent increase[b]	8.7	7.5	6.9	5.6	6.4	11.9	8.3[e]	6.9
7. Real GNP: percent increase[b]	5.3	3.7	3.8	0.4	1.7	2.1	2.6	3.0
8. Excess growth over GNP growth, percentage points:								
a. of short-term loans (4. minus 7.)	4.1	6.5	5.4	8.5	14.4	22.8	(7.1)[f]	3.2
b. of inventories (6. minus 7.)	3.4	3.8	3.1	5.2	4.7	9.7	5.7[e]	3.9

Table 9.1 (cont.)

Notes

a. By USSR State Bank (Gosbank), USSR Investment Bank (Stroibank), and USSR Bank for Foreign Trade (Vneshtorgbank). Regarding the last-named, see note a. to Table 9.3.

b. For 1970 and 1975, average annual rate of increase over five years ending 31 December of the indicated year. For 1978, the same but for three years. For all other years, increase for the year.

c. These figures for 1966-1970 were computed omitting Vneshtorgbank loans, which were less than five percent of all loans in that period.

d. Inventories (zapasy tovarno-material'nykh tsennostei) held by business firms, except kolkhozy.

e. Owing to the resetting of nearly all wholesale prices as of January 1982, the comparability of this figure with those for earlier years is questionable.

f. The figures in parentheses are rates of growth of loans taking into account the 6.0 BR of loans forgiven to kolkhozy in 1982; see note g., Table 9.3.

n.a. = not available

p. Figures in this column may be preliminary.

Sources:

Lines 1., 3., and 5.: official Soviet statistics as reported in various Nar. khoz. volumes, except for our inclusion of data on loans by Vneshtorgbank.
Line 7.: US Central Intelligence Agency, Handbook of Economic Statistics 1984, Washington, D.C., 1984, p. 64.

In 1979 there was an initial significant drop in the rates of growth of inventories, from 6.4 to 5.6 percent per year (if we can trust the statistics), and of loans, from 10.7 to 9.0 percent per year. However, GNP growth fell to a mere 0.4 percent in that year (if the CIA is correct), causing the "excess" rate growth of short-term loans over real GNP to jump to 8.5 percentage points, and over inventories to 5.2, respectively.

After 1979 the picture changes drastically. The rate of growth of inventories turns up moderately in 1980 and sharply in 1981, to 6.4 and 11.9 percent per year, respectively. These figures are surprisingly high for what were depressed years, and may indeed reflect the aforementioned unbalanced-inventories effect under conditions of automatic accommodation by the banking system. And, in fact, the growth of loans—especially short-term loans, which accommodate wage demands and inventory purchases— was extraordinary in 1980 and 1981. Short-term loans increase by 16.1 percent in the course of 1980 and by 24.9 percent in 1981, while the "excess" rate of growth of short-term loans over real GNP jumps to 14.4 percent and 22.8 percent respectively (Table 9.1). Later on, as we analyze in some detail the components of this, as it were, explosion of short-term loans outstanding, we shall relate it to two major factors: the unbalanced-inventories effect, as hypothesized, and a seemingly independent steep rise in short-term loans to the contract construction industry.

In 1982 and 1983 (the latest year for which bank statistics are available at the time of writing) the loan picture shows another sharp turn-around. In 1982 the increase in short-term loans suddenly drops to 8.1 (or 9.7; see line 4. of Table 9.1) percent, i.e., below its average historical level before 1980. And in 1983 it drops even further—to 6.2 percent. But because GNP growth, while clearly improving in 1982 and 1983, is still historically low, the "excess" rate of growth of short-term loans is still historically high in 1982, but notably low (3.2 percent) in 1983. Why the sharp decline in the growth of bank lending, beginning with 1982? We do know that the aforementioned re-financing of contract construction by the banking system was completed by 1981. But could the explanation also lie with mere improvement in the economy's real growth which helped re-balance inventories, break bottlenecks, unclog production lines, and thus speed the repayment of loans? Or was it a deliberate policy of credit tightening supported (as it would have to be) by a determined redistribution of supplies? Or was it the effect of the new, and generally higher, producer goods (wholesale) prices that were introduced across the board on 1 January 1982? The higher prices increased profits in many industries and to this extent should have reduced resort to bank credit.[5] Or, which is likely, each of the three explanations is valid in some measure. Yet we cannot be sure because much of the previously published detail on bank loans disappears from print after 1981.

A closer look at the structure of bank loans during the crucial years 1980 and 1981 can be had in Table 9.2. These are consolidated figures for Gosbank and Stroibank only; no such detail is published for Vneshtorgbank. Only short-term loans are shown in the table. Long-term loans are omitted because they are not germane to our credit-inflation hypothesis, except in the negative sense that they exhibited no unusual behavior during 1980-1981, rising on the average only about 6 percent per year. (The last is worth noting for a different reason. The reform measures of July 1979 provided for a greater role for banks in financing fixed-capital investment; this did not happen, apparently.)

Table 9.2 presents, for each type of loan, the average annual rate of increase during the three years just before 1979 (i.e., 1975–1978), the ruble amount of loans outstanding at the end of 1979, the same at the end of 1981, and the average annual rate of increase over the two years following 1979, i.e., 1980–1981. In addition, the same information is shown for construction (line 5.),[6] and for all activities (sectors) other than construction (line 6.).

The reason for singling out construction in the table is that it attracted a highly disproportionate amount of short-term credit from 1975 through 1981. At the end of 1975 construction accounted for less than 8 percent of all short-term loans to the economy; by the end of 1981 the figure had risen to nearly 26 percent. After 1981 loans for construction increased only at approximately the same moderate rate as loans to the whole economy, as already noted. By channeling so much bank credit into construction during 1975–1981 the authorities aimed to

TABLE 9.2. USSR: Short-Term Bank Loans[a] by Purpose, 1975 - 1981
(amounts at year-end)

		1975 - 1978 Average Annual Increase, % (1)	1979 Million rubles (2)	1981 Million rubles (3)	1980 - 1981 Annual Increase, % (4)
1.	Bank loans,[b] short-term, total	8.7	225,020	327,348	20.6
	of which				
2.	To finance goods inventories	8.2	154,186	234,017	23.2
	2.1 Production materials	5.7	43,663	61,879	19.0
	2.2 Goods in process [unfinished output]	30.5	11,252	59,862	130.6
	2.3 Finished goods	1.9	4,163	4,522	4.2
	2.4 Equipment for installation in construction[c]	17.3	8,177	8,978	4.8
	2.5 Inventories in retail and wholesale distribution[d]	4.8	67,481	77,337[e]	7.1
	2.6 Other goods inventories	21.3	19,450	21,439	5.0
3.	Against payment documents[f]	4.1	33,510	36,319	4.1
4.	For other purposes[g]	17.7	37,324[h]	57,012	23.6
5.	To construction industry	18.7	31,175	84,620	64.7
6.	To the rest of the economy	7.4	193,845	242,728	11.9
	Summary: to finance				
7.	Unfinished output: (2.2 + 2.4)	23.8	19,429	68,840	88.2
8.	Production inputs: (2.1 + 4.)	10.0	80,987	118,891	21.2
9.	Finished goods and trade inventories: (2.3 + 2.5 + 3)	4.4	105,154	118,178	6.0

a. Kolkhozy included
b. Gosbank and Stroibank only
c. Held by construction contractors
d. Tovary
e. This item went up by 15.0 percent in 1981 alone, probably in part owing to retail price increases in that year.
f. Shipment of finished goods
g. For the meaning of this category see text.
h. This item had the largest increase of all items in 1979, 33.3 percent.

reduce sharply the role of customers' advances in financing the notorious "unfinished construction" and "uninstalled equipment" and thereby to bring these wasteful phenomena under better control.[7]

During 1980 and 1981 short-term loans to construction increased by the enormous sum of 53.5 billion rubles, accounting for over one half (52.2 percent) of the absolute increase in total short-term loans to the economy over the two-year period.[8] We can find no evidence that this extraordinary outpouring of credit was substantially offset by net revenue in the (admittedly murky) budget accounts.

But construction alone does not explain the great credit expansion of 1980–1981; loans for all other sectors taken together (line 6.) also turned up considerably after 1979—from an average annual rate of growth of 7.4 percent in 1975–1978 to one of 11.9 percent in 1980–1981. This increase should be seen against the background of the overall slowdown in real economic growth between the two periods. Applying our term in this context, we find that "excess" growth of short-term loans to all non-construction sectors together was 3.6 percentage points per year in 1975–1978, and 10 (!) percentage points per year in 1980–1981.

The next three lines of the table may be of some interest in relation to our hypothesis of credit-inflation during a slowdown. Line 7. combines two types of loan—to finance unfinished output (goods in process) and uninstalled equipment—that would tend to turn up, as we supposed, thanks to bottleneck formation during the slowdown. But these are also types of loan that are in large measure destined for construction and, hence, may be unduly inflated by the special case of that industry. Line 7. does indeed shoot up—from 23.8 percent per year before 1979 to 88.2 percent after 1979—but the heavy influence of construction clouds its meaning for our hypothesis.

Line 8. is the sum of loans to finance production materials and "for other purposes". (The latter is apparently a composite of various types of loan essentially aimed to maintain a firm's solvency.) Thus, the category in line 8. is also of the kind that may be expected to grow relatively fast in response to an unexpected slowdown. On the other hand, the composite loan category in line 9. finances finished goods of various kinds (including those in transit to customers). We expect it to grow relatively less rapidly under the same conditions, and it does. Indeed, as a comparison of lines 8. and 9. indicates, the two categories do behave in a manner not inconsistent with our hypothesis. The average annual rate of growth of line 8. more than doubles between 1975–1978 and 1980–1981; that of line

9. increases only by 36 percent of itself, i.e., only one-third as fast.

Effects of Credit Expansion
on Currency Issue

The Soviet authorities have not published an absolute figure for currency in circulation for nearly half a century, or any relative figure that would permit direct extrapolation beyond 1 January 1958. Igor Birman has estimated currency circulation (actually, household currency holdings) by reconstructing the cash flow between the household and the socialist sectors; his figure for 1979 is 54 billion rubles.[9] In an earlier paper[10] we used the method of partial reconstruction of the consolidated balance sheet of the banking system to obtain changes in net liability residuals which might serve as indications of annual increments in currency circulation—or, more correctly, indications of annual changes in the increments. That paper carried the figures only through 1980 (with a postscript for 1981), but it did already bring out vividly the beginning of what was apparently to be a remarkable surge in currency issue. In the present paper we return to the method, carry the estimates to 1983, and introduce several modifications (see Table 9.3). First, we now complete the coverage of the Soviet banking system by rectifying the omission of the Bank for Foreign Trade (Vneshtorgbank), whose loans, which we assume to be short-term exclusively, add 10 to 13 percent to the total of short-term loans by the other two domestic lending banks, Gosbank and Stroibank, during 1975–1983. Second, for lack of recent data we now omit several minor categories of liabilities,[11] an omission and simplification that hardly affects the larger picture at all.

In cases of ambiguity we try deliberately to err on the "conservative" side, i.e., on the side of understating the suspected increase in currency circulation. Thus, we omit from consideration increases in long-term loans to enterprises on the "conservative" supposition that they are offset by corresponding budgetary appropriations to the banks.[12] We assume that the nominal budget surplus is a true cash surplus which increases the

TABLE 9.3. USSR: Selected Aggregate Financial Data, 1970 – 1983
(billions of rubles)

A. Absolute Amounts (end of year)

	1970	1975	1978	1979	1980	1981	1982	1983
1. Bank loans, short-term, total	110.6	179.4	233.7	254.4	295.4	369.0	398.8	423.5
of which by:								
Gosbank and Stroibank[a] "to the national economy"	(104.7)	(160.5)	(206.1)	(225.0)	(261.4)	(327.3)	(354.9)	(377.4)
Vneshtorgbank[b]	(5.9)	(18.9)	(27.6)	(29.4)	(34.0)	(41.7)	(43.9)	(46.1)
2. "Monetary means of enterprises"[d]	16.5	27.3	33.3	35.0	38.4	40.1	46.6	47.6[p]
3. Savings deposits of individuals[e]	46.6	91.0	131.1	146.2	156.5	165.7	174.3	186.8

TABLE 9.3 (cont.)

B. Annual or Average-Annual Increments

	1971–1975	1976–1978	1979	1980	1981	1982	1983	1980–1983
4. Bank loans, short-term	13.8	18.1	20.7	41.0	73.6	29.8	24.7	42.3
5. Bank loans, short-term, to kolkhozy, cancelled in 1982						6.0^g		1.5
6. "Monetary means of enterprises"	2.2	2.0	1.7	3.4	1.7	6.4	1.0^p	3.0
7. Savings deposits	8.9	13.4	15.1	10.3	9.2	8.6	12.5^h	10.1
8. Budget surplus (for the year or annual average)^f	3.1	5.4	5.1	8.1	10.8	9.9	3.7	8.1
9. Lines 4. + 5. - (6. + 7. + 8.) (Residual)	-0.4	-2.7	-1.2	19.2	51.9	10.9	7.6	22.6
Memoranda:								
10. Goods inventories of enterprises (increments)	14.2	17.4	13.3	22.1	38.5	29.8	26.9^i	31.7
11. Savings deposits plus budget surplus	12.0	18.8	20.2	18.4	20.0	18.5	16.2	18.1

n.a. - not available

Sources: Narodnoe khozyaistvo SSSR, various years, except as stated.

TABLE 9.3 (cont.)

Notes:

a. USSR State Bank and USSR Investment Bank, respectively.

b. USSR Bank for Foreign Trade. All its loans are assumed to be short-term. Figures include "commitments (obyazatel'stva) received against guarantees and acceptances", amount unknown, and to this extent may overstate the amounts of loans proper. Sources: Vneshnyaya torgovlya, 1978 No. 8, 1974 No. 9, 1976 No. 10, 1977 No. 10, 1978 No. 9, 1979 No. 11, 1980 No. 5; Den'gi i kredit, 1972 No. 12, 1973 No. 8; Press Bulletin, Moscow Narodny Bank, (London), 15 July 1980, 18 August 1982, 20 June 1984.

c. We are unable to find Vneshtorgbank balance-sheet data for the end of 1982 (or 1 January 1983). The figure given here is the mean of "total assets" for 1 January 1982 and 1 January 1984, multiplied by 0.84, the ratio of "loans, etc." to "total assets" that obtained fairly steadily for several previous years. The same factor is applied to "total assets" on 1 January 1984 to obtain "loans, etc." at the end of 1983.

d. Not further explained: presumably consist almost entirely of bank money on deposit in the three banks; cf. Finansovo-kreditnyi slovar', Moscow, 1984, vol. I, p. 352, col. 2. Computed from data in the Nar. khoz. yearbooks and Vestnik statistiki (1983 No. 10, p. 76; 1984 No. 12, p. 74) relating to working capital (oborotnye sredstva) of firms, excluding kolkhozy, and to proportion of different liabilities financing the working capital.

e. Includes the very small individual deposits in Gosbank.

f. Actual reported surplus, not increment.

g. In 1982 loans to the amount of 9.7 billion rubles owed by kolkhozy were forgiven as part of the launching of the Food Programme (Pravda, 25 May 1982). Since the loans in question might have been long-term as well as short-term, it is necessary for the present purpose to estimate the short-term component. By casual inspection of the time series of loans (short- and long-term) to kolkhozy outstanding (Narodnoe khozyaistvo SSSR v 1982 g., p. 526, and corresponding data in earlier editions of the statistical yearbook) we conclude that the amount of short-term loans cancelled in 1982 must have been at least 6 billion rubles. If the loans had not been forgiven or nonetheless remained unrepaid, the amount of loan increment in line 4 would have been correspondingly larger, with the same effect on currency in circulation. Hence, we add line 5 to line 4 to compute the residual in line 9.

h. Savings deposit increment in 1984, 15 billion rubles (Pravda, 26 January 1985); average increment for 1980–1983, 11.3 billion rubles.

i. See note (e) to Table 9.1.

treasury's balance with Gosbank, despite strong specialist opinion to the contrary.[13] We overlook the high likelihood—especially in hard times such as those under review—of significant net bank loans to the treasury (which Soviet practice presumably includes and conceals in the budget receipts total); in any case, we have no data for such loans. (Bank loans to the treasury would, of course, be money-creating, like any bank loans.) To the extent that these assumptions are false, currency issue estimates are understated by the method of balance-sheet residuals. (However, the omission of the changes in the smaller types of bank liability mentioned in the footnote to the preceding paragraph works in the opposite direction, though slightly.) Finally, we omit fluctuations in bank holdings of monetary gold and foreign exchange, and in external indebtedness—none of which is likely to be a serious exception to our "conservative" approach to currency estimation.[14]

We are left (Table 9.3, Panel B) with increments of one type of asset, short-term loans (STL), and of three types of liability, "monetary means of enterprises" (MM), presumably nearly equivalent to what we have called here "bank money", savings deposits (SD), a liability of Gosbank since 1963, and the annual budget surplus (BS), which here stands in proxy for (gross) annual increases of the treasury's deposits with Gosbank. For any year or for the average of two or more years: increment in listed assets minus increment in listed liabilities equals residual (R). Or, letting Δ stand for "annual increment of", we write $\Delta STL - (\Delta MM + \Delta SD + BS) = R$; see line 9 of Table 9.3. R can be thought of as unexplained change in net liabilities of the banking system. Its absolute value in itself has little meaning because our reconstruction of the banks' consolidated balance sheet is partial; and it certainly should not be identified with currency issue. But, on the assumption that the increments of omitted assets and liabilities are either largely mutually offsetting or relatively small, we may associate major annual changes in R as being indicative of major changes in the same direction of such a major unpublished item on the liability side as currency in circulation, i.e., the annual currency issue.

The behavior of R in our table is rather striking. From 1971 through 1979, R is small (actually, negative) and changes little—

which does not indicate that annual currency issue is small, only that the year-to-year changes in currency issue may have been small. Then, in 1980, it shoots up by over 20 (= 19.2 − (1.2)) billion rubles and in 1981 by over 30 billion rubles again, to 51.9 billion rubles, only to drop sharply (by 41.0 billion rubles, to 10.9 billion rubles) in 1982, and moderately in 1983 to 7.6 billion rubles; though the last figure is still 9 billion rubles above that of 1979. These large fluctuations in R must have been compensated by fluctuations elsewhere in the bank's consolidated balance sheet, but being so large, could they have by-passed the currency-issue account?

We are left, then, with a presumption that the rate of currency *issue* accelerated considerably in 1980 and further in 1981, and decelerated sharply in 1982 and moderately in 1983. (Note that even in 1983 the value of R, 7.6 billion rubles is 8–10 billion rubles higher than in the pre-1980 years shown in Table 9.3, and thus may betoken a larger annual currency issue than in the period from 1971 to 1979.) In view of the comparatively low real GNP growth during these years, this suggests a considerable increase in the currency overhang—mostly household currency holdings—with regard to the official retail price level. Finally, it should be remembered that the public's savings deposits increased by 40.6 billion rubles (27.7 percent) between 1971 and 1983. Altogether, the household sector would seem to have gained considerably in asset liquidity in the early 1980s.

Unfortunately, Soviet secretiveness in regard to currency circulation precludes a more definitive conclusion. Perhaps some day we shall know more, and shall be able either to confirm our lucubrations or utterly refute them. Yet two pieces of circumstantial evidence do tend to give some support to our deduction from the partial bank data that there may have been a significant acceleration in currency issue in the early 1980s. First, as we noted at the outset, Soviet consumer markets have behaved quite consistently with this conclusion. Second, the specialized Soviet literature of the 1980s on money and credit hints strongly—and, of course, it may do no more in the face of censorship—at a serious problem of currency over-issue, and as often as not connects the development with insufficiently controlled bank lending. Perhaps the most succinct and unambiguous statement of this sort is in a December 1983 article by N. P. Fedorenko, Director of the Central Economic-Mathematical (TsEMI): "Every bank loan is, first, credit creation, and second, because the loan [directly or indirectly–G.G.] pays wages, an act of currency issue".[15]

A paradox remains to be resolved. If indeed currency holdings rose unusually rapidly from 1980 onward, there should have been an upturn in the annual increments to savings deposits as households adjusted their personal "portfolios" in a "normal" way. Instead, after rising moderately in 1979, they declined quite steeply beginning with 1980. The figures are (again, annual increments, in billion rubles): 1978, 14.4; 1979, 15.1; 1980, 10.3; 1981, 9.2; 1982, 8.6.[16] The cumulative decline in annual increment from 1979 to 1982 was 6.5 billion rubles. (However, in 1983 the annual increment rose sharply, to 12.5 billion rubles, and to 15 billion rubles in 1984, thus restoring the whole decline since 1979. We shall return presently to the 1983 upturn.)

The answer to the paradox, of course, lies in the fact that in the Soviet case there are two necessary conditions for depositing currency in savings accounts; namely, the "normal" condition that households have the currency to deposit (according to their portfolio preferences), and second, that the currency be obtained in a legal manner so as not to incriminate the depositor. The second condition is crucial and becomes particularly important at times such as those under review. Anticipating the discussion below, let us point out that at a time of rising black market prices, growing bribery, etc., and redistribution of income, currency tends to gravitate from "honest" to "dishonest" hands, and the average (let alone marginal) propensity to deposit currency holdings in savings banks may well decline. This, then, would resolve the paradox. But what about the 1983 and 1984 upturn? Perhaps it can be explained partly in the same way: a dampening of the redistribution from "honest" to "dishonest" hands, owing to the campaign against economic crime and corruption begun by Andropov and continued by Chernenko, as well as to some improvement in the availability of consumer goods in the first economy.[17]

At this point we might note a *curiosum:* beginning with 1976–1978 and through 1983, the sum of annual increments in savings deposits and the officially stated budget surplus remains virtually constant at 18–20 billion rubles, with the exception of a minor dip in 1982; see line 11 of Table 9.3.

Some Socio-Political Consequences of the Inflation

There surely are many analytical vantage points from which to view and dissect the consequences of the sharp drop in Soviet economic growth that occurred in 1979 and the persistence of relatively low rates of growth since then. Some of them are to be found in this volume. We have chosen a particular point of view, that of the financial and monetary effects of the slowdown. We have argued that a major and unanticipated slowdown under Soviet systemic conditions is likely to lead to an upturn in bank loans so as to allow firms to continue to pay wages and to build up inventories of material inputs (albeit unbalanced owing to shortages), and that the upturn in loans leads to an accelerated issue of currency, rendering the household sector more liquid. We find support for this view in both the sharp rise of the total of short-term loans outstanding and in the structure of the loans, during 1980 and 1981 (though a deceleration of the "credit inflation" in 1982 and 1983). And on the basis of very limited data we have found some presumptive evidence of a likely acceleration of currency issue during the early 1980s, supported by circumstantial indications of a different sort. If our deductions are correct, what further observable, or at least inferrable, socio-political as well as economic phenomena of the early 1980s can our findings help to explain?

Effects on "Plan Discipline". In the socialist sector, faced with growing shortages of inputs and multiplying bottlenecks, firms have been increasingly resorting to illegal methods in order to meet their targets and indicators, such as bartering goods and services; dealing on the black market; acquiring cash by means of padded payrolls and kickbacks; collecting bank-money from other firms for work not done; etc.[18] Illegal transactions on socialist account generate illicit income for individuals. What greases the wheels of the system greases private palms. Pushers, fixers, brokers, and middlemen of all sorts proliferate. More tasks are farmed out by socialist firms to private individuals and groups—*shabashniki* in construction, *gektarshchiki* in agriculture, "non-staff" workers everywhere.

Much of this activity is plan-benign (to use Wiles's phrase): it serves to further official objectives and plans, albeit by illegal means. It also tends to shift a fair amount of the burden of coordination and balancing under conditions of growing economic complexity from the planners to the impersonal adjustment mechanism of the *socialist* underground. It points to a spontaneous decentralizing, marketizing reform of sorts.

But the system of rule suffers from illicit diversion of energies and resources, distortion of official information, slippage of effective governance of the economy, decline in the respect for the plan, the law, and the whole official system, a general spread of cynicism and self-servingness, and, not the least, from an uncontrollable redistribution of private income and wealth and the consequent effects on regime corruption.

The Private Underground and Redistribution of Income and Wealth. In the household sector, the currency inflation translates into a combination of shortages in official outlets and price increases in the free markets, stimulates illegal private activity and augments private income therefrom. And since little underground economic activity takes place in the Soviet Union without paying off some authorities, we can safely assume an upturn in bribes and graft as well. The net result is a substantial redistribution of private income and wealth especially from illegal sources, and not just between individuals but also between social groups, regions, and ethnic groups.

Who has gained from the recent economic slowdown and the attendant inflation? Obviously, all those who have physical or administrative power of disposal over material values and can realize the potential gain, those who (in part for the same reason) are in a position to produce goods and services on their own account, and those authorities, large and small, who are able to extract graft and tribute from the first two groups. Among the gainers may well be many peasants, thanks to the rise in open-market food prices. These, as it were, are "Brezhnev's new rich", a heterogeneous class, to be sure.

Who has lost? Those who lose in any inflation anywhere: students, pensioners, fixed-wage and fixed-salary recipients, provided they have no opportunities for illicit gain and/or privileged access to "closed distributors" of consumer goods. However, ability to benefit from the second economy or from bribes is not sufficient; one must benefit enough to offset the rising cost and difficulty of living.

The resultant redistribution of income—and the even greater redistribution of private wealth—has been a major theme in the Soviet press for the last few years (albeit often obliquely presented), in the emigre press, and in the reports of recent arrivals from and visitors to the USSR. All sources seem to agree that grasping, hustling, wheeling-and-dealing have been gaining ground in everyday life.

Policy Problems. Andropov took over from Brezhnev not only a country in the midst of economic stagnation and major social change, but also one in which public opinion, including elite opinion, was in danger of becoming seriously polarized on issues of socio-economic policy, morality, equity, and ideology. His earliest measures—employing repressive means against indiscipline, lack of order, and corruption—aimed to stem the processes of social dissipation below and loss of control above. Of course, such extreme measures could at best be temporary. Andropov did not live to attempt lasting solutions, if indeed such were within his power to carry out.

Under Chernenko—at the time of writing Gorbachev had barely succeeded to the supreme position—the country returned to "normalcy", but not a static normalcy. Left alone, society will slowly encroach upon *vlast'* (political power) and *poryadok* (order). The second economy will continue to take advantage of the inflation, open and repressed, will steadily push against the limits of the possible, and will grow. Corruption will not stay within its bounds. The monetary overhang does not have to keep expanding in order to continue to corrode the formal economic mechanism, further demoralize the public, and undermine the legitimacy of the official order. The wealth of the "new rich" will breed on itself, as wealth always does. Social tensions will persist, perhaps intensify. Will the regime find within itself the consensus and the courage to perform the major surgical operation of confiscating a large part of the liquid assets in private hands by means of a drastic currency conversion, as in 1947? That it may not is suggested by Jaruzelski's failure to do the same in Poland in the first months after his coup in December 1981, when the need was even greater and the moment certainly more propitious than for Gorbachev today. In good part the new, illicit wealth is concentrated in the hands of the ruling elite and its clients; and moreover, the inter-regional, inter-national, inter-ethnic inequities of any such expropriation will be large and politically serious.

But without such a surgical operation, the chances that effective systemic reform will be attempted, let alone carried out, would seem to be low, though even this necessary step is, of course, far from sufficient. Take, for instance, a modest expansion of the legally permitted scope of private activity; a rather sensible measure on its own merits, if only because it would legalize some of the already existing underground activity. Yet in view of the excess purchasing power, it would look like legalizing wild self-enrichment, inviting more corruption, and upsetting orderly labor markets and stable wage levels. Or take a reform entailing some degree of marketization of the socialist sector. Managerial autonomy under conditions of strong inflationary pressure may be seen as a license for diverting resources from officially desired ends, putting greater strain on price and wage controls (or, alternatively, fueling open inflation), and leading to even more misappropriation of state property, statistical legerdemain, self-enrichment, and corruption.

The economic slowdown would seem to call for radical systemic solutions, but, if our analysis in this chapter is not in serious error, the recent currency inflation, the slowdown's near-automatic consequence, may be placing an additional obstacle to such a reform and its successful realization.

Notes

We are grateful for research assistance to David Sedik and Kathleen O'Brien, and for valuable comments to Joseph S. Berliner, Igor Birman, and Vladimir G. Treml. We are also pleased to acknowledge the financial and material research support of the Ford Foundation and of the following units within the University of California, Berkeley: the Department of Economics, the Center for Research in Management, and the Center for Slavic and East European Studies. All errors and transgressions are the author's.

1. There is, however, a good deal of scattered information to the effect that the quality of foodstuffs sold in official outlets may have appreciably declined.

2. Some transactions between individuals are subject to price control; e.g., dwelling-space rentals, used car purchases. In both cases the controls appear to be widely disregarded.

3. For automatic lending by the State Bank (in the form of the so-called payment credit *(platezhnyi kredit)*) in the event of a firm's lack of funds to pay suppliers, and the fact that such loans in effect are of indefinite term *(bessrochnye)* and are as often as not overdue, see I. Lisitsiyan, "Tovarnoe i denezhnoe obsrashchenie i bankovskii kredit", *Voprosy ekonomiki,* 1984 No. 3, p. 3 and n. 3. For the tendency of State Bank branches automatically to furnish currency for wage payment so as not to hamper production, see P. G. Bunich, "Tol'ko effektivnost' pobedit defitsit", a report in *Ekonomika i organizatsiia promyshlennogo proizvodstva,* (hereafter referred to as *EKO*) 1982, No. 11, p. 9. For a report of bribery of bank officials by enterprises see Radio Liberty, "Soviet Background Notes", 1984, No. 4 (September), pp. 4–5 (processed).

4. Igor Birman, *Secret Incomes of the Soviet State Budget* (The Hague, 1981), Ch. VI, esp. pp. 120–121; Peter Wiles, "Inflation in the USSR 1982", *Jahrbuch der Wirtschaft Ost-europas* (Munich, 1983).

5. Total profits in the economy (excluding kolkhozy) rose from 116,194 million rubles in 1981 to 133,746 million rubles in 1982, up by 22.2 percent. Agriculture's turn came the following year: from 1982 to 1983, net value added of kolkhozy *(valovoi dokhod)* rose from 21.8 billion rubles to 35.4 billion rubles, while profits of state agricultural producing firms (sovkhozy and others) rose from 709 million rubles to 11,579 million rubles, thanks to raised procurement/purchase prices and increased subsidies from the budget *(Nar. khoz. 1983,* pp. 273, 536).

6. In bank statistics, in contrast to inventory statistics, "construction" refers not only to the construction industry proper—the contractor firms—but also to building and installation done by non-construction firms for themselves.

7. Cf. *Rol' banka v povyshenii effektivnosti kapital'nykh volozhenni* (Moscow, 1980), pp. 140–142.

8. The 53.5 billion rubles corresponds to 21 percent of the short-term loans outstanding at the end of 1979, and close to 9 percent of the Soviet 1979 GNP.

9. Birman, *Secret Incomes,* op. cit., pp. 120–121.

10. Gregory Grossman, "A Note on Soviet Inflation", in US Congress, Joint Economic Committee, *Soviet Economy in the 1980's: Problems and Prospects* (Washington, D.C., 1983), Part 1.

11. The following liabilities were included in the calculation of the "residual" in Table 1 of our earlier paper but are omitted in Table 9.3 of this chapter: current accounts of trade unions, social and other organizations; current and special accounts of kolkhozy; "indivisible funds" of kolkhozy; Gosbank inter-branch float.

12. Soviet sources intimate that a large part of the growth in long-term loan balances is offset by deliberate budgetary appropriations to banks. See, for instance, *Finansovo-kreditnyi slovar'* (Moscow, 1984), vol. I, p. 379, col. 2.

13. For example, Birman, *Secret Incomes* op. cit., Wiles, "Inflation," op. cit.

14. Soviet net lending abroad, nearly all to communist countries, CMEA banks, and less-developed countries, is likely to have been positive during 1979–1983, i.e., to have increased the nominal assets of domestic banks, and therefore our residual R. Its omission is yet another contribution to the "conservative" nature of our estimates of R.

15. N. P. Fedorenko, "Planirovanie i upravlenie: kakim im byt'?", *EKO,* 1984, No. 12, p. 17. The clearest conception of the currency-creating nature of Soviet bank credit is A. E. Melkov's; see his "K voprosu o granitsakh kredita", *Den'gi i kredit,* 1983, No. 12, pp. 23–29.

16. *Nar. khoz.,* various years.

17. We are indebted to Professor V. G. Treml for another possible explanation of the decline in savings-deposit increments after 1979; it may lie in the increase in payments to the state for new personal automobiles, in part occasioned by the raising of official car prices in that year. The figures are in billion rubles, rounded: 1979, 7.7; 1980, 8.8; 1981, 10.7; 1982, 19.7; and 1983, 11.7 (*Nar. khoz.* for the various years). The cumulative increase in annual payment for cars between 1979 and 1982 was, thus, 3.0 billion rubles—over half of the cumulative decline in increments to savings deposits of 5.8 billion rubles (Table 9.3). Savings deposits (and currency hoards) compete with cars as a form of wealth, though the relationship between the one and the other need not be 1:1, of course. (However, 1983 witnessed

the opposite: both payment for cars and increment in savings deposits rise, by 1.0 and 3.9 billion rubles respectively.)

18. Gregory Grossman, "The 'Shadow Economy' in the Socialist Sector of the USSR", in NATO, Economic Directorate, *The CMEA Five-Year Plans (1981–1985): Planned and Unplanned Economies* (Brussels, 1982).

10
Political and Moral Aspects of the Two Economies

Peter Wiles

Morality

The writer has little difficulty with the moral aspects of a normal country's second economy.[1] In his experience, too, international conferences of social scientists do not want to hear about morals, let alone the moral stance of one particular contributor. So he will keep this passage short, and therefore very dogmatic. In his view, then, it is immoral to break the law of a "normal" country unless the particular law is by common consent unjust; but individuals in a minority position may break for conscience' sake a law they personally consider unjust provided that they do not attempt to evade the legal penalities of their actions. If pacifists evade war taxes, or the aliquot warmaking part of their general taxes; if marijuana smokers, aware that nicotine and even alcohol are more dangerous, smuggle in their lesser poison; let them accept punishment before the law and the writer will still be honoured to be numbered among their friends.[2] So long as the penalities are not "excessive" neither the offender nor the state is immoral. There must be some government after all, and it is humanly difficult for any government to be at all times responsive even to a majority of the governed. "Normal" governments of course and by definition always repeal in the end laws that the majority considers unjust; and accommodate themselves to the prickly conscience of minority dissidents if they are sincere. A certain responsiveness is part of the writer's definition of "normality" in a government.

Now Second Economists do not break the law for conscience' sake, but for money. It follows that a 2E in a "normal" country is immoral. Brief though I must be about such an unscientific question, I hold this result to be a very solid one, and believe strongly in the immediate and frequent relevance of large moral issues to the social sciences. The immorality of any 2E anywhere colours my whole attitude to it in the USSR.

Take now a government that is out of its people's control, and whose ideals its people do not share. Add that its everyday relations with its people are marked by lies and tyranny. I am in such a case torn, and hope my audience is torn, between the view that such a government should be disobeyed in all possible ways all the time, even by people who do not do it for conscience' sake, and the views that "there must be some government after all", and that illegality is infectious.

These two latter views boil down to nearly the same thing. For when we say we need some government we mean that our interpersonal relations will suffer if there is not some restraint on behaviour. There will, notably, be more private violence and more theft: both of them items condemned in all systems of law whatever. Their connexion with the 2E is evident. As to theft, a black marketer is likely to become a buyer of stolen goods. For although his raison d'être is to buy goods at over the controlled price and resell them at a still higher price, what is he to do when an unknown customer offers him goods at under[3] the controlled price? Refuse them, lest he get into trouble with the law? But he is in trouble with the law anyway, and keeps no records. So he becomes a "fence", a receiver of stolen goods.

Moreover, in the Soviet case there is a great deal of black production. For simple raw materials and tools have all been nationalized as "means of production", so an independent craftsman has no alternative but to steal them. Yet he may well regard (and the writer at least does regard) the right to be an independent craftsman as a natural right: so that the laws nationalizing his raw materials and tools are profoundly unjust, and merit resistance. Yet if a professional thief offers him leather or an awl on the cheap, will he refuse? Will he not become a "fence"? And is he not, if he does it himself, a thief?

Let us go beyond theft to violence. "Honour among thieves" is a mere phrase, having little to do with real thieves. There is much more honour among people who do not steal: partly for the practical reason that contracts are written, and courts, even Soviet courts, enforce them. This puts ordinary people into the habit of honour, which they cannot shake off when the opportunity presents itself. Here again the Second Economist tries to differentiate himself from the thief, but can he succeed? Thieves have no written contracts, and neither does he. Thieves pledge themselves, in friendship, over a drink, and so does he. Thieves go to chosen "godfathers" for arbitration, and so does he. But none of that works very well, so some thieves enforce contracts with violence. . . . Since there is a strong difference of principle between criminals and Second Economists, it may well be that the latter will continue forever to avoid violence, even as embezzlers and other bourgeois thieves avoid it. But I do not feel at all certain.

The last paragraph implies an identity between embezzlers and Second Economists. This is, of course, in the eyes of both parties, not so. But which of them is more likely to bribe the police? In the West, surely the latter: an outright criminal cannot bribe our semi-honest policemen (whereas in the USSR this is not unknown), but a Second Economist probably can. For his is a *victimless offence*. The victimless offence is for us a very important concept. In the West it includes selling alcohol, pornography and the services of gambling and prostitution where these are forbidden. In the USSR we add to this list black production and price control evasion. We might well often add it under capitalism.

So long as the Second Economist does not steal, his customers and (if any) employees only benefit from his activities, and he hurts no one but those vast abstractions the Taxpayer, the Law and (in the USSR) the Plan. "Society", whatever that means, is his only victim. The police are, and should be, lenient towards victimless offences; but just because of that they are open to bribes. Moreover a black business always generates enough money for this, since bribes are part of its overheads.

We must instantly ask whether any good can come of a police force being "on the take", even if only for overlooking victimless offences. The answer is of course no. Illegality is, to repeat, infectious. The Soviet and the US police have ended up taking bribes in respect of all crimes, shaking down those guilty of traffic offences and even, in many US cities, stealing things themselves. An honest police force is as important a contributor to the quality of life as a police force that does not beat up prisoners. Incidentally, if we take bribes why should we not beat people up? If some obvious rules no longer hold, why should others?

> And so you see no end there'll be
> If I once say ABC.

I infer that our moral condemnation of the 2E must be unqualified. It must extend, then, to such legal systems as Prohibition or Soviet detailed planning or simply very high taxation, all of which by their nature create a 2E. There has been far too much talk of its economic merits (below), and so gross a failure to take account of its moral consequences is actually unscientific. For other people's values are facts, and must be studied as such. I hope only not to have excessively intruded my own, and end this section instead with a meditation upon the unfortunate Georgian people. We know that for them the 2E is a form of national liberation from Soviet rule; we know that at heart they are romantics not businessmen; we know that they are comparatively rich on all that black work. Yet now can we refute the wise words of Comrade Shevardnadze: "The Georgian people have become a nation of thieves and liars"? The price they pay for their exemplary 2E is very high.

The Merits of the Second Economy

Moral good is one thing and economic good another: "Not by bread alone. . . ." It is, then, to change the subject to assert that the net economic merits of the Soviet 2E have been exaggerated. Just because it is inevitable, or confirms the prejudices of Western economists, it is not necessarily good. These questions are not within our direct remit. But they are so important that they must not be passed over in silence.

The merits have been listed many times; they are obvious, but not as big as appears, and strongly counterbalanced by demerits. Let us look successively at: inflation, the optimality of resource allocation, economic growth and income distribution. We treat the Soviet case alone.

Inflation. The 2E, it is clear, reacts quickly to changes in consumer demand, and imposes no queues since its prices are flexible. But maybe it only puts up prices: it is quite unclear whether supply is elastic, and fairly obvious that it is not so in the case of new goods. For how, as we see below, could the 2E engage in technical innovation?

Nevertheless it does sell some goods and services, and it therefore at least reduces, in the first round, the queues for the official supplies. This in turn restores to the marginal ruble a certain utility: it becomes again worth earning, which is an important advantage for the official sector.

But we must not forget the second round. The money overhang is not abolished, but falls into new, less legal, hands. What do they do with it? In part they expand their black production, according to their all-important, and possibly quite low, elasticity of supply. If this is done (a) by theft, society's economic gain is only the gain in optimality of resource allocation (below), which may well be negative. But if it is done (b) by extra work the work is voluntary and society is enriched. In case (a) little money is rendered illiquid: it has gone into bribes, the recipients of which want to launder it quickly, so they enter the 2E as buyers—or queue before the official shops! In case (b) the extra production neutralises some at least of the original black money. So the 2E cannot make inflation worse, and it is only a question of how much it really diminishes it.

Optimality. First the 2E diverts stolen materials and therefore lessens official output; again very much of 2E labour is performed on stolen time and therefore lessens official output. But since there is excess demand for the official product at the low official price we have no reason to believe its production is above or below the optimal amount. We can only be sure that it is above if it is piling up in the state shops. This does still occasionally happen, even under today's suppressed inflation, but we have no guarantee whatever that the raw materials and labour will be stolen from precisely these branches! The incidence of steal-ability and lax labour discipline bears no relation to the demand for the product.

Secondly official output is taxed, so the diversion of resources towards the 2E raises the tax rates on what remains official, especially since consumer goods are taxed most. All this con-stitutes an entirely haphazard shift in the relative prices of what is sold, by white and black means, to the population. But in any case the co-existence of taxed and untaxed goods in one competitive category is extremely "irrational", even if the success of the latter does not exacerbate the problem.

Economic Growth. The 2E is much less productive in all those many cases where it substitutes hand work for machine work (machines are dangerous: they cannot run away through the back door when the police knock, they have no sisters to marry inspectors). Again the 2E contributes nothing to R and D, and very little to investment. On the other hand it is much more productive in the skill-and-labour-morale-intensive sectors, such as restaurants, medicine, teaching and repairs of all sorts. Since this is precisely where the Soviet 2E is concentrated, we conclude that it makes in these (statistically unimportant) sectors a sub-stantial contribution of greater than average efficiency. So here at any rate we can make a firm conclusion: the 2E is very positive.

When we say that the 2E contributes very little indeed to research and development, we mean mainly the sectors where the 2E is important. Of course on the other hand sheer R and D as such is hugely dependent on the 2E since it is so difficult to organise in a formal manner.

Income Distribution. One can never generalise about income distribution, since it depends upon the particular centiles, nay the particular social types or even individuals, whom one is considering. Such general averages as Gini's co-efficient are virtually useless. So let us simply make the essential statements about the more important categories concerned in the Soviet case.

First, the 2E produces millionaires, who are in ruble terms richer than anyone in the USSR. But they cannot openly use their wealth, and have little access to the special shops. So the actual utility of their incomes to them is less than the utility of their lower incomes is to the *Verkhushka* or the legal non-Party élite.

Second, Soviet pensioners are distinctly poor, but they have time, that all-important commodity that enables one to queue for other people for a fee (illegally). The 2E is good, then, for these one step above the extreme of poverty—the extreme, as elsewhere, is occupied by single mothers with children.

Third, workers with small legal earnings may be in that position just because their main labour is in the 2E. Here, then, too it equalises the distribution yielded by the official economy.

Fourth, if we take into account the time spent in queuing as a sort of labour, or a negative income, the Nomenklatura is still richer vis-à-vis the average than appears. For only the Nomenklatura need neither queue nor pay someone to queue.

My guess is that the two middle points above raise the income of certain officially poor categories more than the fourth point raises that of the officially rich category named. But we have no good idea of the number of black millionaires, so no idea of the overall effect of the 2E on the proportion between the extremes of wealth and poverty.

In the middle of the distribution everyone profits a little. It is certain that medical and shopkeeping personnel are badly paid because of their high black earnings. This is an interesting and important proposition in its own right, but it hardly affects general inequality statistics.

Summing up the economic balance, the 2E has very substantial faults. It does not seem that the balance of net economic merit is highly positive.

In all these pages on moral and economic loss or gain we have of course taken the standpoint of a friendly, if distant and non-ideological, outsider. One of the main problems of Sovietology is that the writer does not feel, or at least asks himself whether he should feel, friendly. Is it not good for "us" that the Georgian people should have been so thoroughly corrupted by the system? For, illegality being infectious, they may be more willing to sell state secrets, along with everything else. Are not all the demerits of the Soviet 2E more strictly speaking merits from the NATO point of view, since they detract resources from defence? To which indeed the 2E contributes nothing at all.

Effects on Political Power

It is a relief to turn from the normative to the positive: what is the effect of the Soviet Second Economy on Soviet political power? Putting the matter chronologically, the main forces keeping down the 2E were: "War" Communism—terror and idealism; NEP—cooptation, or the inclusion of the 2E within the law à la hongnoise; first FYP, idealism and a little terror; 1932–1941, more terror; 1941–1945, patriotism; 1945–1953, terror; 1953–present, nothing.

It is obvious that the first generation of the new oligarchs saw no redeeming features in the 2E at all. They sought simply to stamp it out, and never themselves participated in it at all. It was simply crime, and a carry-over from capitalism. So the 2E was not a weapon of the government, nor did it corrupt top Communists.

But the 2E under "War" Communism was of course very big indeed, since it included most of the relations of the peasants to the rest of the population, or most of the supply of food. Even party members were hungry, and succumbed, but no one treated the 2E as other than a wholly negative phenomenon. It would be possible, with the hindsight of our new interest in the phenomenon, to explain the NEP as a way of abolishing a very large and very inefficient 2E, which caused great inconvenience and even misery to the people while it exhausted the power of a state hell-bent on suppressing it.

So the NEP legalized the 2E, and the same is true of all considerable decentralizations: they pull a great deal of small black activity back to within the legal market, while thrusting large, socialist, controlled activities into that same area. But in another way the NEP was a 2E, and its relation to state power was of the modern sort: uneasy tolerance and corrupt involvement. No wonder they called it state capitalism! At least however it was legal to be a NEP man, and it was even legal for a party member to be wined and dined by him. The ensuing corruption, that reached fairly near the top of the party, was a minor cause of the abolition of the NEP and the beginning of the Plan Era.

It is my very strong impression—but as usual nothing can be proved—that the 2E was quite small under Stalin, except in collective farms. The kolkhozniki were so oppressed, so disaffected, so difficult to administer that they stole and bribed on a massive scale. But others were subject to equal temptation, yet did not succumb. That is to say, the new planning, which passes every year a law compelling every manager to obey a vast mass of contradictory instructions, absolutely demanded every kind of black behaviour. There was above all, for managers, the bribery of Gossnab and other managers (to provide scarce inputs not planned for, or indeed planned for but still scarce), of higher authorities and planners (to lower one's targets), of bank managers (to relax the wage-fund ceiling, and not to press for loan repayment), of price-setters, party officials, auditors— of everyone, indeed, who can help to iron out the contradictions in the plan and ensure one's bonus. Then, for the consumer, there was the queue, a local excess of demand over supply that actually creates its own bribery fund, which can be used on shop assistants (to keep an article under the counter), professional queuers (the bribe now becomes their wage), and militiamen (not to enforce the law against professional queuers). And for the professional Second Economist there was the black production of unplanned articles. It seems that terror and idealism kept the predictable corruption in check.

It appears to need stressing, every time such a list is drawn up, that Stalinism is no necessary precondition for a 2E. Market economies generate absolutely enormous ones, often exceeding even the modern Soviet effort. In particular, in Latin America drug exports are substantial items in the balances of payments of many countries, and can reach 20 percent of GNP. The tsarist market economy generated vast corruption of officials for permits of one kind and another, or for illegal tax reductions, and a large black production of vodka, for tax evasion. Just the two words "tax" and "drug" sum up most of the pre-communist

2E. Such poor figures as we have suggest that for these two simple motives alone Italy, Colombia and Bolivia have 2Es far bigger than the USSR, which still produces *samogon*.

The surprise, then, is that the 2E under Stalin himself was, to judge by literary evidence, so small. I assigned above three causes to this phenomenon: unexhausted idealism, terror and the absence of suppressed inflation. Of these only terror needs explaining: like illegality (above) terror is infectious. If they are shooting people for writing poems, or for having worked on the Manchurian Railway, why not for speculation—whatever they will decide that means? If a Stalin joke gets me five years how can I be sure that the price of accepting a ten-ruble bribe will be lower? So what if they hint to me they won't do that? "They" are obviously not to be trusted.

That the well of idealism had not yet run dry is very well known from the biographical literature of the first FYP: indeed there was more idealism than in the (allegedly) stand-pat period of the NEP. Terror among managers was already plentiful, with the Promparty trial and the massacre of the meat experts.[4] Later came the Yezhovshchina, a still much greater terror and an End of Ideology indeed. From 1936 it is never again possible to speak of communist idealism. It is wrong to call the Great Purge wholly political: in the dossiers of managerial prisoners were to be found many records (probably accurate) of their illegitimate economic activities, in addition to the 100 per cent fanciful accusations of Trokskyism. That is to say, already the 2E was becoming useful to the OGPU, and so to the regime.

Then followed World War II, for our purposes rightly named the Great Patriotic War. There was real idealism again, though quite non-communist. Terror was relaxed but not stopped: it was not necessary. In 1945–1953 (Stalin died in April), terror substantially increased, but by no means to Yezhovshchina levels. It was of course again political in intention, but terror always slops over into other fields, if only through the inclusion of irrelevant matter in police dossiers. Terror has many side-effects. It is, too, already appropriate to mention that the currency reform of 1947 severely deflated the economies of all households. Spare cash (not inflated enterprise bank accounts) is an essential ingredient in any substantial 2E: there was none.

All this time there was, as we said, a very substantial but in proportional terms negligible 2E in the kolkhozy, which even in severe deflation always have something to barter. Casual reading indicates also some black activity in retail trade and housing allocation.

Stalin's death, and the gradual build-up of an inflationary overhang, have completely changed the picture. There is no idealism any more, no patriotism any more (sufficient to have economic effects), and hardly any terror any more (certainly none in excess of the régime's needs). The citizens' pockets are awash with money they cannot spend, because they have saved for years and years while prices were nearly stable, but cannot securely invest their money anywhere. Under socialism the satisfactory placement of personal savings is rendered nearly impossible by the anti-private-property ideology. So they remain forever liquid, a most inflationary condition that has only recently been appreciated. But the ensuing inflation must remain suppressed, not open, because of the self-imposed policy of stable prices. So the dam has broken, and the USSR has become a very corrupt society.

These large sums enable people to bribe shop assistants, pay professional queuers, afford high black prices, and keep an adequate cash float for an illegal venture into black production. To repeat, the large inflationary overhang of "passive" money for inter-enterprise use in the accounts of enterprises and institutes at Gosbank, is much less important for us. For it to be useful as a bribe it must be somehow prised out of the bank in the form of cash. This is difficult but can be done: one arranges a pay raise for a trusted subordiante and takes it back from him on pay day. It is easier to pay big bribes in kind, and small ones out of one's own unspendable salary. So inter-enterprise bribes have also gone up owing to the suppressed inflation in the retail market.[5]

A striking feature of the Stalin period is the little inter-enterprise corruption that there was, despite the circumstances. I have attributed this above to terror, patriotism and idealism. Detailed plan violation has become neither more nor less necessary or frequent. But take one common form of it, the illicit exchange of productive favours: you give me some of your secret stock of aluminium, and I'll lend you my skilled furnace repairman. Now, the aluminium is exchanged for consumption goods. The prime object was and is to fulfil the general broad plan, properly conceived. In the old days the managers gained only their plan-fulfilment bonuses. Today the one rendering the more urgent favour to the other gains the material personal bribe instead. It need not be said that there are other, simpler cases: bribing one's own accountant, an inspection team and above all superior authority.

The political problem of the 2E, then, begins with Stalin's death, when it becomes big and accepted. Up to that point it was a criminal problem, though of course it was and remains an economic problem. First let us merely state the important points:

1. As we already saw, the militia and OBSKh[6] files on particular people are useful to the KGB for bringing illegitimate pressure to bear on political suspects.
2. The 2E blatantly undermines the credibility of official propaganda on the new Soviet man, and on the economic efficiency of the system.
3. The 2E corrupts nearly all local party officials. This is so universal and goes so deep that provincial political life is thoroughly poisoned.
4. But now the 2E reaches right into the *Verkhushka*, by which I mean the top, say, 200 party apparatchiki and any ministers, generals and policemen of comparable importance. Was not Frol Kozlov's safe found to be full of diamonds?[7]
5. The huge economic privileges of the *Verkhushka* are now a necessity, to keep people honest. But these privileges are very well known and much disliked. They too undermine the regime's credibility. Indeed they too corrupt the *Verkhushka*. These vast privileges are particularly well known to provincial cadres, who try to imitate them, through the 2E, from which they take "protection money".
6. The party never plays an entrepreneurial role in the 2E, they simply "skim the take". Entrepreneurship really is bad party manners, mere corruption is no longer.

7. The wealth of the top Second Economist now equals that
of the Nomenklatura, by which I mean that much larger
circle of those in jobs within the gift of the Central
Committee. This is very undesirable for the party's prestige.
Entertainment and the arts, and medicine, also produce a
peak of wealth which is non-party but legal. Though since
the days of Abel Yenukidze[8] the Nomenklatura has not
been close to such people, they are no threat. The party
can after all build them up or destroy them almost at will,
since they are legal. But to find your favourite restaurant
or beach invaded by a large group of Second Economists
is very irksome. There seem to be no social relations with
this group above oblast' level.

It is impossible to derive a neat, short lesson from these
disparate points. Three larger theses might seem to emerge:

1. All mass phenomena are political and involve the government. Since the Soviet 2E is very big but not counterrevolutionary,
there must be a symbiosis between it and the party elite. This
symbiosis is most virulent at raikom, gorkom and obkom level.
The *Verkhushka* is of course not to be found here, but we do
find the lower ranks of the Nomenklatura: notably the obkom
secretaries themselves, their very close associates and the secretaries of the larger gorkoms. The symbiosis consists in "protection money": the local 2E is "skimmed" as a substitute for
the vast official economic privileges available in Moscow and
the provincial capitals. Party hierarchs never involve themselves
in entrepreneurship.

2. The *Verkhushka* is never (except Kozlov and Mzhavanadze)[9]
directly involved: its economic privileges are too vast. It is indeed
so free of economic care that it can if it wishes resume the
garment of idealism that it cast off on leaving the komsomol.
Its privileges are legal, it has outgrown the grubby intervening
years. So it is permissible to speculate on the existence of an
autumnal, indeed hibernal, idealism that is not all hypocrisy.
Such a garment would be threadbare but not transparent.
Nevertheless the *Verkhushka* was once a gorkom secretary itself,
and it has not forgotten. It will not kick away the ladder it has
climbed, since the next generation is on the rungs.

3. Though by no means at all necessary for the existence of a 2E, Soviet detailed central planning inevitably creates one, and a 2E is necessary for it. The party is very well aware of this, but has its own reasons for perpetuating the planning system. These are (a) all privileges and priorities, personal (caviar for the Central Committee building restaurants) or, say, military (steel for missiles not looms) can be much more easily enforced by orders than by profit if they are sufficiently few;[10] (b) a staggering weight of ideological and propaganda commitment to the present system has built up, so a thorough reform would damage general credibility very severely indeed; (c) systems more nearly approaching a free market like the British and the Hungarian are not doing much better; (d) above all, queues are a source of central power.

This last proposition is a vital one. It means that once the *Verkhushka* has established the few absolute priorities above it has automatically created queues of those with lower or no priority, and these people must come running to the centre to have their own priority upgraded. A market would abolish that power. Needless to say, the whole Nomenklatura and their families never stand in queues. They have their special shops and restaurants, and their chauffeurs and maids can queue for them if it is ever necessary. The queue is in part the evidence that their own personal absolute priority is working. Supplies to the Nomenklatura are to the objects of consumption what supplies to the military are to the means of production.

We may add a more general reflection: Corruption is always conservative. Corruption is very particular, it can hardly be generalised about. It results, of course, from laws and institutions, but its actual operation demands connexions with particular individuals. Old and senior people have developed influence, connexions and prestige throughout their lives: these things are hard-won human capital. Take away the laws and the institutions, and those particular individuals lose their positions. Even if the new laws and institutions create new corruption, the "old and senior" people will have lost their connexions. The post-reform system may threaten to corrupt new people, but these, existing only in posse, have little motivation and no influence. But the prereform system has always powerful allies, even if it has no powerful arguments. Recent changes in the central leadership convincingly illustrate these theses. Stalin was an honest man. He relaxed, to be sure, the maximum party wage and he sharply increased the legal economic privileges of the *Verkhushka*. But that too was legal and, as we have seen, sensible. Khrushchev was a child of the Revolution, a very good Leninist, a firm believer in equality, the near approach of Full Communism, the abolition of the difference between town and country, and much other orthodoxy. He was proud and open about letting these doctrines affect his policies. Few breaths of sexual,[11] none of financial, scandal ever touched him either. The man who chased the ministers out of their Moscow flats to administer Sovnarkhozy in Khabarovsk and Tashkent, who reintroduced the death penalty for economic crime[12] probably did not increase the *Kremlevski paek*.

Brezhnev—*quantum mutatus ab illo*—did increase it. Few breaths of sexual, but a gale of financial, scandal touched him, and his family too. It was in his period that the 2E came to the serious notice of Sovietologists: had they really been asleep before?[13] Andropov the policeman, the Shevardnadze of the Russian people, had too little time to cancel him out.

The way to make a lot of money legally has been, since about 1934, to join the party: you'll finish up in a better paid post. But now it is also the way to the best fringe benefits, and the way to "skimming" the 2E. It is now Leonid Ilyich, not Vladimir Ilyich, who is *zhivee vsekh zhivykh*.[14]

Notes

1. In this chapter, "second economy" includes, as it normally should not, most bribery. It is abbreviated "2E".

2. Though he supports NATO and even cruise missiles, smokes nothing, and drinks alcohol.

3. The thief supplies stolen goods to the "fence" at "theft wholesale price". This is normally lower than even a controlled price. The main "theft cost" is of course not production, but compensation for the risk of arrest. But the fence in his turn risks arrest, and his compensation for that must also come out of the low price he pays the thief. A controlled wholesale price at which substantial business is done sets

an upper limit to the theft wholesale price. But if the former is wholly unrealistic, and no business is done at it, the theft wholesale price can exceed it. The latter will of course always fall short of the theft retail price, which will in turn fall short of the "legitimate" black market price, because in the latter transaction the risk of arrest is small.

4. William Reswick, *I Dreamt Revolution* (Chicago: Henry Regenery, 1952), pp. 294–297.

5. We are bound to ask how effective are bribes and for that matter legitimate wages when there are commonly queues for goods? The answer is, a good deal less than without queues, but still not negligibly. For (1) some people to be bribed are poor and need the money *in order to* queue; (2) the 2E provides nearly everything for money, but at a high price.

6. Otdel bor'by s khishcheniyami (Department of the fight against embezzlement).

7. Konstantin M. Simis, *USSR: The Corrupt Society* (Simon and Schuster, 1982), pp. 48–49.

8. Cf. Reswick, *I Dreamt Revolution,* passim.

9. The third commonly quoted case is Furtseva. But her quoted crime—building a private dacha for her daughter for a measly 120,000 rubles—cannot be taken seriously as a reason for her fall from power, or as, by Russian standards, serious embezzlement. Simis, *USSR: The Corrupt Society,* op. cit., pp. 49–57.

10. At a slightly lower level of priority nearly everything has priority, and the word becomes meaningless.

11. Merely a romantic association within the Politbureau.

12. Indeed, the notorious Rokofov case, an execution before there was any law allowing it.

13. Brezhnev had one piece of objective bad luck; the monetary overhang first attained serious dimensions under him.

14. "More alive than all who live" (Mayakovsky).

Economic Relations as an Instrument of Soviet Hegemony Over Eastern Europe?

Klaus von Beyme

Introduction

The Soviet Union has no doubt a hegemonial position in the Eastern bloc. It accounts for some 65 percent of the Comecon nations' total income. This position—which is not quite as overwhelming as the Soviet predominance is in the military sphere—makes it, however, difficult to accept the idea of cooperation on an equal footing between the member states of Comecon, in contrast to the European Community, of which the predominant power in its political camp is not even a member. Nevertheless the Western literature is careful not to imply a dependence relationship between the Soviet Union and its satellites. Even the leftist literature, usually the most critical literature on the Soviet Union available in the West, no longer talks about "exploitation". A Marxist definition of exploitation in the sphere of socialist international economic relations could easily make the term inapplicable, because the penetration by foreign capital and the dominance of multinational corporations over the economy do not exist in the socialist camp. But even the leftist literature accepts other criteria and normally suspects price discrimination and political dominance as being sources of "exploitation".[1]

For the early phase of the post-war relationship in the Eastern bloc, Western Marxists have listed instruments of economic exploitation such as reparations, joint ventures in Bulgaria, Hungary and Romania, or the purely Soviet corporations in the

214

GDR, discrimination in the price system and the role of the Soviet Union as an intermediate trader of international goods, enabling it to earn extra profits.[2] This last mechanism has also been frequently identified in the case of Soviet sugar purchases from Cuba at prices favourable to Cuba but with the effects of ruining other sugar-exporting economies and even of undermining Cuban economic prospects in the long run by undermining the world sugar market by sustaining dumping prices. Pettifogging quarrels about whether this is a new form of imperialism are as common as they are barren in this type of literature.[3] For the later stages of economic development, even the Neomarxists usually have not assumed that there is economic exploitation of its satellites by the Soviet Union.[4] The thesis of this chapter is that the debate on the question of expolitation can hardly be decided empirically, since most of the arguments put forward are based on a number of value judgements which cannot be evaluated in a scientific way.

Comecon: An Instrument of Hegemony?

The first problem is that the Soviet economy probably needs an instrument such as Comecon to support its foreign economic relations even less than the Soviet Union needs the Warsaw Pact for its military dominance in Eastern Europe. It has been clear from the genesis of the socialist system that the bilateral pacts of friendship and assistance are a good equivalent and make verbal moves towards dissolution of the bloc organizations rather more significant than mere propaganda manoeuvres.[5] An assessment of the question whether economic relations serve as an instrument of Soviet hegemony over Eastern Europe has therefore to rely as much on an examination of the individual bilateral relations as on research on Comecon. Comecon has had many aims, but basically it has remained an organization for the conclusion of long-term trade agreements among member countries.[6] Despite a common ideology, significant differences exist in the steering systems of individual countries and despite manifold declarations, plan coordination has largely remained confined to *bilateral trade*.[7] The Soviet literature, too, does not deny the dominance of bilateral relations. Comecon simply claims to be a major centre for integration.[8] During the period when experiments with new planning methods were being conducted, the Soviet Union had the least inclination to allow far-reaching economic reforms and, indeed, has the least cause for giving priority treatment to reforms promoting foreign trade, since it is least dependent upon this trade.[9] Following the phase up to 1956 during which costly prestige projects, such as steelworks, were built, which later proved to be unprofitable, Comecon has been assigned to promote a form of specialization which will benefit all Comecon countries.[10] In the Soviet literature nothing is said about the many conflicts that have developed (particularly with Romania) over this form of specialization. Western economists rate the benefit of the intended division of labor in Comecon very differently from Soviet sources. At the outset particularly the least developed countries (Bulgaria and Romania) and the most advanced countries (the GDR and Czechoslovakia) seem to have derived a certain advantage from cooperation. For countries at an intermediate stage of development, such as Poland, Comecon had neither a positive nor a negative impact.[11]

One cannot, however, attribute all the successes and failures of socialist economies directly to Comecon, or indirectly to Soviet foreign economic policy. Some countries had been more strongly oriented towards the Soviet economy (e.g. Poland) and others have deliberately oriented their economies towards the West (Romania). Poland has even combined both features. Other countries, such as Bulgaria (with little ideological independence), have not fared badly with their specialization (agriculture). The individual countries' literature generally attributes the indisputably impressive growth rates achieved during the post-war period to the party of that particular country, whilst the Comecon literature ascribes it all in blanket fashion to Comecon. In contrast to the European Community, Comecon measures are not concentrated on the agricultural market but on industrial planning stead. When it comes to agriculture, the emphasis is, in turn, on the integration of industries that process agricultural produce.[12]

TABLE 11.1. Diversion of Trade Flows of Comecon Countries Toward the Soviet Union

Soviet Trade in Million Rubles at Present-Day Exchange Rate		1933	1946	1950
Bulgaria	Exports	0.2	75.5	90.0
	Imports	–	46.5	62.2
Germany/GDR	Exports	67.2	36.9	167.2
	Imports	116.1	45.3	144.1
Hungary	Exports	0.9	26.1	198.4
	Imports	3.8	29.0	181.4
Poland	Exports	4.0	95.8	217.3
	Imports	10.2	97.6	189.0
Romania	Exports	0.1	27.3	102.5
	Imports	–	20.2	125.3

Source: RGW-DDR.   25 Jahre Zusammenarbeit, Berlin (East), Akademieverlag, 1974, p. 45.

Second, the integration of a number of developing countries outside Europe cannot hide the fact that cooperation in Comecon is for the most part concentrated on Europe. The inclusion of new countries has had more the function of a political signal within the community than any effective economic significance. Mongolia marks an exception here. Its intensive cooperation is so strongly focussed on the Soviet Union, however, that Comecon becomes of marginal importance because of the very extent of Mongolia's dependence on Soviet supplies of machinery and industrial equipment[13] (See Table 11.1). Suspicions that the most recent accession, namely Vietnam (1978), had political, declamatory overtones are confirmed by the fact that the majority of Comecon countries only learned of Vietnam's application at the start of the XXXII Council Meeting—if Yugoslav information on this is correct.[14]

The consequential economic burden of this policy of annexation on the Soviet Union is considerable, as was made clear by Cuba. The price was accepted for political reasons. It is suspected that the containment of Chinese influence in Southern Asia was behind the admission of Vietnam. Comecon will presumably put up resistance if the Soviet Union tries to take on further burdens. In the West, Afghanistan, South Yemen and Ethopia have been named as further candidates for Comecon membership.[15] It should at all events be remembered that the cost-benefit calculation of a great power, which has committed itself to the growth of world socialism, cannot be assessed solely on criteria of economic rationality. The Soviet Union is, however, increasingly trying to get its CMEA-partners to "share the burden", as well as "share the blame" for this expansion of influence.

Third, there is a much wider range in the degree of linkage of foreign trade between the socialist countries than between the countries within the European Community. When Comecon and the socialist camp were set up there was an unparalleled diversion of foreign trade flows. Countries, such as Cuba, which had earlier on only purchased marginal goods like Christmas tree decorations from Czechoslovakia, suddenly became entwined in much closer trade relations. A national domestic market even had to be torn apart in the case of the GDR. Most of the Comecon countries had a traditional relationship with Western Europe which they then had to sever. Only Poland and Germany had had a considerable level of trade with the Soviet Union prior to 1945 (see Table 11.1). It proved impossible to conjure up foreign trade from ideological exuberance. The consequence was systematic "undertrading",[16] which produced greate drawbacks for some of the socialist economies. It was not until the 1970s that this shortcoming was ironed out.

Fourth, one factor of dependence could lie in the Russia-centered price system. The currencies of the socialist countries are all internal currencies. The Comecon economies lack any arrangements to align domestic prices with international price levels, either through a fixed or a flexible rate of exchange. The "anarchical formation of prices" on the world market is rejected but at the same time it is stressed that the prices on the socialist market cannot be completely unrelated to world market prices. The Soviet literature highlights the two-fold character of the system, with national independence of each currency system on the one hand and coordination within the socialist division of labour on the other.[17]

Comecon's price policy protects the socialist camp from the capitalist world market. Since the 1973 oil crisis the Soviet Union has had to pass on part of the cost increase to the Comecon countries. It based this price alignment on world market prices over a period of five years. In 1975, however, the Soviet Union still granted the Comecon countries considerable relief.

The socialist price system makes it difficult to pinpoint the price discrimination and "exploitation" repeatedly claimed by authors criticizing Comecon from the "right" or from the "left". Western authors are also coming to view the problem in increasingly differentiated terms. At most there is evidence of a certain price discrimination for all concerned, although this stems from the lack of a uniform socialist price system[18] and cannot be seen as an evil intention on the part of individual actors or even Soviet foreign policy.

Fifth, Comecon has no free market for the factors of capital and labor comparable to that of the European Community which might create dependence relations among the developed and less developed countries in the West and which would stimulate the economy. The socialist market is largely construed in terms of commodity of trade. Criticism of this concept in the earlier Comecon literature still delineated the socialist concept of market from the "bourgeois" concept in detailed terms.[19] In the more recent literature, however, dogmatism concerning the differences has become considerably weaker.

Instead of having a capital market the Comecon countries practise a type of "investment creation in kind". This has been fittingly described as "counter-trading extended over time".[20] Joint ventures between socialist countries largely focus on tapping sources of raw materials. The country providing the finance needs to have a direct demand for a product before it can invest in another socialist country, since there is no scope for purely monetary profit from investment inside Comecon. The foreign trade doctrine does not even admit rationalisation as an argument for countries to join together to produce cheaper goods. Instead, it is stressed that the chief concern is the "satisfaction of needs in terms of *use value*".[21]

It is frequently assumed that the Soviet Union derives greater advantages from joint ventures than do the peoples' democracies.

The joint projects of the 1970s have tended to be more broadly multilateral than their predecessors, and have more directly involved Western contributions to the production systems. Since 1979 the member countries of CMEA no longer participate in the development of Soviet resources on the former joint venture investment basis, but rather invest individually in industries within their own economies. These investments are primarily aimed at developing export capabilities through the help of which Eastern Europe can better compensate the USSR for future deliveries in energy and raw materials.[22]

Finally, Comecon does not aspire to any supranational institutions, and this sometimes is regarded as further proof that there is no push towards more hegemony from the Soviet Union. Nevertheless debates on the limits of sovereignty in the case of further integration of the economies were apparently held on the eve of the Comecon summit of June 1984.[23] But even the renunciation of supranational institutions, which also includes particular procedural care to avoid majority decisions in Comecon, is no protection against possible dangers of hegemony, but rather a protection of the Soviet Union's discretionary power since majority decisions would mean that Moscow gave up its veto power.[24]

The supranationality of the EEC is sharply criticised by the East and denounced as an example of hegemonial dominance of the monopolies (particularly the American monopolies) over the smaller national economies.[25] This rejection of the EEC model, however, has made a virtue of necessity. The Soviet Union today does not mention the fact that from 1962 to 1964 it was all in favour of allowing the Comecon organs to make binding *ex ante* decisions rather than simply engaging in *ex post* coordination of the plan decisions made by the individual countries. At that time, however, the Soviet initiatives failed, primarily due to resistance from Romania.[26]

How far can Soviet foreign policy be shown to be a driving force behind Comecon? It would be wrong to take the hegemonial foundations of the institutions and conclude from them that Comecon is still merely an instrument of current Soviet foreign policy. In this age of polycentrism the regional Comecon organizations have been gaining an increasing momentum of their own. The policy of association has frequently been taken as evidence of a one-sided interest on the part of Moscow in this matter, illustrated by the minimal process of consultations through which the Soviet Union prepared the other members for the accession of Vietnam in 1978. Even the policy of penetration of the African states, however, is no longer regarded as a single-handed action on the part of the makers of Soviet foreign policy. Emphasis is instead placed on the growing interests the smaller Comecon states have in cooperating with the Third World countries "of socialist orientation".[27]

Hegemony Through Bilateral Trade Relations?

The bulk of economic relations within the socialist camp are bilateral trade relations. The following is a checklist of alleged exploitative features in these trade relations:

The first criticism is directed against the imposition of the Soviet economic model, which has created more economic dependence because of the necessity for Soviet deliveries of raw materials.[28] This basic decision could be taken for granted if it had been a majority decision, which it was not, probably even in Bulgaria and Czechoslovakia, where it came closest to being one. Once this decision was irreversible for the satellite economies, however, it can hardly be argued that the Soviet Union exploited the peoples' democracies by imposing its model—on the contrary, although there was exploitation in some respects in the late 1940s, the Soviet Union on the whole had to invest in order to make the new socialist economies work. This, however, does not mean that Soviet sacrifices to assist their new allies were generally beneficial to the peoples' democracies. Even authors, like Marrese and Vaňous, who have promoted the much-debated hypothesis that the Soviet Union has been subsidizing the East European countries in their trade relations, viewed the "dynamic Soviet impact as negative because Eastern Europe would probably have been more productive in the 1960s and 1970s without Soviet influence".[29]

This basic decision to orient the economy towards one country has been rightly compared with the dependence of East European economies on Germany before World War II. This dependence is said to have been beneficial to both sides. Germany was ready to absorb the surpluses of East European economies for which there was hardly any other market, but on balance Germany reaped greater advantages from the exchange than its partners did.[30] There is a striking parallel to the Soviet dominance of Eastern Europe after World War II. But it is likely that the long-term disadvantages after World War II were considerably greater since the options for the East European economies would have been wider as economic exchange became diversified on a world scale in an unprecedented way. The emphasis on intra-Comecon trade lured Eastern Europe into the development of technologies which are not cost-efficient from the point of view of the world market. In the short run the protection against competition from the world market was beneficial; in the long run it was detrimental. It has even been argued that this one-sided fundamental option for a Soviet-type economy introduced new distortions into East European development which have finally necessitated the reintegration of the region into the capitalist world economy.[31] Indeed, this basic design led all the East European economies to face the conflict between growing demands for consumption and the tendency to over-accumulation as a consequence of their socialist ideologies and ambitious plans. Whereas leftist analysts of the basic option in favour of socialism argue that most of these economies have been demarginalized and have avoided a lot of detrimental developments they would have experienced under capitalist conditions (e.g. over-urbanization, mono-culture, vulnerability through dependence on world markets controlled by a few Western multinational corporations),[32] they tend to overlook the fact that these gains are more appreciated by underdeveloped socialist countries, such as North Korea or China, which also fit the image of self-centered development so dear to this school of thought better than semi-developed countries do. For highly developed areas, such as the GDR, the imposed basic option could be still more devastating if the country had not been developed and disciplined enough to make any system work. In a long-term perspective the new losses incurred by attempting too rapid reintegration into the capitalist world market, and the concomitant indebtedness, can be seen as predetermined by the one-sided decision of the communist elites to buy the Soviet model wholesale.

Second, the benefits derived from the Soviet Union's purchasing of the goods manufactured by the East European countries, which are well below what is frequently called the *"mirovoi uroven"* or *"Weltniveau"* and which could *not compete on world markets*, are not easily assessed against the drawbacks of this exchange. Hungarian economists have demonstrated that increasing investment in joint ventures with the Soviet Union has forced Hungary to import Western inputs.[33] The longer integration within the CMEA continues, the more difficult it becomes to undertake the necessary reforms and to achieve the technological innovation which would lead to a standard of production competitive on the world market.

Third, on the other hand, Soviet trade with the East European and other Comecon countries shows no indication of a typical exploitative relationship, since the hegemonial power is exchanging raw materials and fuel for manufactured goods. Even in the case of less developed socialist countries, such as Bulgaria and Poland, half of their exports to the Soviet Union consist of machines and technological equipment. In the case of the GDR it amounts to two thirds. Only the underdeveloped Comecon countries offer raw materials or food in exchange for machines and fuel, such as rubber (Vietnam), sugar and fruit (Cuba) and meat (Mongolia) (see Table 11.2). The share of oil in imports from the Soviet Union to this group of countries tends to be lower than to more highly developed countries, since these countries import a greater share of manufactured goods than the Soviet Union does (Table 11.2). But whilst the supply of fuel and gas at below world market prices gives some advantages, it does not help to stimulate technological innovation. The quantity-oriented "ideology of tons" has at times also been nurtured by the easy and cheap access to raw materials from "Big Brother".

The Soviet Union pays fairly good prices for the manufactured goods of the East European countries, but certain inputs used by these countries have to be bought by them for hard currencies because of their use of Western technological equipment, even

TABLE 11.2. Main Products Exchanged in Soviet Trade (in billion rubles)

		Soviet Exports		Soviet Imports		
		1982	1983	1982	1983	
Bulgaria		4885	5510	4288	5053	
	fuel	1546	1784	2105	2599	machines and industrial
	gas	444	540			equipment
Czechoslovakia		5047	5871	4731	5420	
	fuel	2067	2433	2585	3168	machines and industrial
	gas	771	950			equipment
GDR		6419	6797	5776	6595	
	fuel	2414	2749	3792	4405	machines and industrial
	gas	596	716			equipment
Hungary		3707	4058	3746	4007	
	fuel	1120	1156	1613	1921	machines and industrial
	gas	362	437			equipment
Poland		4812	5274	4097	4786	
	fuel	1889	2185	1856	2202	machines and industrial
	gas	521	663			equipment
Romania		1423	1639	1683	1665	
	fuel	66	185	510	643	machines and industrial
	gas	138	194			equipment
For comparison						
Cuba		3131	3399	2709	2693	
	fuel	1086	1184	2476	2408	sugar
	machines	858	969	24	39	fruit
Mongolia		918	993	313	351	
	machines	600	616	96	97	meat
	fuel	103	139			
Vietnam		804	904	206	234	
	machines	255	288	12	16	rubber
	fuel	263	328			

Source: Vneshnyaya torgovlya SSSR v 1983 g. Moscow, 1984, pp. 46ff.

though their manufactured goods are mostly not competitive on the world market. These goods may have limited "exchange value", but for the Soviet Union their use value—to use their own terminology—generally is as high as commodities of Western origin.

Fourth, the terms of trade offered by the Soviet Union to its Comecon partners are fair. Whilst in January 1975, one year before the expiry of the Comecon price agreement, the Soviet Union nearly doubled oil prices to its neighbours, and it has been calculated that the effect of this deterioration in terms of trade amounted to roughly one per cent of GNP for the GDR, Hungary and Bulgaria,[34] the prices charged were still favourable for the satellites. A 50 per cent reduction in Soviet deliveries between 1980 and 1985 would have reduced the growth rate in the GDR, Czechoslovakia and Hungary to one per cent or less.[35]

But even without this extra subsidy to cushion the impact of the rise in world energy prices and the ensuing slump on the East European countries, the implicit Soviet trade subsidies to Eastern Europe are considerable. Marrese and Vaňous have calculated the much debated sum of 87 billion dollars from 1960 to 1980. Some critics regard this as "unrealistic".[36] The most common arguments are that the authors have neglected the Western-made components of Soviet imports from the Comecon countries and East European credits for the development of Soviet natural resources. Though the "economist manqué" will hardly be capable of challenging the figures by statistical counter-operations, the political scientist will be more appreciative of the political gains obtained in return for these subsidies. Even Marnese and Vanous come to the conclusion that "Despite the large and generally increasing magnitude of the subsidies, we argue that the Soviet Union has been better off by subsidizing Eastern Europe in exchange for nonmarket benefits than by not paying subsidies at all."[37] In creating long-term integration or even dependence these gains are politically hardly less relevant than certain benefits *à fonds perdu* from the United States to her most faithful satellites in the Third World. The subsidies have the same impact as drugs have on addicts: the more one gets, the more one depends on them. Intra-Comecon trade is an aim of the Soviet Union, not only for economic purposes, but also in order to avoid the umbrella obligations for the Soviet Union in case of additional Polish debts.[38]

The Soviet Union as a hegemonial power retains a number of options even in times when her own energy resources no

longer suffice to cover the increasing demands of the whole
socialist camp, but all of the options are likely to be detrimental
to the East European countries, whether the choice is to import
from the Western world, to reduce oil exports to the West, or
to attempt to break the energy bottleneck by massive imports
of Western technology for oil exploration and production.[39]
　But the Soviet Union also emphasizes the need for greater
integration within the socialist camp for ideological reasons too.
Even before the end of the euphoric period of détente, about
1975, a trend towards consolidation of trade within Comecon
started because of the increase in energy costs. The Soviet Union
itself set a good example by increasing the intensity of its trade
relations with Comecon partners up to 1978. In 1980, however,
the proportion of Soviet trade with Comecon fell below the 50
per cent mark again (see Table 11.3). After 1975 countries, like
Cuba, which had concentrated their foreign trade most heavily
with Comecon became the most dependent countries. Even
Romania, the Comecon country with the smallest share of
Comecon trade, increased the proportion up to 1977, only to
fall back again below the 1974 level by 1980. When it comes
to trade with the West, Soviet comparisons show that the highest
rate of increase was registered in Poland in 1965.[40] Romania's
trade with the West was greater than her Comecon trade at
the start of the 1970s. Only Hungary did not let itself be blown
off course and still had a rising percentage of Western trade
after the 1973/74 crisis. The degree to which Comecon countries'
foreign policy is dependent on Soviet foreign policy thus cor-
relates to a certain extent with the level of their Western trade,
reflecting political rather than economic dependence on the
hegemonial partner.

Conclusions

　It is a unique situation in recent history that the hegemonial
power of an area is less developed than some countries in its
sphere of influence; but *sub specie eternitatis* this dependence
relationship is the rule rather than the exception: since the days
of Ancient Rome militarily dominant powers have frequently

TABLE 11.3. Comecon Member Countries' Intra-Comecon Trade (turnover in %)

	1972	1973	1974	1975	1976	1977	1978	1979	1980	1981	1982
Bulgaria	78.1	77.2	70.2	73.8	76.6	78.0	78.4	75.7	72.8	70.6	73.0
Cuba	61.2	60.9	52.2	55.4	64.0	71.8	78.9	n.a.	n.a.	n.a.	81.5
Czechoslovakia	67.1	65.2	61.0	66.0	67.8	67.5	68.5	65.0	65.5	67.1	70.0
GDR	67.8	65.9	61.0	66.2	63.9	67.9	68.8	65.8	62.7	63.4	63.1
Hungary	65.0	63.2	59.0	66.1	54.3	53.4	52.1	52.0	49.6	51.3	51.7
Mongolia	95.4	95.1	95.9	96.2	97.2	96.2	96.8	96.9	97.7	97.1	96.9
Poland	59.4	53.4	47.0	49.7	50.2	53.2	54.7	54.7	53.3	59.7	54.3
Romania	46.6	43.2	34.7	38.0	39.2	41.9	39.7	35.4	34.0	38.7	43.7
USSR	59.6	54.0	48.9	51.8	50.8	52.5	55.7	51.9	48.6	47.6	49.1

Source: Statisticheskii ezhegodnik stran-chlenov SEV, Moscow, 1983, p. 315, and earlier editions.

held sway over economically more developed areas. It is therefore likely that the hegemonial relationship is more a political than an economic one.

A purely economical calculation can show that the satellites also benefited from this asymmetric relationship: they had a guaranteed market for their goods which had a high use value for the Soviet Union but a limited exchange value on the world market and they got favourable conditions for the import of raw materials and fuel. Indeed, the Soviet Union has subsidized trade and contributed to part of the costs of developing Soviet-type economies in the peoples' democracies. The Soviet Union has offered these favourable short-term conditions for political and for economic reasons. But short-term gains have to be weighed against long-term losses since the East European economies had no incentive for developing technology that meets the standards of the world market, and had to make sacrifices by importing this technology from the West. Even some of their exports to the West are unthinkable without Western technological contributions.

A final assessment of the mutual advantages and disadvantages is not possible on a purely statistical basis. A judgement finally depends on whether the fundamental (and in most cases not voluntary) decision to opt for a Soviet-type economy is seen as an advantage. Even the Neomarxist literature is divided on this issue. On the one hand authors accept the basic ideas and "achievements" of "real socialism", on the other hand they resent the lack of participation in bringing about these decisions. For underdeveloped countries, such as North Korea or China, this basic decision is easier to accept than for the more developed countries in Eastern Europe. In spite of all its progress one could ask whether Bulgaria is really less marginalized and better off than Portugal? For the more highly developed areas of the northern tier, however, the fundamental option for a Soviet-type economy has in the long run probably been an obstacle to innovation and autonomy. But since this fundamental option for the time being is irreversable it is certainly useful to comfort them by showing that the widespread belief among the population of the peoples democracies that these countries are being exploited by the Soviet Union has little foundation in economic reality.

Notes

1. Klaus Jürgen Gantzel, "Zu herrschaftssoziologischen Problembereichen von Abhängigkeitsbeziehungen in der gegenwärtigen Weltgesellschaft," in Dieter Senghaas ed., *Imperialismus und strukturelle Gewalt: Analysen über abhangige Reproduktion* (Frankfurt: Suhrkamp, 1972), pp. 105–120, 119.

2. Renate Damus, RGW: *Wirtschaftliche Zusammenarbeit in Osteuropa* (Opladen: Leske, 1979), pp. 61f.

3. See Klaus von Beyme, *Economics and Politics Within Socialist Systems: A Comparative and Developmental Approach* (New York: Praeger, 1982), pp. 238ff.

4. Christopher K. Chase-Dunn, "The Transition to World Socialism", in Christopher K. Chase-Dunn, *Socialist States in the World System* (London: Sage, 1982), pp. 271–296, 278.

5. See Jens Hacker, *Der Ostblock* (Baden-Baden: Nomos, 1983), pp. 806ff.

6. See Giuseepe Schiavone, *The Institutions of Comecon* (London: Macmillan, 1981), p. 51.

7. J. Bethkenhagen and H. Machowski, *Integration im Rat für gegenseitige Wirtschaftshilfe* (Berlin: Berlin Verlag, 1976), p. 26.

8. M. Senine, *L'integration socialiste* (Moscow: Progress, 1974), p. 176; cf. A. Lebahn, "Alternativen in den EG-RGW-Beziehungen", *Aussenpolitik*, 1980, pp. 147–166, on p. 151.

9. P. Marer and J. M. Montias eds, *East European Integration of East-West Trade* (Bloomington: Indiana UP, 1980), p. 32.

10. V. P. Sergeev, *Mezhdunarodnoe sotsialisticheskoe razdelenie truda: pokazateli i tendentsii razvitiya* (Moscow, 1979), p. 187.

11. Marer and Montias, *East European Integration of East-West Trade*, op. cit., p. 381.

12. Yu. F. Kornov ed., *Agrarno-promyshlennaya integratsiza stran SEV* (Moscow 1976), p. 6ff.

13. Ts. Davaadorts and V. Tsedenbal, MNR. *Itogi shestidesyatiletiya sotsial'noekonomicheskogo razvitiya* (Moscow: Progress, 1981), p. 107.

14. H. Bräker, "Die Aufnahme Vietnams in den RGW und die Politik der Sowjetunion und der VR China in Südostasien," *Berichte des Bundesinstituts für Internationale und ostwissenschaftliche Studien*, No. 7, 1979, p. 9.

15. P. Summerscale, "Is Eastern Europe a Liability to the Soviet Union?" *International Affairs*, 1981, pp. 585–598.

16. P. Hanson, "Soviet Trade with Eastern Europe", in K. Dawisha and P. Hanson eds., *Soviet-East European Dilemmas: Coercion, Competition and Consent* (London: Heinemann, 1981), pp. 90–107, on p. 93; Yu. A. Konstantinov, *Mezhdunarodnaya valyutnaya sistema stran-chlenov SEV* (Moscow, 1982), p. 3.

17. A. M. Alekseev et al., *Sotsialisticheskaya integratsiya i ee premimushchestva pered kapitalisticheskoi* (Moscow, 1975), p. 385.

18. B. Meissner and P. Farkas, "Preisdiskriminierung innerhalp des RGW?" *Jahrbuch der Wirtschaft Osteuropas* (Munich: Olzog, 1973), Vol. 4, pp. 295–318, on p. 316.

19. A. I. Levin, *Sotsialisticheskii vnutrennyi rynok* (Moscow, 1973), p. 20; V. E. Tybalkin, *Mezhdunarodnyi rynok SEV* (Moscow, 1978), p. 35.

20. Bethkenhagen and Machowski, *Integration im Rat*, op. cit., p. 68.

21. G. Proft et al., *Planung in der sozialistischen Integration* (Berlin (East): Staatsverlag der DDR, 1972), p. 154.

22. John Hannigan and Carl McMillan, "Joint Investment in Resource Development: Sectoral Approaches to Socialist Integration", in U.S. Congress, Joint Economic Committee, *Economic Assessment: Part 2: Regional Assessments* (Washington, D.C., 1981), pp. 259–295.

23. Franz-Lothar Altmann, "Der Moskauer RGW-Wirtschaftsgipfel vom Juni 1984", *Berichte des Bundesinstituts für internationale und ostwissenschaftliche Studien*, 1984, No. 26.

24. B. Bracewell-Milnes, *Economic Integration in East and West* (London: Croom Helm, 1976), p. 184; Hacker, *Der Ostblock*, op. cit., p. 886.

25. V. I. Kuznetsov, *SEV i obshchii rynok* (Moscow, 1978), p. 60.

26. Marer and Montias, *East European Integration*, op. cit., p. 22.

27. Ch. Choker, "Adventurism and Pragmatism: The Soviet Union, Comecon, and Relations with African States", *International Affairs*, 1981, pp. 618–633.

28. Damus, *RGW*, op. cit., p. 62.

29. Michael Marrese and Jan Vanous, *Soviet Subsidization of Trade with Eastern Europe* (Berkeley: University of California, Institute of International Studies, 1983), p. 145.

30. Andrzei Korbonski, Foreword to Marrese and Vanous, *Soviet Subsidization*, op. cit., p. XIIf.

31. Arpad Abonyi, "Eastern Europe's Reintegration", in Chase-Dunn, op. cit., pp. 181–201, on p. 189.

32. See Dieter Senghaas, "Sozialismus—eine Interpretation aus entwicklungs-geschichtlicher und entwicklungstheoretischer Perspektive", in Dieter Senghaas ed., *Von Europa lernen: Entwicklungsgeschichtliche Betrachtungen* (Frankfurt: Suhrkamp, 1982), pp. 277–320, on pp. 302ff.

33. L. Csaba, "Kelet-nyugati egyuttmudodes es gazdasagi mechanizmusa", *Közgazdasagi Szemle*, 1980, pp. 452–466, quoted in Abonyi, "Eastern Europe's Reintegration", p. 192.

34. Martin J. Kohn and Nicholas R. Lang, "The Intra-CMEA Foreign Trade System", U.S. Congress, Joint Economic Committee, *East European Economies post Helsinki* (Washington, D.C., 1977), p. 139.

35. Robin A. Watson, "The Linkage Between Energy and Growth: Prospects in Eastern Europe", in Joint Economic Committee, *East European Economic Assessment, Part 2, Regional Assessments*, op. cit., pp. 476–508, on p. 477.

36. Werner Beitel, "Belastung der UdSSR durch Wirtschaftshilfe und aussereuropäische und osteuropäische Klienten", in *Sowjetunion 1982/83*, op. cit., pp. 191–200, on p. 199.

37. Marrese and Vanous, *Soviet Subsidization*, op. cit., p. 149.

38. See Klaus von Beyme, *The Soviet Union in World Politics* (Boulder: Westview Press, 1985), Chapter 5.

39. See U.S. Central Intelligence Agency, *The International Energy Situation: Outlook to 1985* (Washington, D.C., 1977); Robert W. Campbell, "Implications for the Soviet Economy of Soviet Energy Prospects", *The ACES Bulletin*, 1978, No. 1, pp. 37–52; Paul Marer, "The Economies of Eastern Europe and Soviet Foreign Policy", in Seweryn Bialer ed., *The Domestic Context of Soviet Foreign Policy* (Boulder: Westview Press, 1981), pp. 271–312, on pp. 298f.

40. I. I. Orlik, *Politika zapadnykh derzhav o otnoshenii vostochnoevropeiskikh sotsialisticheskikh gosudarstv* (Moscow, 1979), p. 152.

12
Economic Reform and Soviet Foreign Policy

Jerry F. Hough

Most Western discussion of economic reform in the Soviet Union focuses on the domestic stimuli for it and especially the domestic political obstacles to it. The pressure for reform is seen as coming from the growing Soviet consumer dissatisfaction with long lines and a poor choice of consumer goods and from a decline in the rate of economic growth that threatens the steady rise in the standard of living—and with it, perhaps, the political stability of the system.

The political resistance to reform is correctly thought to be multi-dimensional in character. The institutional opposition of the ministries has long been recognized, as has the ideological suspicion of market mechanisms. In recent years, scholars have also gained an increasing appreciation of the painful obstacles to reform posed by the popularity of long-standing social policy. The guarantees against unemployment and inflation, together with the drive for greater egalitarianism, would all have to be sacrificed to some extent if a thorough economic reform were to be instituted. The Polish experience suggests that this could be not only ideologically distasteful, but also politically dangerous. The workers, of course, want all of the benefits of economic reform, but they do not want to pay the "taxes" that it costs.

In addition to the domestic aspects of economic reform, however, there are also a number of external aspects to it, and these deserve greater emphasis. The basic purpose of this chapter is to initiate the exploration of this subject. It begins with a discussion of the foreign-related requirements for and obstacles to reform and ends with speculation about its possible foreign policy implications.

Stability, Nationalism, and Economic Reform

Obviously many Soviet citizens grumble about their economy, as citizens of all countries grumble about theirs. Nevertheless, to a considerable degree, Westerners have exaggerated the severity of the short-term problems of the Soviet economy and the malaise in the Soviet population resulting from them. Even at its low point, the Soviet economy was growing at 2 percent a year, and in the last three years the rate of growth has risen to the 3–4 percent level.

The very real malaise that was observed in the Soviet Union was surely associated, first of all, with the fact that the Soviet Union had not had a healthy leader for nearly a decade and that the leadership was unwilling or unable to take any decisive policy initiative in any direction. The popular response to Andropov, who actually did almost nothing substantively in the policy realm but only talked of change and replaced some personnel, was a clear sign that the population had not yet given up on the system. The response to Gorbachev points in the same direction.

The crucial question is whether a healthy leader and a continuing marginal improvement in the present economic situation would suffice to maintain political stability in the long run. Let us imagine that Gorbachev remains healthy until the year 2000 and continues to try to court public opinion, that living standards rise at some 2 percent a year, that the quality of goods improves very slowly, but that the Soviet Union still fails to make the transition that Japan did in the 1960s to an economy capable of competing with the West in the production of items of advanced technology. Would such a scenario produce continuing political stability into the twenty-first century?

Few questions are more difficult to assess than the likelihood of long-term political stability and especially the timing of instability. Right-wing dictatorships have proved to be unstable in the face of industrialization, but it has been very difficult to predict how long a specific dictatorship would survive. Representative democracy has been quite stable over the last 40 years—an outcome not always foreseen by those who feared that the fall of Weimar showed a mass susceptability to demagogic appeals—but here too the periods of relative instability have not been foreseen. American political scientists of the 1950s had no sense of the impending unrest of the 1960s, and few would have predicted the stability of the 1970s and early 1980s had they known the severity of the post–1973 economic problems.

Communist regimes have a mixed record. Those which have been imposed from without have, despite totalitarian controls, often been quite unstable, but those that essentially were the product of internal forces have been very stable. The major reason for this difference seems to be the relationship of the respective regimes to nationalism and patriotism. In Eastern European countries where communism was imposed by the Soviet Union, communism entailed a loss of national independence, and the forces of nationalism have been opposed to it. (Frequently the communist leaders of such countries have tried to re-establish this link by taking actions independent of Moscow.) In countries where communism was largely produced by domestic revolutionary forces—Russia, China, Vietnam, Cuba, Yugoslavia, and Albania—the communists allied themselves with local nationalism and, indeed, made national independence one of their major themes. In the Third World, the communists treated the socialist revolution as the inherent second stage of the national-liberation movement, a stage that was necessary for the achievement of national "economic independence", and thereby tried to link communism and nationalism even ideologically.

In the Soviet Union, the Communist Party associated itself with Russian nationalism in three ways. First, the concept of a strong, centralized party implied Russian control over the non-Russian borderlands. Despite ideological assertions about world revolution and the withering away of the state, people must have assumed from the beginning that this was irrelevant utopianism and that Lenin was really talking about a Russian revolution. The Bolsheviks quickly gained the support of the

Russian workers, while the Mensheviks were supported by the non-Russian workers. The workers must have sensed that the competing images of the party meant competing images of the relationship of Russians and non-Russians after the revolution. Today even those Soviet liberals who favor democratization for Russia are deeply worried that a Western-style electoral system would lead to twenty Quebecs, and hence they tend to prefer liberalization within a single party system. The unrest in a country such as India does nothing to reassure them.

Second, the Communist Party achieved a major increase in the power and status of Russia as a nation. Russia performed abysmally in the Russo-Japanese War and World War I. While Lenin did not support the war effort in World War I, he identified the party with national defense against foreign intervention in the Civil War, and Stalin intensified this identification in the 1920s and the 1930s. The party did, in fact, lead Russia to victory in World War II, to the establishment of control over Eastern Europe after the war, and then to the achievement of superpower status and approximate military equality with the West.

Third, the Communist Party created a distinctive way of organizing society, which became a model for other societies and thus a source of national pride. In the nineteenth century the Slavophils had argued with the Marxists and other Westernizers about whether Russia had to follow the Western pattern of industrialization. While Lenin insisted that Russia had to have industrialization based on large factories as in the West, he established an industrial system and industrial society that was radically different from the West. This associated the Bolsheviks with some of the deepest traditions in Slavophil nationalism, and those with a Russo-centric point of view could glory in the sense that Russia had decided "not to borrow dogmatically the achievements of Western European civilization, not to assimilate them 'in the manner of India', but to create a more advanced social structure which better answered the interests of the masses than Western European civilization".[1]

These three factors combined to forge a link between Russian nationalism and communist power that is a powerful explanation for the stability of the Soviet Union over the decades. They also must be kept in mind when we consider the political consequences both of the defects in the Soviet economy and of economic reform.

On the one hand, the question of nationalism raises two major political problems for the proponents of economic reform. First, a Marxist is inclined to believe that political power flows from economic power. If economic power is decentralized from the Moscow ministries, a Russian communist may, rightly or wrongly, fear that Moscow's political control over the non-Russian republics may also be weakened. If reform integrates the Soviet Union into the world economy, as it must if it is to be successful, then Soviet Moslems are the natural salesmen of Soviet technology in the Middle East, and Russians may fear that this will infect them with dangerous political and religious ideas.

Second, a movement away from the present Soviet economic system towards one that uses more market mechanisms is a movement away from a system created by Russians towards a system associated with Russia's major adversary. Even to the extent that the model is perceived to be the Hungarian, or even worse, the Chinese, model of socialism rather than capitalism, the same problem tends to rise. It is a particularly bitter pill to be seen as following the Chinese lead.

On the other hand, the importance of the link with Russian nationalism means that the problems created by Soviet economic performance are, in the long run, far deeper and more threatening than consumer dissatisfaction with long lines and a narrow choice of consumer goods. The inability of the Soviet Union to move to the forefront of the technological revolution—indeed, even to keep up with countries such as Japan and now Taiwan and South Korea—raises the most serious questions about the ability of the system to maintain Russia as a world-class power, let alone as the beacon to the world. It would be unpleasant for the Soviet leaders to be accused of following the Chinese model; it would be a total disaster for them if people began to think that China was making a Japan-like transition to a modern economy while Russia was not.

The problem with economic performance extends even to the old claim of achieving military equality with the West. Whatever may be said about overall numbers of weapons, clearly the United States has been the first to introduce weapons incorporating technological innovations, and the Soviet Union has often been very slow in catching up. It was not until the mid-1980s that the Soviet Union acquired an ability to produce a reliable solid-fuel intercontinental ballistic missile of the type that the United States acquired 20 years ago with the Minuteman. Only a few years before, again some 20 years behind the United States, the Soviet Union began to place its important satellites in high orbit and to catch ejected film from satellites rather than to be forced to bring down the entire satellite.

At the present time the United States is introducing not only a series of more accurate nuclear missiles, but is planning a new generation of conventional weapons of great technological sophistication and is accelerating its research on space weapons. A spate of articles and statements have appeared in the Soviet media on these weapons, and many convey a real sense of urgency and alarm about the conventional weapons in particular. For example, Marshal Nikolai Ogarkov, in his famous interview of 9 May 1984 in *Krasnaya zvezda*, downplayed the danger of a nuclear first strike and seemed to suggest that both sides would be reluctant to use nuclear weapons in a war, but then went on to emphasize that the new conventional weapons were nearly as powerful as nuclear ones.

To some extent, such articles may simply be part of the budgetary battle over the priority to be given to the ground forces in comparison with the strategic rocket forces, but inevitably they raise the possibility that the Western technological advantage may lead to some American military breakthrough that will put Russia at a grave disadvantage. Thus, Ogarkov pointedly included in his interview a quotation from Engels about the dependence of the military upon the economy, while in February a military observer in *Izvestiya* had referred to "the use of the technological achievements of the West in the realm of conventional weapons".[2]

As a result, the Soviet argument about technology and economic reform is far more complex than usually understood in the West. Bruce Parrott has identified two broad tendencies in the traditional Soviet attitudes towards Western technology, and he has linked them with foreign policy and military posture:

> The traditionalist tendency has emphasized the aggressiveness of the USSR's capitalist competitor and treated the development of Soviet military technology as a matter of overriding priority.
> . . . The nontraditionalist tendency, on the other hand, has muted the theme of imperialist aggressiveness and sometimes shown a concern that heavy stress on Soviet military technology unduly hampers technological progress in nonmilitary spheres.[3]

If the Soviet autarkical economy limits the Soviet technological capability even in the military sphere, then this equation becomes very different. Five days after the *Izvestiya* comment, the defense minister, Dmitrii Ustinov, apparently felt compelled to reassure the readers of *Pravda* that "the contemporary level of production and of science and technology in our country permits us to create any kind of armament if this is needed to answer the challenge of imperialism".[4] On 21 May, twelve days after the Ogarkov interview, Ustinov gave an interview to TASS in which he emphasized "the irreversible change in the correlation of forces in the international arena in favor of socialism" which ensures that "imperialism has no chance to achieve its class goals by military means". The "insurmountable obstacle", in Ustinov's view, is "the powerful economic potential and the invincible defense might of the USSR".[5]

Ustinov was not able to convince the head of the General Staff, and it is quite likely that Ogarkov was removed for his position on this issue—and for his earlier support of Andropov, which was associated both with a congruence of views on economic reform and with their common war experience in Karelia. The issue will not, however, die, and if doubts about the ability of the Soviet economy to match American weaponry were to grow, the military pressure for economic reform would grow dramatically, and at some point a military intervention would occur.

The problem goes even deeper, however. The fundamental promise of communism was not one of catching up with the West militarily, but of surpassing the West economically and socially. In the mid-1950s, the Soviet leaders and most Soviet economists still assumed that the West was about to enter a period of more serious depressions and that the Soviet Union had the most effective economic model. In fact, in the wake of the launching of the Soviet Sputnik in 1957, many in the West feared that the Soviet Union might have a technological advantage that would make the Soviet model attractive to the Third World.

Today virtually all Soviet economists writing about the Third World find it hard to hide their contempt when they write about the effects of autarky and complete nationalization on economic development. They advocate the preservation of a private sector in the Third World, at least in the services, and they insist on the need for foreign capital. When they assert that the Soviet Union does not have the necessary resources, that the Third World has to accept Western investment, and that political dependence tends to flow from economic dependence, the Soviet economists are implicitly saying that the Soviet economy is having an adverse impact on Soviet power in international relations.[6]

The issue is also implicitly raised in some of the discussion of Japanese foreign policy. Thus in May 1984, the benign explanation of Nakasone's actions was described by the *Pravda* correspondent as "the conduct of the policy of Japan in correspondence with its economic might".[7] The *Pravda* correspondent in Malaysia spelled out the point:

> Japanese propaganda long ago claimed that it has the role of teacher and mentor of the developing countries. *Disposing of huge resources* [my italics], it tries to impose on them 'the model of movement into the future' on a 'purely Asiatic path', based on Japanese experience. Its essence is that following the experience and example of the Japanese capitalist will, without fail, give Malayan business the ability to compete and will secure its mastery of contemporary technology and knowledge.[8]

This analysis is not challenged directly. Rather, the more conservative position is that, as in the case of the Tokyo correspondent, Nakasone is going beyond an economic policy to develop a military threat as well. Or, as in the case of the correspondent in Malaysia, it is that Japanese investment abroad has negative social consequences. He referred to exploitation, a driving out of local businessmen, and Japanese use of their own architects and engineers instead of local personnel. Similarly, an article on European alarm at the Japanese referred to the bankrupting of local firms and the Japanese use of "Japanese methods of administration" in their own firms in Europe: "strengthened exploitation, a limitation of trade union activity, and paternalism".[9] Such articles may create fears in the Soviet Union about Japanese investment inside the country, but they never suggest that the Japanese model is anything other than effective in producing economic growth.

Ultimately, though, the central question for the Soviet population is not power in the Third World, but the general position of Russia in the world. It is easy for the Soviet leaders to explain away the success of the United States because of its early lead in industrialization and its avoidance of war on its homeland. Japan, however, began industrialization at about the same time as Russia, and it too suffered during World War II. When the Soviet citizen continually reads that Japan no longer simply copies Western technology but is in first place in a series of contemporary technologies,[10] that it has become a "world economic state" and has surpassed the USA as the "symbol of youth and dynamism in the Western world",[11] the effect must be chilling. If the population gains the sense that other Third World countries such as South Korea and Brazil are going to follow the Japanese path and that communism will leave Russia in an increasingly backward position, the consequences for stability will be serious.

In short, a zero-growth scenario that involved the end of the slow, steady rise in standards of living would obviously pose a real danger for political stability, but it should not be assumed that a steady 2 or 3 percent increase in standards of living would solve the political problem. The ability to meet world standards of technological innovation and production is just as crucial in the long run.

As Brezhnev knew that he would not live past the mid-1980s, there was no incentive for him to take the risks of reform to solve a long-term problem. Gorbachev hopes to rule Russia as it enters the twenty-first century, and his incentives are very different. Hence it is hardly surprising that he has been talking about technology, technology, technology, and the need to raise it to world levels. He has called for "a deep reconstruction of the whole economic mechanism", "a decisive revolution in the economy", "a fundamental perfecting of the system of price formation", "a major reconstruction in the minds of economic managers". He has specifically pledged not to allow deeds to lag behind words, and he asked the rhetorical question to one audience, "Are we not turning too sharply?" His answer was direct: "No . . . a different, calmer approach would not suit us. The time dictates that this is exactly how we must act".[12]

Economic Reform and the Attack on Protectionism

Both the drive for equality with the West and the reluctance to abandon a system developed by Russians are important factors in the decision whether or not to have a major economic reform that incorporates market mechanisms. These factors in and of themselves have relatively few implications for the type of foreign policy that the Soviet Union would follow if it were to introduce economic reform. Indeed, to some extent, the best solution to the problem of reconciling the opposing political pressures generated by nationalism might be a chauvinistic foreign policy, with the reform being justified by the need for defense and with it being accompanied by stronger political controls established over the borderlands in the name of an external threat.

When the imperatives of reform itself are considered, however, the situation becomes much more complex. The Western literature on reform focuses on the various steps required domestically in the Soviet Union and the political obstacles that these encounter, and other chapters in this volume have the responsibility of exploring this side of the question. While this side of the question deserves emphasis, there is one aspect of economic reform that has been given little attention in the scholarly literature and almost none in the American public discussion.

This is the need to attack protectionism, to subject Soviet industrialists to foreign competition, and to integrate the Soviet economy more fully into the world economy.

Westerns do not talk much about Soviet protectionism, for the Soviet economists do not use that term to describe their foreign economic policy. Yet, in fact, the Soviet Union has had a policy of protectionism that extends far beyond anything found in the industrial or industrializing world. The system of autarky and the monopoly of foreign trade meant that outsiders had no independent access to the Soviet market. When foreign trade was conducted, Soviet manufacturers faced no threat of a loss of business, for they continued to have their own captive market. Hence they did not have to raise the quality of their goods to meet the competition. In addition—and perhaps even more important, for the Japanese have had strong protectionism as well—Soviet producers have normally had little incentive or need to export their manufactured goods. As a consequence, they have not had to meet world standards in product design, in quality, or in cost of production in the markets abroad. This has had very important consequences in the Soviet Union. If one lists the familiar criticisms of the Soviet economy—low quality of goods, lack of responsiveness to consumer demand, sluggishness in technological innovation—it is striking how similar they are to the consequences of protectionism predicted by the proponents of free trade.

Although Westerners often talk about the integration into the world economy that Brezhnev initiated in the early 1970s, it was an extremely conservative step. Soviet leaders knew for some time that the Soviet economy had real problems, and Khrushchev thought that some magical reorganization would solve them. By the early 1960s it was clear that administrative reorganization was not a panacea, and an economic debate developed in the early 1960s on what to do. Just as Brezhnev took a very cautious alternative in the domestic reforms, so he took the cautious alternative in foreign economic policy. (Indeed, the two were tied together, for an attack on protectionism would require a major change in the incentive system under which industrialists worked.) He assumed, or at least hoped, that the importation of advanced technology would itself have a qualitatively positive impact on the Soviet economy.

Undoubtedly the imported technology had some benefits for the Soviet Union, but, in essence, the policy failed. After it was launched, the Soviet Union received unexpected windfalls in a ten-fold increase in the price of its two main export items—petroleum and gold—but, despite the fact that available foreign currency was greater than expected, the rate of growth continued to decline. As the Polish experience demonstrated very clearly, imported Western technology that must be manned and managed under the Soviet incentive system will not function as productively as it did in a system in which managers have the incentive to economize on labor and other costs.[13]

What the Soviet economy really needs, as many Soviet economists have come to emphasize, is not so much the importation of Western technology *per se* as the importation of technology that competes with the production of Soviet managers. Even more, it needs measures that compel Soviet managers to export technology. Only if Soviet managers are forced to produce goods that can compete in the world market will they produce goods of world-level quality and cost for the domestic market. Clearly Gorbachev and Shevardnadze understand this well.[14]

The attack on protectionism that must be part of any thorough economic reform has a series of implications that have not been fully understood in the West, and these will complicate the already difficult task of building support for reform.

First, integration of the Soviet Union into the world economy increases the social costs of reform. In very broad terms, economic reform requires some sacrifice of "social justice", as traditionally understood in a socialist society, in exchange for economic growth and especially technological advance. Income inegalitarianism will increase, subsidized food prices will have to be attacked, and an incentive system that encourages managers to economize on labor will lead to greater job insecurity. All of these steps will arouse fears on the part of those with low incomes, the pensioners and the industrial workers, and in Poland the raising of meat prices actually led to riots. Integration into the world economy will expose the Soviet Union more to the Western business cycles, and this will increase the dangers of inflation and unemployment even more than domestic measures alone.

Second, the attack on protectionism will make managerial political support for reform more ambivalent than it already is. Essentially, economic reform in the Soviet Union entails the same sacrifice of social policy for economic growth that is involved in Reaganism and Thatcherism, and this aspect of reform is going to be as popular with Soviet managers as with their American and British counterparts. In the public discussion of the 1977 Soviet Constitution, the article on the duty to work received the greatest attention, and the discussion revealed a deep anger at what was perceived to be widespread laziness. Reform would give the managers greater authority to discipline workers and even to fire them, and managers as a group would benefit from an increase in income inegalitarianism.

Nevertheless, no automobile manager in the United States and Western Europe is eager to compete with Toyota, and any attack on protectionism is going to be no more popular with the central and plant managers of the Ministry of the Automobile Industry of the USSR. Raising the quality and the efficiency of Soviet goods to world levels is going to be very difficult. Unquestionably there are managers who would like the challenge—especially if they were to be given the challenge by being promoted to replace the many older managers—but the challenge is great enough that it must produce great anxiety among most managers.

Third, integration of the Soviet Union into the world economy would almost inevitably involve greater integration of the Soviet Union into world civilization. By itself, an expansion of international business contacts makes it difficult to prevent ideas from crossing the border as well as goods, but the problem goes much deeper. It will be hard for the Soviet Union to compete effectively in the world market until a broader segment of the Soviet elite gains a feeling of the West: how its institutions work, the sales techniques that Western business uses, the changing tastes of Western publics and the differences from country to country.

A narrow group of scholars specializing on the West has become quite sophisticated, but the problem of diffusing such knowledge to a broader elite has hardly begun to be addressed. Even officials in charge of selling goods to foreigners inside Russia have not perceived how popular T-shirts (even T-shirts with pro-revolutionary motifs) would be as souvenirs and do not sell them. Russia will not gain this knowledge until it sends far more people abroad (China sent tens of thousands of students when it launched its modernization drive), until it uses Western consultants, until it allows its personnel abroad to mix fully into local society, and until it allows far greater access to Western magazines and journals. The problem is not only exposure to Western ideas. The Soviet Union should be a major commercial force in the Middle East, but for this its Moslems need to develop contact with and a feel for Middle Eastern society.

The conservatives' fear that economic reform would result in subversion by Western ideas is further heightened by an understanding of the fact that the cutting edge of the technological revolution is at present the information revolution. The Soviet Union will never master the computer and the management of information on a broad scale unless it gives a broad range of citizens, especially among the young, substantial access to them. It cannot do this while maintaining the same controls over the private reproduction of politically unacceptable material that it now does.

Coalition-Building and Foreign Policy

Any examination of the costs of economic reform makes it perfectly obvious why Brezhnev did not have the energy or the inclination to introduce it. Gorbachev's inclinations seem very different, and his age gives him a different set of interests. The problems of reform are also easier for him, for there is a widespread recognition of the problem of stagnation, a yearning for strong leadership of almost any type, and a willingness to give a strong new leader some leeway in doing things.

For all of Gorbachev's advantages, however, the problems are still great, and the problem of building a shifting set of coalitions that will minimize opposition at each stage will be a complex one. As in China and Hungary, serious reform should really begin in the countryside and in a few of the services. Reform there is not as complicated, and Gorbachev would have the authority of his own expertise—and the successes of Hungary and China to support him. Tatyana Zaslavskaya has explicitly—and correctly—stated in *Izvestiya* that the path to take is to turn the already-existing contract brigades into family units.[15]

Agricultural reform does not, unfortunately for Gorbachev, solve the problem of technological innovation. (Of course, difficulties in an agricultural reform would give the General Secretary the excuse for radical changes in the system by which tractors, fertilizers, and the like are produced and distributed.) Meaningful industrial reform will be much more difficult, and the coalition difficult to forge because so many interests are involved.

The obvious first step in building a coalition is to mobilize higher officials and lower ones against the ministries in the middle. Zaslavskaya specifically does this in her article, writing about the undue expansion of the power of the second (ministerial) link in the Soviet system and warning about the ministries as the major source of opposition. Although she (rather disingenuously) describes the plant managers as the lower link and the major beneficiary of reform, these men have little political power. The basic core of the coalition for reform will have to rest on the republican and obkom first secretaries, who do sit on the Central Committee. As was the case in 1957 when Khrushchev used their support to dismantle the industrial ministries, they continue to detest the ministries, and they are the only powerful actors who have a self-interest in the decentralization of power.

As the General Secretary talks to other groups, he should be emphasizing benefits at each stage and deemphasizing costs. To the managers (both in the ministries and the plants), he should emphasize the change in social policy and the leisure-time advantages of greater integration with the West (the joys of skiing in St. Moritz), and he should be saying little at first about an attack on protectionism. For the workers, he should emphasize immediate consumer gains and deemphasize social policy and foreign competition. It is an extremely delicate balancing act.

The fact that reform will almost surely come in stages and that the attack on protectionism should come relatively late in the process (greater incentives for exports are another matter), because of the technical problems and the imperatives of building political support, means that reform does not have absolutely necessary foreign policy preconditions at the beginning.

Nevertheless, in the long run, and to some extent in the short run, the political problems of economic reform do tend to have foreign policy implications. First, of course, any difficult program calling for sacrifices is facilitated if it can be justified in the name of national defense against a foreign threat. Since the real impetus for reform actually is the effect of the technological lag on the Soviet defense and foreign policy posture, it makes double sense to use this as the public justification for the sacrifices. Second, the need to increase investment and the danger of cutting consumption in the face of a change in social policy make restraint on military spending highly desirable. Third, the attack on protectionism is incompatible with a Stalin-like policy of isolation and autarky, but requires guaranteed access to world markets.

Unfortunately for Gorbachev, these implications of economic reform for foreign policy are rather contradictory. Any emphasis upon a foreign threat may serve as a justification for increased military expenditure rather than restraint, and it tends to retard the process of opening to the outside world. Indeed, in the Soviet Union the foreign threat has been the traditional justification for a garrison-state mentality with respect to the West.

Two solutions to these dilemmas suggest themselves. The first is to distinguish between the long-term threat and the short-term one. It is the latter that implies the need for expenditures on readiness and on procurement—the expenditures that are extremely counterproductive. The long-term threat is best handled by industrial investment, computerization, and military research-and-development in high technology fields. This is precisely what is needed to correct the technological lag.

In the mid-1980s two perfect long-term threats existed. One was President Reagan's Star Wars program, and the other was

Chinese modernization. Neither posed the slightest danger to the Soviet Union over the next decade or so, but each looked extremely frightening from a twenty-year perspective. Star Wars in particular focused attention precisely on the high-technology research and development that was needed.

The second potential solution to the foreign policy imperatives of economic reform is to move away from the bi-polar policy that Gromyko pursued towards a multi-polar policy with special attention to Western Europe and Japan. In that way, the United states could be used as the threat, and Western Europe and Japan could be used to guarantee access to the world economy.

The latter solution is not a hypothetical one imagined by an American scholar. If the Soviet debates over the years were examined carefully, it is likely that the appeals for a multi-polar policy have long been present,[16] but the theme became particularly strong during Andropov's year in office. It was particularly strong in the writings of the two major foreign policy appointments of Yurii Andropov—Alexander Yakovlev, the director of the Institute of the World Economy and International Relations (IMEMO) and Lev Tolkunov, the editor of *Izvestiya*. (Both Yakovlev and Tolkunov were obviously associated with Andropov: Yakovlev worked for years in the Yaroslavl party organization out of which Andropov came, and Tolkunov was deputy head of the socialist countries department of the Central Committee in the early 1960s when Andropov was its head.[17]

Both Yakovlev and Tolkunov took a very similar position in 1983 and early 1984. Both condemned the view (associated with the Americanists in the pro-detente group such as Georgii Arbatov and Alexander Bovin) that the problem in Soviet-American relations is a cyclical one associated with President Reagan.[18] Both suggested that American policy was hostile on a long-term basis, but both put great emphasis upon the divisions existing within the West—the traditional way of saying that the Soviet Union should engage in flexible diplomatic manoeuvering to take advantage of these divisions.[19]

Thus Tolkunov, in a major article in a journal on International Affairs in 1983, took an extremely negative view of the United States, asserting that President Nixon, the apostle of detente, and President Reagan, the apostle of crusade, thought in analogous ways. Nevertheless, the article ended with a fervent declaration that there was no alternative to detente.[20] Even after the deployment of the Pershing missiles in Germany, *Izestiya*, which he was editing in early 1984, carried few articles about a military threat from Europe and many articles on divisions in the West, especially economic divisions. The man whom he hired as the leading *Izvestiya* commentator, Valentin Falin, was one of the most vociferous of the anti-American and pro-German figures in the foreign policy establishment. The *Izvestiya* pattern of coverage, and the Falin commentary in particular, strongly implied that the Soviet Union should court Europe on a governmental and economic basis more than rely on the peace movement against a threatening Germany, which was governed by a man who was said to be encouraging revanchism (the overall *Pravda* line).

Yakovlev, for his part, wrote in scathing terms about the United States, its political culture, and even its citizenry, specifically criticizing "some politicians and public figures" (no doubt, Arbatov but also probably Andrei Gromyko) who "with a certain complacency are inclined to consider this an accidental moment in history, a moment of irrational character, attributing it to the personal characteristics of President Reagan".[21] In an article in *Pravda* in March 1984, Yakovlev wrote of a relative levelling (*nivelirovanie*) in the strength of the three centers of power: the USA, Western Europe, and Japan, and he added that "in any case it is self-evident that in the historically foreseeable future the centrifugal tendency in the capitalist world will grow".[22] As befits an institute deeply dedicated to economic reform, Yakovlev put his greatest stress on Japan. It was he who made the earlier-cited statement about Japan becoming a "world economic state" and the symbol of youth and dynamism in the Western world.[23]

This is not the place for an elaborate analysis of various Soviet options and for a prediction about the timing of economic reform and any foreign policy change. Rather it is enough here to insist that foreign policy and domestic policy are very closely linked. It was no accident that Yakovlev and Tolkunov were appointed (and that Andropov himself wrote off relations with the United States in September 1983) in a period in which the

General Secretary was moving towards significant economic reform. It was no accident that one of Chernenko's first actions was to remove Tolkunov from his editorship, that the press began accelerating its coverage of German revanchism (as a way of supporting Gromyko's policy of dealing with the United States to control Germany), that the Honnecker trip was cancelled, that Ogarkov was fired, and, of course, that the General Secretary stopped economic reform in its tracks. All of these fit together. And it was also no accident that the Gorbachev who emphasized economic reform stopped the emphasis on revanchism, removed the architect of the bipolar foreign policy as his foreign minister, and made Yakovlev one of his chief advisers.[24] At this time the degree to which economic reform will be pushed and to which foreign policy will be changed are still not certain, but a multi-polar policy with an emphasis on the Star Wars danger is so useful for domestic reform that for the next few years at least, it is likely that the speed of reform and the speed of a shift from a bipolar policy will be highly correlated.

Notes

1. M. Evchuk, "Klassiki russkoi filosofii XIX veka," *Bol'shevik*, 1944 No. 20, p. 26.

2. *Izvestiya*, 18 February 1984, p. 5.

3. Burce Parrott, *Politics and Technology in the Soviet Union* (Cambridge, Mass.: The MIT Press, 1983), pp. 5–6.

4. *Pravda*, 23 February 1984, p. 2.

5. *Ibid.* 21 May 1984, p. 4.

6. For the Soviet debates on the Third World see Jerry F. Hough, *The Struggle for the Third World: Soviet Debates and American Options* (Washington, D.C.: The Brookings Institution, 1985).

7. *Pravda*, 19 May 1984, p. 4.

8. *Ibid.* 5 April 1984, p. 4.

9. *Ibid.* 18 April 1984, p. 5.

10. *Ibid.* 7 February 1984.

11. Alexander Yakovlev, the then director of IMEMO, *ibid.* 23 March 1984, p. 3.

12. *Pravda*, 27 June 1985, p. 2.

13. For the Soviet experience see Jerry F. Hough, *The Polish Crisis: American Policy Options* (Washington, D.C.: The Brookings Institution, 1982).

14. In April 1984, under Chernenko, Shevardnadze held a Georgian Central Committee session on economic reform at which he called for "daring decisions," and also a Central Committee conference on the need to export manufactured goods, *Zarya vostoka*, 7 April 1984, p. 3 and 11 April 1984, p. 3. While chairman of the Foreign Affairs Committee of the Supreme Soviet, Gorbachev held an unprecedented session on expansion of foreign economic relations with the Third World, and everyone knows this requires the export of manufactured goods.

15. *Izvestiya*, 1 June 1985.

16. See the discussion of the differences in the analysis of Europe and NATO in Michael J. Sodaro, "Soviet Studies of the Western Alliance," in Herbert J. Ellison ed. *Soviet Policy towards Western Europe* (Seattle: University of Washington Press, 1983), pp. 234–265.

17. The early biographies of both men can be found in *Ezhegodnik Bol'shoi Sovetskoi Entsiklopedii* (Moscow 1971), pp. 632 and 643.

18. See Bovin's article in *Izvestiya*, 16 November 1983, p. 4.

19. For the classic analysis of this technique of debate see Franklyn Griffiths, "Images, Politics and Learning in Soviet Behaviour Toward the United States," doctoral dissertation, Columbia University, 1972.

20. L. Tolkunov, "Ideologicheskaya bor'ba i mirnoe sosushchestvovanie na sovremennom etape," *Mezhdunarodnaya zhizn'*, 1983, No. 12.

21. *Izvestiya*, 7 October 1983, p. 5. For a similar line of argument see the interview with him in *Komsomol'skaya pravda*, 25 December 1983, pp. 1 and 3.

22. *Pravda*, 23 March 1984, p. 3.

23. A broader discussion about Europe and the bi-polar policy can be found in Jerry F. Hough, "Soviet Perspectives on European Security," *International Journal* (Toronto), Vol. XL, No. 1 (Winter 1984–1985), pp. 20–41.

24. See Jerry F. Hough, "Gorbachev's Strategy," *Foreign Affairs*, Fall 1985, pp. 1–23.

13
Developing Countries in the Foreign Economic Relations and Foreign Policy of the USSR

Heinrich A. Machowski

Introduction

During the phase of basic industrialization before and immediately after World War II, the Soviet Union considered foreign trade of limited importance. The country was indeed one of the very few with a large enough domestic market and abundance of raw materials to make autarkic industrialization possible. But even so the Soviet Union soon had to recognize that, with time, such a policy would ultimately result in lower living standards than could otherwise be achieved. In the post-Stalin era, under Khrushchev, this recognition, together with a new foreign policy objective, brought about a change in the Soviet assessment of the importance of foreign trade. Cooperation between the CMEA countries was now to be intensified, partly in reaction to the initial success of the EEC. The Soviet Union also sought to accelerate development of its chemical, and later its automobile industry, with the help of Western technology. The first large-scale imports of Western grain also occurred at about this time. Finally, trade and development aid were used for the first time to gain political influence in the Third World.

Since the mid-1950s the Soviet Union has intensified its efforts to develop ties with the non-communist countries of the Third World and has endeavoured increasingly to assert its political influence in these parts of the world. Whereas Khrushchev's efforts were classed by the West as "commitment and adventurism", Brezhnev's later policy has been praised as "highly rationalistic, realistic, pragmatic, and, until Angola, cautious".[1] The reference to Soviet-Cuban intervention in Angola from 1975 is an expression of growing Western fear that the spectacular spread of Soviet power in the Third World could inflict damage on the economic interests of Western industrialized countries (possible Soviet control over deposits of natural resources in South Africa). The Soviet military invasion of Afghanistan in 1979 not only heightened these fears; it further triggered (primarily in the United States) an outright "revolution of perception"[2] with regard to the future goals of Soviet policy towards the Third World and, indeed, the very nature of Soviet foreign policy (was the USSR a world order power or an expansionist imperialist state?).

Analysis of political and economic relations between the Soviet Union and the developing countries encounters fairly serious difficulties. There is no more public discussion of goals and resource commitments in this regard than there is of profits and losses, or of costs incurred by the Soviet Union through its relations with "the South". Soviet public policy statements and press coverage are chronically afflicted by excess ideology and propaganda; they are often empty slogans that do not lend themselves well to analysis. Furthermore, published Soviet economic statistics, compared with corresponding Western standards, have only limited information value and are very incomplete; and the gaps cannot in every case be filled by Western estimates. For these reasons, Soviet options, priorities, and positions often may only be speculatively described.

Soviet Interests and Objectives in the Third World

Soviet policy towards the Third World has a politico-strategic, an economic, and an ideological dimension. The main objective of Moscow's foreign policy over the past twenty-five years, and thus also the chief determinant of its policy in developing regions, has been "its claim to act, and to be treated, as a superpower equal to the United States".[3] This exalted claim (in view of the clear relative weakness of Soviet economic power compared with the United States) explains the nuclear armaments effort and the development of a globally operating naval fleet; for genuine superpower equality with the USA requires not just corresponding military strength, but an equal worldwide presence, at least in key regions. A large portion of Soviet commitment in the Third World may be explained by this necessity. "Anticolonialism" and "anti-imperialism" were catch-words for the Soviet effort to build up its own position in the Third World at the expense of Washington and its allies. To reduce the serious risk of direct confrontation with the USA, Moscow allowed "representatives" to act in its place (as Cuban actions in Africa demonstrate).

A further important goal of Soviet policy in the Third World is the struggle against the "Chinese threat";[4] since the late 1950s the People's Republic of China has become Moscow's rival as it is attractive to a number of developing countries viewed by Moscow as candidates for "socialist development" and therefore potential allies. Thus Moscow carries out its policy of restraint taking account of the Poeple's Republic of China, not only in Asia but in the Third World generally, though the policy met with difficulties after the invasion of Afghanistan. Finally, the Soviet Union and China are both currently indirectly engaged in hostilities in Kampuchea.

Since the mid-1970s the Soviet Union has increasingly tried to include the CMEA as an institutional factor in relations with developing countries. The obvious purpose of these efforts is to strengthen coherence within the "socialist community of nations" while at the same time reinforcing its claim to the leadership of this community. A further factor may be that after the admission of Cuba (1972) and Vietnam (1978), the CMEA has also faced an internal "North-South problem".[5]

Since the early 1970s particular stress has been laid in the Soviet Union on the economic dimension of relations with Third World countries. At the XXIV CPSU Congress in 1971 Kosygin, then head of the government, declared:

> In the coming five-year period, the further expansion of the USSR's foreign economic ties with the developing countries of Asia, Africa, and Latin America is planned. With respect to

many of them—India, Afghanistan, Iran, Pakistan, the United Arab Republic, Syria, Iraq, Algeria, and others—our trade and economic cooperation are entering a stage in which we can speak of firmly established mutually advantageous economic ties. Our cooperation with these countries, based on the principles of equality and respect for mutual interests, is acquiring the nature of a stable division of labor, counterposed to the system of imperialist exploitation, in the sphere of international economic relations. At the same time, through the expansion of trade with the developing countries the USSR will receive the opportunity to satisfy the requirements of its own economy more fully.[6]

Richard Lowenthal saw it as a "distinct shift from old-style anti-imperialism to a new concept that can best be described as 'counter-imperialism'—a strategy of fighting Western imperialism by using the familiar 'imperialist' methods of establishing zones of political and economic influence linked to the Soviet Union's firm ties".[7]

General Trade Trends

This section presents the main results of an analysis of Soviet trade relations with the non-European, non-socialist developing countries (among the developing countries, only China, Vietnam and North Korea are here considered to be socialist countries). The period under examination was 1970 through 1982, though in some cases data are available only to 1983 or even 1982 (the terms "developing countries", "LDCs" and "Third World" will be used interchangeably for simplicity. According to Soviet sources the USSR maintained trade relations with a total of 89 countries in the Third World, with 73 of which it concluded long-term (presumably five-year) trade treaties.[8]

Soviet exports to the LDCs over this period increased by over 6.5 times in nominal terms and in 1984 amounted to more than 13.7 billion dollars. Soviet imports from this group of countries went up by more than 7 times over the same period to more than 9 billion dollars. Over the past fourteen years the share of Soviet trade directed to the non-socialist developing countries has remained rather steady at about 15 percent of exports and 11 percent of imports (see Table 13.1).

From Soviet sources one can conclude that the overall growth in real Soviet exports to and imports from the LDCs was impressive too: real exports increased from 1970 to 1975 by more than 20 percent, whereas the growth of real imports was in the range of 60 percent. This relationship changed dramatically in the following five-year period 1976–1980: real Soviet exports went up by a further 45 percent, whereas the growth of real imports declined to only 15 percent. From this it follows that the Soviet terms of trade declined over the period by 15 to 20 percent (incidentally, this is the only region where the Soviet Union suffered a deterioration of its terms of trade during those years).

Table 13.1 documents the long-recognized significance of the "unspecified" exports in Soviet-LDC trade: 47 percent of the total Soviet exports over the years 1970 to 1984 cannot be identified either by country of destination or by kind of commodity. The relative share of "unspecified" exports increased from 39 percent in 1970 to over 51 percent in 1984, i.e. these deliveries were by far the most dynamic part of Soviet trade with the LDCs.

The Soviet foreign trade statistics offer the following three sets of data: total exports and imports, exports and imports specified by country, and exports and imports identified by country and commodity. The difference between the total trade and the identified trade consists of the "residual" trade. This residual trade accounted for as much as 57 percent of total Soviet exports to the Third World over the years 1970 through 1983, though there are inconsistencies in the figures given in the sources, possibly because of changes in definition (the lower figure of 47 percent, cited above, is also found. The size of the import "residual" was 7.5 percent, much less significant than for exports.

So the data problems are formidable and even growing. While the gaps in official Soviet statistics on trade with the LDCs have always existed, the quality of these data has deteriorated sharply since the mid-1970s. For instance, since 1977 it has been impossible to calculate unit values for virtually all Soviet exports

TABLE 13.1. USSR Foreign Trade with the Third World* 1970 - 1984

	Exports FOB			Imports FOB			Export Surplus			Share in Total Trade in %	
	Total	Unspecified	Specified	Total	Unspecified	Specified	Total	Unspecified	Specified	Exports	Imports
				(Billion US Dollars)							
1970	2.04	0.80	1.24	1.27	0.01	1.26	0.77	0.79	-0.02	16.0	10.8
1971	2.03	0.70	1.33	1.41	0.03	1.38	0.62	0.67	-0.05	14.7	11.3
1972	2.45	1.09	1.36	1.63	0.01	1.62	0.82	1.08	-0.26	15.9	10.1
1973	3.97	2.15	1.82	2.36	0.08	2.28	1.61	2.07	-0.46	18.6	11.3
1974	4.49	2.05	2.44	3.16	0.05	3.11	1.33	2.00	-0.67	16.4	12.7
1975	4.60	1.91	2.69	4.17	0.04	4.13	0.43	1.87	-1.44	13.8	11.3
1971/75	17.54	7.90	9.64	12.73	0.21	12.52	4.81	7.69	-2.88	15.8	11.4
1976	4.96	2.37	2.59	3.78	0.09	3.69	1.18	2.28	-1.10	13.3	9.8
1977	7.27	3.92	3.35	4.09	0.05	4.04	3.18	3.87	-0.69	16.0	9.8
1978	8.41	4.17	4.24	4.17	0.03	4.14	4.24	4.14	0.10	16.0	8.2
1979	9.65	4.32	5.33	4.87	0.05	4.82	4.78	4.27	0.51	14.8	8.4
1980	10.55	4.74	5.81	7.82	0.20	7.62	2.73	4.54	-1.81	13.8	11.5
1976/80	40.84	19.52	21.32	24.73	0.42	24.31	16.11	19.10	-2.99	14.8	9.6
1981	12.03	5.05	6.98	10.79	0.21	10.58	1.24	4.84	-3.60	15.1	14.8
1982	12.04	6.58	7.46	9.25	0.22	9.03	4.79	6.36	-1.57	16.1	11.9
1983	14.19	7.04	7.15	9.67	0.28	9.39	4.52	6.76	-2.24	15.5	12.1
1984 #	13.75	7.05	6.70	9.19	0.37	8.82	4.56	6.68	-2.12	14.7	11.7
1981/84	54.01	25.72	28.29	38.90	1.08	37.82	15.11	24.64	-9.53	15.4	12.6
1971/84	112.39	53.14	59.25	76.36	1.71	74.65	36.03	51.43	-15.40	15.2	11.3

*(Asia (without China, Japan, Korea, Mongolia, Vietnam), Africa (without South Africa), Middle East (without Israel), America (without Canada, Cuba, USA). #) Preliminary.

Source: USSR Foreign Trade Yearbook, various editions.

and imports of fuels, metals and minerals. Beginning with 1977 it is consequently almost impossible to calculate price and real trade trends for Soviet trade with the Third World. Tom Wolf in a recent study tried to calculate this kind of data; his findings, however, are not very convincing: "Soviet net barter terms of trade are estimated at worst to have declined (cumulatively) by 14 percent over this six-year period 1975–1981 or at best to have improved by about 5 percent".[9] This development is largely a reflection of the more general deterioration of official Soviet trade statistics over this period.

Global and regional analysis of USSR-LDC trade is greatly affected by these data problems. The significance of the Third World as a trading partner to the USSR is relatively small. Among the twenty-five most important partner countries, which accounted for 86 percent of total Soviet foreign trade in 1983, there are only four non-communist developing countries: India, Argentina, Libya and Iran. Tables 13.2 and 13.3 show the importance of the first ten LDC partners in Soviet trade over time and the countries' shares of the identified total trade with LDCs. The first main feature is that Soviet trade is extremely concentrated. In 1983 three-quarters of Soviet exports went to ten countries, the corresponding figure for imports being almost 85 percent. The concentration of Soviet trade with LDCs is thus even higher on the import than on the export side. Extreme concentration is a traditional feature of Soviet trade with LDCs.

From a global LDC perspective, the USSR has never been an important market for their exports nor an important supplier of goods to them. Moreover, its share both of LDC exports and of LDC imports fell during the period 1970–1980. A reversal of this trend seems to have occurred in the early 1980s, the respective shares going up to 2.4 and 3.9 percent in 1982. In comparison, just over one fifth of LDC trade was conducted with the EEC in 1982, 18 percent with the USA and 14 percent with Japan.

Of the countries for which one could make rough estimates of trade shares, only in the case of Afghanistan, Argentina, Ethiopia, India, Libya, Sudan, Syria and North Yemen did 10 percent or more of their reported exports go to and/or imports come from the USSR, and for six of the countries this was true

TABLE 13.2. Main USSR Trading Partners in the Third World
(in percent (total exports = 100))

EXPORTS

	1970		1975		1980
Egypt	2.9	India	1.2	India	2.1
Iran	1.5	Iran	1.2	Iraq	0.9
India	1.0	Iraq	1.1	Turkey	0.7
Iraq	0.5	Egypt	1.1	Iran	0.5
Turkey	0.5	Algeria	0.5	Afghanistan	0,5
Algeria	0.5	Syria	0.4	Egypt	0.3
Afghanistan	0.3	Brazil	0.4	Syria	0.3
Syria	0.3	Afghanistan	0.2	Libya	0.3
Pakistan	0.3	Morocco	0.2	Pakistan	0.3
Morocco	0.3	Turkey	0.2	Ethiopia	0.2
Share 1)	47.8	Share 1)	47.1	Share 1)	42.5
Share 2)	78.6	Share 2)	80.6	Share 2)	77.2

	1981		1982		1983
India	1.9	India	1.7	India	1.9
Iraq	1.6	Iraq	1.6	Iran	0.8
Iran	0.7	Iran	0.9	Afghanistan	0.6
Afghanistan	0.6	Afghanistan	0.7	Iraq	0.5
Turkey	0.6	Nigeria	0.4	Nigeria	0.5
Syria	0.5	Libya	0.4	Libya	0.4
Egypt	0.4	Egypt	0.4	Egypt	0.4
Libya	0.3	Syria	0.3	Syria	0.3
Nigeria	0.3	Ethiopia	0.3	Ethiopia	0.3
Ethiopia	0.2	Brazil	0.3	Algeria	0.2
Share 1)	46.7	Share 1)	42.1	Share 1)	37.7
Share 2)	80.5	Share 2)	79.2	Share 2)	74.6

1) Ten top-ranking partner countries as % of total exports to the Third World.

2) Ten top-ranking partner countries as % of specified exports to the Third World.

Source: USSR Foreign Trade Yearbook, various editions.

of the early but not the late 1970s. What evidence exists thus does not suggest widespread high Soviet trade shares in the Third World. This development suggests that any fundamental deepening of Soviet-LDC economic interdependence over the past decade may have been less than is often perceived in the West and claimed by the Soviet authorities.

In order to examine the trends in Soviet trade with different groups of developing countries, three groups by standard economic criteria, i.e. OPEC members, LLDCs and NICs (Newly

TABLE 13.3. Main USSR Trading Partners in the Third World
(in percent (total imports = 100))

IMPORTS

1970		1975		1980	
Egypt	2.7	Egypt	1.7	Argentina	3.0
India	2.3	India	1.5	India	2.0
Malaysia	1.0	Iraq	1.2	Libya	0.6
Iran	0.6	Brazil	1.1	Iraq	0.6
Algeria	0.6	Argentina	1.1	Afghanistan	0.6
Ghana	0.4	Iran	0.9	Brazil	0.6
Afghanistan	0.3	Malaysia	0.4	Malaysia	0.4
Pakistan	0.3	Syria	0.3	Thailand	0.3
Turkey	0.3	Afghanistan	0.2	Syria	0.3
Indonesia	0.3	Turkey	0.2	Philippines	0.3
Share 1)	79.1	Share 1)	76.0	Share 1)	73.3
Share 2)	79.8	Share 2)	76.8	Share 2)	75.2

1981		1982		1983	
Argentina	4.5	India	2.6	Argentina	2.2
India	2.5	Argentina	2.3	India	1.8
Brazil	1.0	Libya	2.0	Libya	1.7
Iran	0.9	Brazil	0.7	Brazil	1.0
Libya	0.7	Syria	0.5	Iraq	0.6
Afghanistan	0.6	Egypt	0.5	Iran	0.6
Thailand	0.6	Afghanistan	0.5	Egypt	0.6
Egypt	0.5	Malaysia	0.4	Syria	0.5
Syria	0.5	Iran	0.3	Afghanistan	0.5
Malaysia	0.3	Thailand	0.2	Malaysia	0.4
Share 1)	82.1	Share 1)	85.4	Share 1)	82.2
Share 2)	83.7	Share 2)	87.5	Share 2)	84.7

1) Ten top-ranking partner countries as % of total imports from the Third World.

2) Ten top-ranking partner countries as % of specified imports from the Third World.

Source: USSR Foreign Trade Yearbook, various editions.

Industrialized Countries), and a fourth group based on presumed political orientation, have been distinguished, though such distinctions are always somewhat arbitrary (see table 13.4). One third of the specified Soviet exports to the LDCs over the period examined went to OPEC members, and the share of the LLDCs increased significantly. The role of the DCSO as a market place for Soviet exports increased sharply over the thirteen years. The bulk of specified Soviet imports from the Third World stem from OPEC members and NICs respectively. The increase of the NICs' share is especially spectacular. This, of course, is due to the grain imports from Argentina and Brazil. This tends to confirm one's intuitive impression that the pattern of Soviet exports to the Third World is more heavily influenced by political factors and less by economic factors than is the pattern of Soviet imports from the developing countries.

The Soviet Union has achieved an export surplus on trade with the Third World every year since 1970. For the whole period it amounts to a cumulative surplus of more than 36 billion dollars. This results entirely from the "unspecified" trade, on which the cumulative surplus was about 51 billion dollars (see table 13.1). Since most Western observers believe the "un-reported" exports comprise arms deliveries, the Soviet surplus would consist of these shipments. To put it the other way round: on its "civilian" trade with the LDCs the Soviet Union has incurred a cumulative deficit of more than 15 billion dollars. From table 13.5 one can see that the USSR tends to run relatively large surpluses in "civilian" goods with oil producers, LLDCs and with the socialist-oriented countries, and a very large deficit with the NICs as a group. Again, the latter includes large agricultural exporters like Argentina to whom the USSR sells relatively little.

Soviet literature is equally deficient in information about whether the USSR has provided credit for financing its export surpluses on terms that would qualify them as development aid. Further, it is not known exactly with which developing countries the Soviet Union transacts payments on the basis of convertible currency. Presumably this would apply to its dealings with OPEC countries; the USSR has achieved an export surplus of more than 4 billion dollars with these partners over the past thirteen years, making trade with OPEC countries an important source of convertible currency income for the USSR.[10]

The meaning of these balances would certainly be clearer if all payments were effected in hard currencies. But this is not the case. Right from the beginning of its relations with LDCs, the Soviet Union established bilateral clearing accounts with most of them which allowed settlements in accounting dollars or even, as in the case of India, in accounting local national

TABLE 13.4. Regional Structure of Soviet Trade with the Third World, 1970 - 1983
(in percent)

	1970	1975	1980	1981	1982	1983
Total Specified						
Exports	100	100	100	100	100	100
OPEC Members[1]	30.3	37.4	29.8	36.8	41.1	31.9
LLDCs[2]	9.8	10.0	15.3	14.0	15.4	16.8
NICs[3]	0.8	5.9	2.1	2.0	4.6	2.9
Residual	59.1	46.7	52.8	47.2	38.9	48.4
DCSO[4]	4.1	4.4	14.7	15.2	16.2	20.1
Total Specified						
Imports	100	100	100	100	100	100
OPEC Members	11.2	27.1	15.1	13.2	21.7	29.3
LLDCs	8.0	4.1	8.0	6.4	5.9	5.3
NICs	4.8	20.5	29.9	39.2	26.7	28.1
Residual	76.0	48.3	47.0	54.4	45.7	37.3
DCSO	3.2	2.4	6.3	4.8	4.9	4.6

1. Algeria, Ecuador, Gabon, Indonesia, Iraq, Iran, Kuwait, Libya, Nigeria,
   Qatar, Saudi Arabia, United Arab Emirates and Venezuela.
2. 36 countries according to OECD classification, including: Afghanistan,
   Ethiopia, Yemen (PDR), and Laos.
3. Argentina, Brazil, Hong Kong, Korea (South), Mexico, Singapore and Taiwan.
4. Developing countries having a "socialist orientation": Afghanistan,
   Angola, Congo (PR), Ethiopia, Laos, Mozambique, Nicaragua and Yemen (PDR).

Source: as Table 13.1.

TABLE 13.5. Regional Distribution of Soviet Trade Balance with the Third World[1]
(in billion US dollars)

	1970	1975	1980	1983
Total Specified				
Trade	-0.01	-2.97	-6.52	-13.07
OPEC Members	+0.23	+0.08	+2.64	+ 4.47
LLDCs	+0.02	+0.49	+1.65	+ 3.29
NICs	-0.05	-1.36	-5.87	-14.39
Residual	-0.21	-2.18	-4.94	- 6.44
DCSO	+0.01	+0.10	+1.42	+ 3.76

Soviet surplus: +, Soviet deficit: -.
1) Cumulated since 1970.

Source: as Table 13.1.

currency. The advantages for both parties were obvious: they saved hard currencies, secured essential imports for their economies while at the same time finding markets for their own products (capital goods from the USSR, raw materials from LDCs, with the possible partial exception of India's manufactures). In an epoch of falling raw materials prices, LDCs found the long-term agreements with the USSR particularly attractive because they offered them both stability of prices and of markets. As far as the stability of Soviet trade with the developing countries if concerned, however, a western study concluded: "the USSR can only claim to have become a market of rather average overall stability".[11]

Along with the changes in the world economy i.e. rising prices for some primary products, there has been a growing tendency to include more and more convertible currency payments in the settlements. This new method of payment which was introduced mainly by LDCs, has not been strongly opposed by the USSR, which saw in it new possibilities of selling its manufactures for cash. The number of clearing agreements between LDCs and the USSR rapidly diminished: from 20 in 1970 to 16 in 1975 and down to 9 at the end of 1983 (calculated from IMF data). In fact, by early 1982 the USSR declared officially that it had bilateral clearing accounts with only seven countries: India, Afghanistan, Iran, Bangladesh, Pakistan, Syria and Egypt. In 1983 these countries accounted for more than one-third of identified imports and more than one-half of identified exports respectively.[12]

In 1982 49 percent of the identified Soviet exports to the LDCs were of machinery, vehicles and equipment in the CMEA Trade Classification; in 1970 the figure was 61 percent (see table 13.6). The second most important export item was fuels and industrial raw materials, whose share more than doubled to 37.5 percent in the past thirteen years—a development that may be primarily attributed to energy price rises. The share of this commodity group also increased on the import side, by almost 20 points, to 27.5 percent, for energy purchases from the Third World have also increased in importance to the Soviet economy, even though the USSR has remained a major net energy exporter. Identified Soviet imports from the Third World remain, however,

264

TABLE 13.6. USSR Trade with the Third World (in percent (all commodities = 100))

CATEGORIES[1]	EXPORTS				IMPORTS			
	1970	1975	1980	1982	1970	1975	1980	1982
I. Industrial machinery 2)	60.8	49.6	47.1	48.8	0.2	0.7	1.0	2.6
II. Fuels, metals 3)	17.8	27.2	37.8	37.5	8.2	25.3	19.6	27.5
III. Chemicals 4)	1.8	5.7	3.4	4.6	12.0	4.2	5.7	2.7
IV. Building materials 5)	1.4	2.0	1.4	0.9	0	0.1	0	0.3
V. Raw materials of vegetable origin 6)	5.5	8.1	6.8	4.7	36.3	19.1	13.9	13.4
VI. Raw materials for the production of food	1.8	0.3	0.2	0.5	15.8	29.7	36.0	27.3
VII. Footstuffs	7.8	5.2	2.5	2.2	16.9	11.1	15.6	15.6
VIII. Consumer goods	3.1	1.9	0.8	0.9	10.6	9.8	8.3	10.6

Classification

1. CMEA trade
2. And equipment (including spare parts).
3. And mineral raw materials.
4. And fertilizers and rubber.
5. And construction parts.
6. And animal origin (not food).

Source: USSR Foreign Trade Yearbook, various editions.

dominated by agricultural products of all kind (55 percent to 60 percent). Among them the foodstuffs (categories VII and VIII) increased in importance by 10 points to more than 42 percent. Here Soviet grain imports from Argentina are primarily responsible: because of the American partial embargo on grain enacted by President Carter in January 1980, and lifted again by President Reagan in April 1981, the USSR bought ca. 15 billion tons of grain from Argentina: this made the USSR an important trade partner for Argentina; in 1981 its share of the country's exports amounted to 83 percent for grain, 88 percent for corn, 63 percent for barley, 100 percent for rye, 22 percent for soybeans, and 24 percent for meat.[13] The growing role of food in Soviet imports from the LDCs could partly be seen as an aberration, reflecting the series of bad Soviet grain harvests in the late 1970s and early 1980s, combined with a diversion of grain imports as a result of restrictive policies.

The picture of the commodity structure of Soviet exports to the developing countries differs significantly if one uses UN foreign trade data (see Tables 13.7 and 13.8). The exports were dominated by arms, while the role of machinery and transport equipment (SITC category 7), that made up one third of all Soviet exports in 1970, declined steadily in subsequent years. To quote Tom Wolf again:

> Taking the export and import development together, one is struck by a commodity composition of Soviet-LDC trade which appears to be increasingly dominated in real terms by arms and petroleum exports and the import of food. For the 1970s as a whole, there is little evidence of a significant "deepening" of the international division of labour between the Soviet Union and the Third World. Soviet exports of "civilian" manufactured goods to the LDCs have been growing at relatively moderate rates, while imports by the USSR of Third World manufactures have largely stagnated.

Given this picture of the commodity composition of Soviet trade with the Third World, which still shows predominantly the traditional pattern of exchange between North and South, no great change in this structure seems likely. Even if the value

TABLE 13.7. Commodity Composition of Soviet Trade with the Third World
(in percent of total exports and imports)

SITC CATEGORY		1970	1975	1980	1982
		EXPORTS			
Mineral fuels, lubricants and related materials	(SITC 3)	5.6	13.6	18.4	20.2
Machinery and transport equipment	(SITC 7)	33.7	24.7	24.1	20.8
Not reported by kind of commodity		36.8	37.5	43.8	45.7
		IMPORTS			
Food items, including beverages, tobacco and edible oils and seeds	(SITC 0 +1+22+4)	49.9	62.5	67.4	75.9
Textile fibres, textile yarn and fabrics and clothing	(SITC 26 +65+84)	24.7	13.0	9.1	8.3
Mineral fuels, lubricants and related materials	(SITC 3)	2.0	12.3	8.8	4.3
Agricultural raw materials	(SITC 2 Less 22, 27, 28)	23.6	9.2	7.2	5.3

Sources: UN, Statistical Yearbook, 1975 and 1983; Monthly Bulletin of Statistics May 1977, May 1981 and May 1984.

TABLE 13.8. Commodity Composition of Soviet Trade with OPEC Countries
(in percent of total exports and imports)

SITC CATEGORY		1970	1975	1980	1982
		EXPORTS			
Machinery and transport equipment	(SITC 7)	63.2	55.8	49.1	40.6
Manufactured goods	(SITC 6+8)	13.7	9.0	5.6	1.8
Not reported by kind of commodity		7.8	21.6	38.8	50.3
		IMPORTS			
Mineral fuels, lubricants and related materials	(SITC 3)	3.6	65.4	74.4	41.2
Food items, including beverages, tobacco and edible oils and seeds	(SITC 0 +1+22+4)	55.0	25.4	11.1	26.6
Agricultural raw materials	(SITC 2 Less 22, 27, 28)	21.9	5.0	10.7	22.6
Manufactured goods	(SITC 6+8)	11.2	1.7	3.2	8.9

Sources: UN, Statistical Yearbook, 1975 and 1983; Monthly Bulletin of Statistics, May 1977, May 1981 and May 1984.

of imports of manufactured goods from LDCs should rise substantially in the future, their share may remain constant, due to the considerable amounts of food and raw materials that the USSR will need to import. There may be a growth of trade, but its pattern will remain rather traditional, hardly making for a new international division of labour. As a consequence, there is little reason to anticipate a change from a complementary to a competitive trade pattern.

Economic Aid

The Soviet Union publishes a few sporadic and very generalized reports, but no systematic account of its own assistance to the Third World. For a detailed analysis of the volume and structure of Soviet aid it is necessary to rely on Western estimates. These are marred by a high uncertainty factor (danger of double and multiple counting of credit commitments and actual payments; unclear definitions of development aid in the narrow sense, i.e., services on preferential terms, and commercial credit and military aid).[14]

According to an American source,[15] the volume of Soviet aid measured as credit commitments increased from 200 million dollars in 1970 to 2.3 billion dollars in 1983. Soviet development aid is characterized among other things by the fact that it has been subject to heavy fluctuations. However, this is not always an expression of Eastern donor countries' changing political stance towards the Third World. It is much more the reflection of a twofold situation: the earmarking of new, typically large aid projects does not go on continuously; and framework agreements on economic and technical cooperation only result in concrete plans after some time has elapsed. According to this estimate the aid actually drawn, based on an average over several years, is probably slightly less than half of that pledged. This rate of utilization is unusually low. On the whole, the discrepancy between the amount of credit extended and that actually drawn is probably due to the donor country's limited ability to deliver as well as the receiving country's inability to offer appropriate development projects, or in the case of joint projects, to fulfill its part of the agreement.

TABLE 13.9. Soviet Aid-Related Deliveries *) to the Third World, 1970 - 1983 #)

	Billion Rubles	Percent of Total Specified Exports	Percent Of Total Identified CMEA Category I Exports
Total Developing Countries	8.13	20.88	54.56
Of which			
Iran	1.27	29.88	67.52
Iraq	0.92	16.08	40.03
Nigeria	0.81	74.65	92.68
India	0.77	11.13	74.18
Egypt	0.56	16.74	38.89
Turkey	0.54	28.77	76.71
Afghanistan	0.50	22.64	46.08
Pakistan	0.49	58.97	73.79
Algeria	0.46	25.09	81.42
Libya	0.34	28.96	33.37
Total Reported Countries	6.65	17.08	44.62

*)"Equipment and materials delivered for projects built abroad with technical assistance of the USSR".
#) Cumulated data.

Source: USSR Foreign Trade Yearbook, various editions.

An important indication of the volume of the flow of Soviet concessional resources to recipient countries (gross disbursements) is the item in the Soviet foreign trade statistics, "Equipment and Materials for Projects Built Abroad with Technical Assistance of the USSR" (see table 13.9). Proof of the high status of this technical assistance is the fact that it is planned and administered, not by the foreign trade ministry, but by the equally high-ranking State Committee for Foreign Economic Relations, especially founded for this purpose in 1957. According to this source, the USSR provided technical aid valued at more than 8 billion foreign trade rubles to developing countries between 1970 and 1983. That is the equivalent of roughly 11 billion dollars, two billion dollars more than American estimates of Soviet credit provisions in these thirteen years.

Tom Wolf has tried to examine econometrically whether Soviet imports from major Third World recipients of Soviet economic aid have been systematically influenced by these past aid-related deliveries. His results yield little if any evidence, either for individual trade partners or for his sample of countries as a group, of a systematic relationship between Soviet aid-related exports and subsequent Soviet imports.[16]

Traditionally, measures in the state sector of the economy and heavy-industry projects such as iron and steel production, the metals industry, and heavy machinery, are in the forefront of the USSR's aid program. Increasingly, however, funds for prospecting and exploring mineral resources, particularly oil and natural gas, are being committed. Soviet self-interest, plus a fall in developing countries' enthusiasm for the massive project packages of the earlier style of Soviet commitment, probably combine to produce this new orientation. To a certain extent, a tendency is also observable away from the single project to comprehensive (horizontally or vertically integrated) measures involving more than one branch of production.

As in the West, various motives also prompt Soviet development aid; foreign policy is of course important, but economic, ideological, and purely humanitarian considerations are also involved. Economic motivation may be said to be gaining in importance, and the desire to expand its raw materials base and secure the procurement of strategic products may be added. Interest in gaining foreign policy ground and reducing the other superpower's influence may be said to be equally strong in East and West.

According to official reports, credit agreements have an average duration of about ten to twelve years, and interest rates as a rule amount to 2–2.4 percent per year. In addition, socialist creditors do not calculate commissions for loans agreed but not drawn. Repayment obligations can begin immediately after completion of the project; in special cases the first repayment installments may be delayed until up to three years after project completion.

In general, capital aid from the USSR and other socialist countries is characterized by the fact that, due to the predominance of payments and services in kind, it is almost entirely tied to deliveries. What is advantageous to developing countries is that the debtor is generally allowed to pay back the loan largely with products of the facility built on the credit, though deliveries of traditional export goods are also used. Only a few Eastern European countries require partial repayment in convertible currency. Except for scholarships, services within the framework of technical assistance may also be included as payments. A common feature of the entire Eastern development aid is the almost total absence of multilateral aid—the result of close interlinking of trade and aid and a reflection of the bilateral trade structure.

Any comparison of the USSR's (and the other CMEA countries') and Western donor countries' development aid is subject to narrow limitations. Soviet (and Eastern European) aid is to a certain extent differently defined; the data base is very shaky; and the available Western estimates cannot be tested for quality. Soviet representatives at UN ECOSOC claimed the USSR gave 30 billion rubles (44 billion dollars) in net aid to developing countries during 1976–1980, rising from 0.9 percent of GNP in 1976 to 1.3 percent in 1980.[17] (Net disbursements are the gross disbursements less the developing countries' amortisation of previous aid loans. It is the most frequently quoted measure of aid volume performance, and the UN used net disbursements when setting the aid volume target of 0.7 percent of donors' GNP. Most DAC countries accept this target in principle. The USSR and East European donors do not accept the UN's 0.7 percent target.)

UK estimates suggest total Soviet net disbursements were 8.3 billion dollars during 1976–1980.[18] This contrasts with the Soviet claim that its net aid was 44 billion dollars during the period. These estimates of Soviet net aid, combined with World Bank estimates of Soviet GNP, suggest the net aid/GNP ratio was 0.19 percent in 1980, the year for which the USSR claimed an aid/GNP ratio of 1.3 percent. The Soviet net aid/GNP ratio probably remained at 0.19 percent during 1981–1982.

According to OECD estimates in 1982 more than 74 percent of net aid in the framework of official development assistance (ODA) came from Western industrialized countries and 18 percent from OPEC countries. The CMEA countries' share was a scant 6.5 percent, 5 percent of which came from the USSR. This figure includes Soviet assistance to communist developing countries (Cuba, North Korea, and Vietnam), though such subsidy elements as might derive from favorable price calculations in commercial transactions between the USSR and some of these countries are not included.

Concluding Remarks

The former Soviet party leader, Andropov, in his speech to the Central Committee of the CPSU in November 1982, particularly stressed continuity with past Soviet foreign policy. He added, "Solidarity with countries that have liberated themselves from colonial oppression, and with people who are defending their independence, was and remains one of the fundamental principles of Soviet foreign policy". At the same time he called the recovery of the Soviet economy an "international duty" of the party and supported this with the following Lenin quotation: "We exercise our greatest influence on the worldwide revolutionary process through our economic policy".

However, it may be argued that it has been the inadequacy of Soviet economic power that has limited its commitment as well as its attractiveness to the Third World. Over the last thirteen years it has become more and more evident that Soviet economic capabilities do not match Soviet political aspirations. In other words, the developing countries are primarily economically orientated towards the West, and many of these countries use their ties with the USSR (and with other CMEA countries) mainly to bolster their negotiating positions vis-à-vis the West—and this is not likely to change in the foreseeable future.

But the relative economic weakness of the Soviet Union also determines the Soviet posture towards the new international economic order;[19] the demands of developing countries in the North-South dialogue will be supported readily and loudly as long as they do not involve any obligations. But if this dialogue generates demands that require financial or organizational assistance, they will be flatly rejected by the USSR. This posture entails a conflict for Soviet policy with the Third World which is likely to intensify in the future.

Notes

1. Joseph G. Whelan, ed. *Soviet Policy and United States Response in the Third World* (Washington, D.C., 1981), pp. 37–38.
2. Astrid von Borcke, "How Expansionist Is the Soviet Regime? Domestic Determinants of Foreign Policy Decisionmaking of the Soviet

Leadership," in *The Soviet Union 1980–81* (New York: Holmes & Meier, 1983), p. 90.

3. John C. Campbell, "Introduction: The Role of the Soviet Union in World Politics in the 1980s," in Lawrence T. Caldwell and William Diebold, Jr., *Soviet-American Relations in the 1980s, Superpower Politics and East-West Trade*, 1980s Project and Council on Foreign Relations, 1981, pp. 12–13.

4. Helmut Hubel and Siegfried Kupper, *Sowjetunion und Dritte Welt*, *Arbeitspapiere zur Internationalen Politik*, No. 14, Forschungsinstitut der Deutschen Gesellschaft fur Auswärtige Politik, 1981, pp. 88–91.

5. According to the CMEA's basic documents Mongolia (a member since 1962), Cuba and Vietnam enjoy the status of developing countries. Nothing has been said, however, about the amount of aid they receive, and from whom.

6. *Pravda*, 7 April 1971.

7. Richard Lowenthal, *Model or Ally? The Communist Powers and the Developing Countries* (New York: Oxford University Press, 1977), pp. 360–361.

8. A. Kodachenko, "Wirtschaftliche Zusammenarbeit zwischen RGW und Entwicklungsländern," *Deutsche Aussenpolitik*, 1981, No. 1, p. 55.

9. Thomas A. Wolf, "Soviet Trade with the Third World: A Quantiative Assessment," May 1984, pp. 10–11.

10. See Heinrich Machowski and Siegfried Schultz, *RGW-Staaten und Dritte Welt*, *Arbeitspapiere zur Internationalen Politik*, 1981, No. 18, Forschungsinstitut der Deutschen Gesellschaft fur Auswärtige Politik, pp. 18–20.

11. Thomas A. Wolf, "An Empirical Analysis of Price Discrimination, Stability, Aid and Bilateral Clearing in Soviet Trade with Developing Countries," op. cit., p. 41.

12. Giovanni Graziani, "Commercial Relations Between Developing Countries and the U.S.S.R. Recent Trends and Problems," Universita' Degli Studi Della Calabria, Working Papers, 1984, No. 5, p. 9 ff.

13. Olga Zhuravlewa, "Der Nahrungsgüteraspekt der wirtschaftlichen Zusammenarbeit zwischen den sozialistischen Ländern und den Staaten Lateinamerikas," *Aussenhandel der UdSSR*, 1983, No. 1., p. 46.

14. Machowski and Schultz, *RGW-Staaten. . .* , pp. 35–36.

15. CIA, *Handbook of Economic Statistics*, 1984, p. 109.

16. Thomas A. Wolf, "An Empircal Analysis of Price Discrimination, Stability, Aid and Bilateral Clearing in Soviet Trade with Developing Countries," May 1984, p. 41.

17. First put forward at UN ECOSOC by Soviet representative Makeev on 12 July 1982, repeated by Plechko at the UN 2nd Committee on 20 October 1982.

18. *Soviet, East European and Western Development Aid 1976–1982*, Foreign Policy Document, 1983 No. 85 (mimeographed), p. 6 ff.

19. Oleg Bogomolow, "The CMEA Countries and the New International Economic Order," in Christopher T. Saunders, Ed. *East-West-South Economic Interactions Between Three Worlds* (London: Macmillan Press, 1981), pp. 246–256.

14
The Politics and Economics of Soviet Arms Exports

Roger E. Kanet

Since the beginning of the 1970s the Soviet Union has increased dramatically its sales of conventional military equipment to countries in the Third World. The value of Soviet deliveries of military equipment to the non-communist developing countries in 1970 amounted to approximately $1 billion (slightly more than 22 percent of total imports from the USSR by all developing countries); by 1979 the figure had increased to almost $11 billion (more than 45 percent of total imports) (see Table 14.1). During the early years of the 1980s Soviet arms exports levelled off at an annual average of $9 billion (approximately 33 percent of all armaments purchased by Third World states). It is important to recognize that the expansion of the percentage of arms provided to the developing states by the USSR occurred during a period in which Third World countries greatly increased both the total amount of armaments imported and their share of global arms imports.

Military assistance and arms transfers have been an integral part of Soviet policy toward developing countries ever since the shift in Soviet policy toward these countries in the mid-1950s. However, since the early 1970s the military aspects of Soviet policy toward the developing world have far outstripped in importance most other forms of contact. Military support, including the provision of increasingly sophisticated weapons systems and of military training, has become the single most important element in Soviet relations with a substantial number

TABLE 14.1. Soviet Military Relations with Non-Communist Developing Countries,
1955 - 1983
(in millions of current US dollars)

	New Agreements Concluded	Deliveries
Total 1955-83[a]	93,300	78,505
1983[b]	4,165	7,815
1982[b]	12,575	9,945
1981[b]	7,935	8,730
1980[b]	16,040	9,540
1979[b]	9,815	10,875
1978[b]	3,570	7,195
1977[b]	10,075	5,065
1976[b]	6,550	3,445
1975[c]	3,655	2,390
1974[d]	5,735	2,225
1973[d]	2,890	3,135
1972[d]	1,680	1,215
1955-71[d]	8,615	6,920
1971[e]	1,590	865
1970[e]	1,150	995
1955-69[e]	5,875	5,060
1969[f]	350	450
1968[f]	500	500
1967[f]	525	500
1966[f]	450	500
1965[g]	260	
1964[g]	875	
1963[g]	390	
1962[g]	415	
1961[g]	830	
1955-60[g]	1,285	
1960[h]	570	
1959[h]	40	
1958[h]	470	
1957[h]	240	
1956[h]	290	
1955[h]	110	

Note: The figures are based on estimates. Since more recent estimates update
earlier ones and since the data in the table come from different sources,
the columns do not total.

TABLE 14.1 (cont.)

Sources:

[a]Totals have been calculated by using data from source "d" for 1955-1974 and from sources "b" and "c" for 1975-1983.

[b]Richard F. Grimmett, Trends in Conventional Arms Transfers to the Third World by Major Suppliers, 1976-1983. Congressional Research Service, Report No. 84-82F, 7 May 1984, pp. CRS-16, CRS-22.

[c]Richard F. Grimmet, Trends in Conventional Arms Transfers to the Third World by Major Suppliers, 1975-1982. Congressional Research Service, 11 April 1983, pp. CRS-10, CRS-13.

[d]US Department of State, Soviet and East European Aid to the Third World, 1981: February 1983, p. 4.

[e]Central Intelligence Agency, National Foreign Assessment Center, Communist Aid Activities in Non-Communist Less Developed Countries, 1979 and 1954-1979: A Research Paper. ER-80-10318U, October 1980, p. 13.

[f]Central Intelligence Agency, National Foreign Assessment Center, Communist Aid to Less Developed Countries of the Free World, 1975. ER-76-10372U, July 1975, p.1.

[g]US Department of State, Bureau of Intelligence and Research, Communist States and Developing Countries: Aid and Trade in 1972. Research Study, RECS-10, 15 June 1973, Appendix, Table 9.

[h]US Department of State, Bureau of Intelligence and Research, Communist States and Developing Countries: Aid and Trade in 1970. Research Study, RECS-15, 22 September 1971, p. 17.

of developing states, in particular those that the Soviet Union views as "progressive".

The growth of international sales of modern military equipment expanded almost exponentially during the 1970s and early 1980s. Between 1970 and 1982, for example, the value of total world arms exports rose from $4.1 billion to $36.5 billion.[1] While the United States and Western Europe have played major roles in the growth of international arms sales, the Soviet Union has played an even greater role. Ever since 1960 the USSR had ranked, behind the United States, as the second major world supplier of armaments. By 1978, however, the Soviet Union became the major source of armaments. During the period 1978-1982 the USSR transferred arms to all markets valued at almost $50 billion compared with US arms exports of $37 billion for the same period.[2]

One of the most distinctive characteristics of the growth of the international arms trade during the past decade and a half was the dramatic shift in the market. By far the most dynamic portion was that among developing countries. The substantial increase in purchasing power among the OPEC countries and the rise in the intensity of a number of regional rivalries among Third World states generated a new market for sophisticated weaponry. As a result the developing countries' share of total world arms imports rose from an annual average of 56 percent for 1963–1966 to 73.2 percent in 1972–1976 and reached 81.9 percent for 1982.[3] The Soviet Union has expanded its share of this growing market for armaments in the Third World and for the period 1978–1982 provided 37.0 percent of all weapons shipped to Third World states ($44,500 out of $120,200 million).[4]

The purpose of this chapter is to examine the place of arms transfers and other forms of military support in overall Soviet policy toward the Third World—in particular the countries of Africa and Asia. We shall be interested in showing how the Soviet military program has developed over the past thirty years, how that program relates to other aspects of Soviet relations with the Third World, and the apparent goals that the Soviet Union hopes to achieve through the provision of military equipment to Third World "clients" and "allies".

The Evolution of Soviet Policy Toward the Developing Countries

At the time of Stalin's death in 1953 the Western opponents of the Soviet Union maintained political, economic and military relations with all areas of the world—much of which was still under European colonial control—while Soviet international contacts were limited primarily to the countries that formed their newly-created empire in Eastern Europe and to their allies in China. The Soviet ability to project military—and in most cases political—power was limited to those regions under direct control of the Soviet army. The United States and its European allies had already become engaged in a process of expanding a network of military bases from Europe through the Middle East to East Asia as part of the policy of containment. To counter these efforts, the Soviet Union initially entered upon a policy of "denial" aimed at ensuring the neutrality of those developing countries—especially Afghanistan, India and Egypt—

which professed a non-aligned approach to foreign policy and
opposed the intrusion of military alliances into their region. The
USSR sought to expand ties with such countries in order to
prevent the uncontested growth of Western political and military
influence, to ensure that gaps would remain in the US sponsored
alliance network, and to win the support of the non-aligned
states for international political issues of importance to the Soviet
Union.[5] Measured in terms of political contacts, economic relations (including assistance), or military aid, Soviet involvement
in the areas of special strategic concern along the southern
borders of the USSR expanded rapidly.[6] In addition, however,
the Soviet Union did attempt to take advantage of a number
of opportunities in other areas, such as the civil war in Zaire
(then Congo-Leopoldville) and the radicalization of the governments of Sukarno in Indonesia, Nkrumah in Ghana and Touré
in Guinea.

Although the initial Soviet push toward expanding contacts
with the countries of the Third World was accompanied by
optimistic statements about the prospects for the development
of a revolutionary climate in these countries, the immediate
Soviet goal was the reduction of Western influence in regions
of strategic significance for Soviet security. This at times led to
a contradiction between the imperatives of Soviet policy and
the USSR's ideological assessments of these countries, since the
leaders involved could no longer be depicted as reactionaries
who ought to be swept away by the tide of revolution. At the
authoritative level, this change in doctrine was heralded at the
XX Party Congress in 1956 with Khrushchev's introduction of
the concept of the "zone of peace". The non-aligned states were
no longer to be regarded as mere outposts of Western imperialism
but as independent proponents of peace and, therefore, worthy
of Soviet support and assistance. Thus, despite rhetoric about
support for the construction of "scientific socialism" in developing countries, the Soviet Union was willing to provide support
to such evidently non-socialist countries as monarchical Afghanistan and the Ethiopia of Emperor Haile Selassie in an
attempt to undermine the Western position.

By the time of Khrushchev's overthrow in late 1964, however,
Soviet policy toward the developing countries was in partial

disarray. The optimism of the 1950s was already under attack and was being replaced by a growing realism concerning prospects for political and economic developments in most of the Third World. Although the USSR had ended its isolation from these countries, it had not succeeded in establishing significant influence relationships. Where Soviet goals had been partially accomplished—e.g., the reduction of the Western presence in the Middle East—success resulted far more from the initiatives of the developing countries themselves than from Soviet policy. Soviet hopes that many of the emerging nations would be willing to cut or reduce their economic and political ties with the West proved unfounded. Rather than emulate the Soviet Union as an alternative socio-political model, the majority of leaders in Asia and Africa chose instead to use the Soviet Union as a means to lessen their dependence on the former colonial powers and give them an additional source of military and economic assistance. Additionally, the USSR's capacity to provide support to friends, such as Lumumba, Nkrumah and Keita, in periods of crises was made difficult by its inferior position vis-à-vis the West—particularly by the virtual absence of an ocean-going navy.

Despite shortcomings, the Khrushchev years were not without successes upon which future Soviet policy could be built. In South Asia, India had already begun to depend heavily upon the USSR for both military assistance and for support in the development of heavy industrial projects in the state sector of the economy. In the Middle East both Egypt and Syria were now indebted to the Soviet Union for military and economic assistance, while Turkey and Iran had begun to expand their ties with their northern neighbor as a means of lessening their dependence on the United States. Throughout Asia and Africa the Soviet Union had become a force to be dealt with by the US and its allies, even though the West still commanded more influence and was able to exert more military capabilities in most areas of the developing world.

The first few years of the regime of Brezhnev and Kosygin saw a continuing reassessment of Soviet attitudes and policies.[7] Confidence in the development of Soviet-type socialist systems and an emphasis on economic "show projects" were replaced by the effort to establish firmly-based relations with Third World countries that would begin to provide the USSR with bases of operation from which it could expand contacts and attempt to increase its activities and build up influence. Even more than in earlier years Soviet policy focused on countries and political groupings that had inherent importance for their own purposes. First, they re-emphasized close ties with those countries along the southern boundaries of the Soviet Union, from India to the Arab countries of North Africa. The importance of this area for the strategic security interests of the Soviet Union is self-evident, as Soviet commentators have repeatedly noted.[8] Support for minor revolutionary groups and for activities in Sub-Saharan Africa was generally downplayed in the late 1960s—to the point where some Western commentators mistakenly argued that the Soviet Union had virtually lost interest in that continent.[9]

Since the early 1970s the USSR has continued to provide substantial support to groups or countries of potential importance to their strategic and global interests, despite what seems to be a preference for supporting "progressive" regimes and movements. In spite of the recent upsurge of Soviet involvement in Sub-Saharan Africa, Soviet interest is still concentrated heavily in the arc of countries that border the southern flank of the USSR. Here the Soviet goal continues to be the reduction of Western influence and military capabilities and the concomitant expansion of the military and political capabilities of the Soviet state. This has meant the continued provision of military and political support to such countries as Iraq, Syria and South Yemen. In several cases the USSR has signed treaties of friendship and cooperation with important South Asian and Middle Eastern countries, such as Iraq and India. In fact, during the 1970s it increased its efforts to improve relations with countries formally allied with the West, such as Turkey and Iran (prior to the overthrow of the Shah) by offering economic assistance and military sales as a means of reducing these countries' dependence on their Western allies, in particular the United States. Another important element in Soviet policy has been the search for access to both naval and airport facilities that would enable the country to expand the reach of its military capabilities, as we shall see in greater detail below.

Throughout the last thirty years Soviet policy toward the developing countries has relied heavily on the provision of economic and military assistance as a means of developing and consolidating relations. In general the terms of Soviet assistance are favorable when compared with commercial loans available to emerging nations on the international market, though the Soviet Union offers virtually no non-repayable grants and all aid is provided in the form of credits for the purchase of Soviet goods and equipment. Soviet trade with Asia and Africa has grown rapidly as well, though an important aspect of this trade has been the degree to which it has been related to the provision of economic assistance. With few exceptions (e.g., the sale of military equipment to Libya and the purchase of rubber from Malaysia) trade has resulted from agreements between the Soviet leaders and their Afro-Asian counterparts which include the commitment of Soviet economic and technical assistance. Examples of this type of agreement have been those with Egypt and India which called for the Soviet Union to provide capital equipment on the basis of long-term credits. These loans were to be repaid with the products of the recipient country over a period of twelve years at an interest rate of 2.0–2.5 percent. Such agreements have been especially attractive to those countries which have had problems obtaining the convertible currency necessary to purchase on the world market machinery and equipment needed for economic projects.

By the early 1980s, then, the relative position of the two major power blocs in the Third World had changed markedly. The collapse of the Western colonial empires and the ensuing rise of numerous anti-Western political regimes in the developing world, voluntary Western military retrenchment, and various other developments have resulted in the contraction of the Western military presence and of Western political influence throughout most of Asia and Africa. At the same time the Soviet Union has been able to establish a network of economic, political and military relationships that permits it for the first time in its history to play the role of a global power with worldwide interests and the capabilities to pursue many of those interests effectively. The change in the relative position of the Soviet Union in the international political system stems in part from the continued build-up of Soviet military power and the willingness and ability of the Soviet leadership to take advantage of the conflicts between the less developed states and the major Western powers.[10] By the 1970s the Soviet leaders were able to employ their newly developed military power—including an ocean-going fleet and long-range transport aircraft—in conjunction with access to port and air facilities in order to support distant and dispersed political and strategic goals.

The Expansion of Soviet Military Relations with Developing Countries

One of the most important changes in Soviet policy toward the Third World since the late 1960s has been the increasing emphasis on the expansion of military relations between the Soviet Union and individual developing states. Throughout the period 1955–1969 the USSR delivered an average of slightly more than $330 million worth of military equipment per year to developing countries. Beginning with the decade of the 1970s this amount began to rise substantially, reaching $995 million in 1970, $2,225 million in 1974, and $7,245 million in 1982. While deliveries of Soviet economic assistance to developing countries averaged about $510 million from 1972 to 1978,[11] deliveries of military equipment and supplies averaged more than six times as much—$3,164 million per year, with average annual deliveries for the entire 1972–1982 period amounting to $4,579 million. The major recipients of the increased Soviet arms transfers have been Libya and Algeria, which pay for weapons with hard currency earned from oil exports, Iraq, Ethiopia and Angola. Not only have Soviet sales and deliveries increased significantly since the 1960s, but the regional distribution of deliveries has also been extended. Until 1974 approximately 84 percent of all Soviet arms commitments and deliveries went to a few countries in South Asia and the Middle East. With the expansion of Soviet involvement in Sub-Saharan Africa during the 1970s, especially in Angola and Ethiopia, Africa became a more important recipient of Soviet military equipment. Between 1975 and 1978 agreements for military

TABLE 14.2. Soviet Military Relations with Developing Countries, By Region, 1955 - 1981
(in millions of US dollars)

	Total 1955-79	1955-74	1975	1976	1977	1978	1979	1980	1981	Total 1955-81
Agreements (Total)	48,440	18,905	3,205	6,100	9,335	2,520	8,360	13,915	6,060	68,415
North Africa	10,960	2,805	535	0	4,650	770	2,200		0	
Sub-Sharan Africa	4,635	715	220	840	1,510	980	370		1,910	
East Asia	890	890	0	0	0	0	0		0	
Latin America	970	205	70	335	110	0	250		105	
Middle East	24,445	11,980	1,195	4,105	1,735	325	5,105		3,505	
South Asia	5,410	2,330	1,305	220	705	390	410		535	
Deliveries (Total)	36,680	13,495	2,045	3,085	4,740	5,705	7,615	6,290	6,445	49,415
North Africa	7,165	685	450	1,010	1,265	1,685	2,090			
Sub-Saharan Africa	3,530	410	270	285	55	1,400	615			
East Asia	885	885	0	0	0	0	0			
Latin America	675	30	70	95	370	95	15			
Middle East	18,675	9,375	1,080	1,235	1,720	1,890	3,375			
South Asia	4,410	2,130	170	460	800	380	520			

*Values are based on estimated Soviet prices in rubles converted into dollars.

Source: CIA, Communist Aid Activities in Non-Communist Less Developed Countries, 1979 and 1954-79: A Research Paper. ER 80-10318U, October 1980, p. 14. US Department of State, Soviet and East European Aid to the Third World, 1981: February 1983, p. 2.

Note: The recent source does not provide any breakdown by region for 1980 nor a regional breakdown for new agreements in 1981. The totals for all agreements and deliveries come from the 1982 source and do not agree exactly with the total given in the 1980 CIA data.

support to Sub-Saharan Africa comprised 12 percent of total new commitments, while deliveries came to about 11 percent of total deliveries.

Despite the expansion of the number of recipients of Soviet military equipment and support in recent years, the number of such countries is still relatively restricted. Of the twenty-four countries reportedly receiving Soviet military support prior to 1967, fifteen received cumulative amounts of $40 million or less.[12] Although the number of recipients of Soviet military supplies has grown significantly in recent years, relatively few have received deliveries totalling more than $100 million during the most recent period for which data are available, 1978–1982.[13]

The arms export program of the USSR has differed in composition from that of the United States. Most important is the substantially greater role of military services in the American program. US deliveries of such services have been estimated to be nearly four times as great as those of the USSR, at least through the late 1970s, as a result of a larger provision of training and technical assistance and of a military construction program unparalled by the Soviet Union. On the other hand, Soviet deliveries of weapons systems had been larger than those of the United States and made up a significantly greater portion of total Soviet arms exports than was the case in the US program.[14] By the late 1970s, however, Soviet military-related services, in particular training and technical assistance, grew markedly. In addition, this growth was complemented by the services provided by Soviet allies—in particular the GDR and Cuba.[15] The number of military personnel from developing countries being trained in the USSR has averaged about 1,900 per year, with most receiving instruction in air defense systems, or as pilots, tank operators, and maintenance technicians.[16]

Finally, Soviet weapons are generally delivered to Third World customers much more rapidly than are those of the United States. The time elapsed between Soviet sales and deliveries has been averaging twelve to eighteen months; US leadtimes have averaged approximately three years.[17]

Before turning to a discussion of the place of Soviet military relations with developing countries in overall Soviet foreign relations, note should also be made of the types of weapons that have been supplied by the Soviet Union to several major Third World customers. Ethiopia, during 1977–1978 alone, received an estimated 500 Soviet tanks, 60 MiG-21 fighter aircraft and 20 of the more sophisticated MiG-23s, more than 300 armored personnel carriers and larger numbers of rocket launchers and 155 and 185 mm. guns.[18] Libya has received immense amounts of Soviet military equipment—especially considering the small size of the Libyan military. It is one of the very few countries to which the Soviet Union has sold the sophisticated MiG-25 fighter and the SA-9 air defense missile system.[19] Algeria, Iraq, and Syria have also received the most up-to-date Soviet equipment—often even before Warsaw Pact states have obtained them. The Soviet Union has also been willing to facilitate the development of arms production capabilities in India. For a number of years India has produced under Soviet license various versions of the supersonic MiG-21 fighter. Most recently the USSR signed an agreement with India to produce the MiG-31, which is still in the development stage. They have also agreed to provide the Indians with updated technology for T-72 and T-80 tanks and new submarines.[20]

No matter how one measures the Soviet arms support program in the Third World, the evidence indicates its growing importance during the past decade. In the following section we shall examine the factors that have apparently influenced the Soviet leaders in their decisions to expand the sale of military equipment to Third World states and the benefits for their overall foreign policy position that they hope to gain from arms transfers.

The Place of Military Support and Arms Transfers in Soviet Foreign Policy

In the earlier sections of this chapter we have surveyed the evolution of Soviet relations with the countries of the Third World and asserted that military assistance and arms transfers have played an important role in those relations. At this point we shall attempt to assess the precise function of military support in overall Soviet policy. Before examining Soviet goals, however, it is important to understand a number of factors inherent in the Soviet economic-political system which affect the ability of the Soviet Union to engage in the type of military support operations that they have developed. First of all, the Soviet Union has become the largest producer of conventional military equipment in the world. Exports have become the most efficient method of disposing of this huge surplus of weapons and, as we shall see below, have become a supplementary method of earning hard currency.[21] Moreover, given the focus of the Soviet economy on military production, this sector has become the most efficient and competitive. Soviet military equipment is generally qualitatively equal to, or even superior to, comparable equipment obtainable from other potential suppliers.[22] The USSR has, therefore, large stockpiles of surplus weapons of good quality and current vintage that it can make available to Third World states. The growing availability of such weapons has coincided with the phenomenal expansion of the market for weapons throughout Asia, Africa and Latin America.

Another factor relevant to Soviet arms transfers policy has been the growth of the Soviet navy and its operation in waters far from Soviet territory. By the beginning of the 1970s this fleet was operational and required access to facilities throughout Asia and Africa.[23] Arms transfers to certain Third World states have been a "bargaining" factor in Soviet attempts to acquire access to such facilities.

Political Factors in Soviet Military Support

The major purpose of Soviet arms assistance and sales, however, has been political. It should be borne in mind that it is not always possible to separate clearly the military-security aspects of Soviet objectives from the purely political. To a substantial degree the two are intertwined, for the growth of military capabilities may well bring with it an enhanced ability to achieve political goals. It is also important to note that military support is merely one of a number of instruments employed by the USSR—or by other countries, for that matter—in the effort to achieve foreign policy objectives. Diplomatic contacts, trade relations, economic and technical assistance, cultural policy and propaganda, and subversion are additional methods employed by the Soviet leaders in their relations with Third World states during the past quarter of a century. In any particular set of circumstances one or other of these instruments may predominate. The focus on military relations in the present discussion should not be interpreted to mean that these relations alone comprise the totality of Soviet policy toward the developing countries.

Initially the primary concern of the Soviet Union in extending military assistance to developing countries was the desire to undermine Western influence and strategic interest in regions of primary concern for Soviet security. Closely related to this goal was the desire to establish and extend the presence of the Soviet Union itself. In all cases where Soviet military equipment was supplied to developing countries, Soviet military technicians arrived along with the equipment in order to instruct the local military in its use. The corollary to this policy was the bringing of officers to the Soviet Union for extended periods of training.

Probably the most extreme example of the growing role of the Soviet Union in the affairs of a client state—at least the example that is most completely documented—is Egypt by the beginning of the 1970s. After the disastrous Six-Day War of June 1967 the entire Egyptian military was reorganized, largely by Soviet military advisors. Prior to their expulsion by President Sadat in the summer of 1972, approximately 21,000 Soviet military technicians were present in Egypt.

More recent examples of large-scale Soviet presence in Third World states have occurred in Angola, Somalia (until 1977), Ethiopia and, at a totally different level, Afghanistan since the Soviet invasion of that country in late 1979. In all of these cases the provision of military equipment and technical support has been one of the most important means employed by the Soviet Union in gaining a presence and in attempting to influence the course of political events in the recipient country.

Throughout the 1970s and 1980s Soviet policy in the Third World seemingly followed two paths—support for "progressive" regimes that are entering upon a path of socialist construction and a more pragmatic approach of dealing with "non-progressive" Third World states whose strategic location or raw materials base makes them of potential importance to the USSR. Military support has been among the most important elements in both of those sets of relationships. However, it appears most crucial in the case of those radical Third World states which have turned overwhelmingly to the Soviet Union for support. Bruce Porter has concluded that:

Although lasting influence may always be somewhat elusive, it would seem that the USSR's diplomatic influence over a Third World client is apt to be greatest when the client is a radical, left-wing regime intent on establishing a Socialist state. When such a client is also embroiled in a conflict and almost totally dependent on the Soviet Union for its very survival, conditions may be favorable for transforming it into a highly loyal ally.[24]

Among those states termed "progressive" by the Soviet authorities, virtually all receive the vast majority of their military equipment from the USSR. In addition, the USSR has lent great support to various national liberation movements, primarily in Africa, and, along with its East European and Cuban allies, became the major source of military support for rebel organizations in Angola and Mozambique prior to independence. In Zimbabwe they transferred military equipment to Joshua Nkomo's forces prior to independence, and both SWAPO (in Namibia) and the African National Congress (in South Africa) receive most of their military supplies from the Soviet Union and its allies. The "liberation" struggle carried out in Oman also has received support, at least indirectly through South Yemen, from the Soviet Union. Such military support, as in former Portuguese Africa, is expected to bring to power regimes that are not only favorably inclined toward the Soviet Union, but are also dependent upon it for their very survival.

The provision of military supplies has also been a way by which the Soviet leaders seek to ensure the stability of countries turning to them for support. Well-trained and loyal security forces are viewed as essential to stabilize the existence of budding Marxist-Leninist regimes, particularly given the experiences of several "progressive" governments in the 1960s. The position of the Soviet Union and its allies in Ghana, for instance, changed drastically with the overthrow of Kwame Nkrumah in 1966. This emphasis on the training of elite "palace guards" and domestic security police has become especially important as an element of Soviet policy in Africa where the USSR and its East European and Cuban allies have provided not only military equipment, but even the military personnel needed by revolutionary movements and regimes, as in Angola and Ethiopia, to seize power or to consolidate that power.

However, not only "progressive" or self-proclaimed Marxist-Leninist governments have been the recipients of major Soviet military support. In fact, much of Soviet military assistance and sales over the course of the past thirty years has gone to countries which, though often anti-Western (or at least anti-American), were hardly "progressive" in their domestic policies, at least in the Soviet sense of that term. Soviet military support to most of the Arab states in recent decades has had as its major focus the competition for political and military influence with the United States in the oil-rich Middle East. The continuation of the Arab-Israeli conflict has provided the Soviet leaders with conditions favorable to their involvement. To date, however, there is little evidence that they have been able to translate this involvement into influence. So long as the Soviet Union is willing to support Arab initiatives, relations remain cordial. When the interests of the Arab states and those of the Soviet Union diverge, however, the Soviet leaders generally find themselves incapable of changing the policies of the Arab states.

One final political purpose of Soviet military policies in the Third World should be mentioned prior to our discussion of military and economic motives. Throughout the 1970s the Soviet authorities have emphasized repeatedly the fact that the international environment has changed, that the role of the capitalist West in the international system is receding, and that a new international correlation of forces has emerged. However, only by playing a role in events on a global scale can the Soviet leaders demonstrate to leaders throughout the world that their assessment of the changing international balance is indeed accurate. If nothing else, the Soviet leaders have shown in recent years that they have both the ability and the willingness to provide support to their allies. The success of the MPLA in Angola or of the central government in Ethiopia can largely be attributed to Soviet (and Cuban) military support. The provision of various forms of military assistance throughout Asia and Africa has been among the most important means employed by the Soviet Union in verifying the claim that a changing balance of forces has already emerged.[25] The image of the Soviet Union as an equal, or even superior, to the United States may well influence leaders in Asia and Africa to work out a *modus vivendi* with the Soviet Union and its clients, given the apparent dominant future role of the country in the international system.

Military-Security Considerations in Soviet Military Support

Closely related to the Soviet desire to strengthen its global role is the continuing competition with the United States—and with the People's Republic of China. Over the course of the past fifteen years or so, Soviet policy in the Third World has been based, in part, on the desire to expand the capabilities to project power abroad in support of Soviet state interest. These projection capabilities depend upon two separate, but unrelated, developments. First, there was the need for the Soviet Union to produce the military equipment necessary to exert military power in regions beyond the territory controlled by the Soviet army. Again the Soviet leaders have conducted a constructive program that has now given them a large, modern ocean-going navy and long-distance transport aircraft.[26]

The second requirement was access to military facilities throughout the Third World at which to refuel, repair, and refurbish the newly-developed military capabilities. In this portion of our analysis of Soviet military support to developing countries, we wish to demonstrate the relationship between arms transfers and the Soviet acquisitions of access to such facilities.

We do not wish to become involved, however, in the fruitless debate concerning the precise definition of a military base or the various distinctions that can be made between bases and other types of military facilities.[27] Although we shall distinguish between facilities over which the Soviet forces have exercised virtually complete, albeit often temporary, control and facilities to which they have had only limited access, our major concern will be between the general relationship between access and the provision of military support to the host government. Robert E. Harkavy has argued that the Soviet Union "has accelerated the use of arms transfers for acquiring strategic access, expanding a once limited basing network to near global dimensions during an era which is witnessing the withering of previous ideological bars to many arms-transfer client relationships".[28] The evidence points to the acquisition of military facilities in areas of strategic interest to the Soviet Union as one of the primary motivating factors for Soviet economic assistance and military transfers to the Third World. During the past fifteen years or so, the Soviet leaders have been especially successful in creating a network of such facilities throughout the Indian Ocean area, the Middle East, and various parts of Africa that now permits them to influence developments far from the territory of the Soviet Union. It must also be noted that the development of the Soviet network of facilities has depended upon the support that they have been willing to provide to host countries, either in local conflicts or in conflicts with the West.

Among the most important developments that have enabled the Soviet Union both to export military equipment and to acquire basing facilities has been the Arab-Israeli conflict. Initial direct Soviet involvement in the Middle East was directly related to the provision of military assistance to the Arab states. By the early 1970s the Soviet Union had developed a position in Egypt that appeared to be especially strong. Egypt was largely dependent upon the USSR for both development assistance and military equipment, and the Soviet forces had gained access to port and air facilities throughout Egypt. These facilities, which were under complete Soviet command, provided them with the opportunity to conduct air surveillance activities throughout the Eastern Mediterranean and to maintain their growing naval strength in the region. Similarly, the Soviet forces were also able to gain access to various types of military facilities in Syria and Iraq, though they have never exercised the type of control over these facilities that they maintained in Egypt prior to their expulsion in 1972.

The conflict between Somalia and Ethiopia has afforded the Soviet leaders with a dual opportunity; first, the acquisition of large-scale military facilities in Somalia and later, after their decision to opt for support for the new revolutionary regime in Addis Ababa and the loss of the Somali military facilities, the acquisition of facilities in Ethiopia.

The civil war in Angola in 1975 and the war between Somalia and Ethiopia in the Horn of Africa have indicated both the extent of existing Soviet military facilities and their importance to the Soviet Union in supporting its allies and clients throughout the Third World. Without access to air facilities in Algeria, Benin, Congo, Guinea, and elsewhere in West Africa, the rapid and large-scale shipment of Soviet military equipment and Cuban troops essential for the MPLA's victory would have been impossible. Soviet access to facilities in Iraq, South Yemen and Libya were indispensable for the movement of massive amounts of Soviet military equipment and large numbers of Cuban troops to help the new friends of the USSR in Ethiopia.

It should be noted, however, that not all major recipients of Soviet arms have provided the Soviet Union with military facilities. India, for example, has provided only limited servicing and repair facilities for the Soviet fleet. In the case of Iran it seems clear that the primary Soviet expectation at the time that arms were sold was to lessen Iran's dependence on the United States—not to acquire any type of military facilities.

A final point must also be emphasized concerning the weakness of the Soviet Union's position in many of the countries in which it has acquired military facilities. Both Egypt and Somalia expelled the Soviet forces when their goals and those of the Soviet Union clashed. During the 1976 civil war in Lebanon, Syria restricted Soviet access to naval facilities in that country in order to show its displeasure with Soviet opposition to Syrian intervention against the PLO and the Lebanese leftists.[29] The Soviet leaders have apparently been quite aware of the tenuous nature of their military presence in the developing countries and have generally followed a policy of establishing parallel, or backup, facilities. For example, throughout the late 1960s and early 1970s they simultaneously courted North Yemen, South Yemen, Somalia and Egypt. When Somalia expelled the Soviet forces as a result of Soviet military support for Ethiopia in 1977, they were still able to use the facilities in Aden, South Yemen. In West Africa the Soviet Union seems to have developed a parallel set of facilities in Benin, Guinea-Bissau, Equatorial Guinea, Congo and Mali.[30] A related example can be seen in the increased deliveries of military equipment to Syria immediately after the expulsion of Soviet forces from Egypt in 1972 and the resulting extension of access to Syrian naval facilities. Later, during the deterioration of Soviet-Syrian relations as a consequence of disagreements over policy in the Lebanese civil war, the Soviet Union began to concentrate its arms supplies in Iraq, where it also reached an agreement for the expansion of access to Iraqi air and naval facilities.[31]

To date Soviet military capabilities in the Third World have been employed for a variety of purposes. First, they have been used to support an ally or client state against a regional opponent—e.g. the Arabs versus Israel, India versus Pakistan, and Ethiopia versus Somalia—or to support one faction in a domestic civil war, as in Angola. As has already been noted, the Soviet Union has also provided substantial military assistance to revolutionary movements committed to the overthrow of "colonial" regimes, as in southern Africa. Finally, their overseas military capabilities have provided the Soviet forces with the opportunity to monitor the activities of Western civil and military shipping in the major shipping lanes from the oil-rich Persian Gulf region through the Indian Ocean and the South Atlantic to Europe and North America.

Economic Factors in Soviet Arms Transfers

In a 1973 analysis of the economic costs to the Soviet Union of its arms supplies in the Middle East, Gur Ofer concluded that the delivery of these weapons constituted "a heavy and ever-increasing supply burden, an increase that creates even heavier claims on increments of new available resources".[32] Ofer based his conclusion on the fact that by the beginning of the 1970s military aid to the Middle East alone represented a total of 1.8 percent of total machinery production in the Soviet Union—more than double the percentage for the years 1955–1966.[33] Up through the early 1970s virtually all Soviet military equipment shipped to Third World states was provided on the basis of medium-term credits. These credits generally carried relatively low interest rates—when compared with private Western credit—and were repayable with traditional exports of the recipient country or in local currency.[34] Moreover, the sale price of Soviet weapons has generally been heavily subsidized. According to one estimate, approximately 40 percent of the value of Soviet military equipment has been written off as grants. Even without discounts the list price of Soviet weapons has usually been below the price charged for comparable Western equipment.[35]

Yet recent developments in Soviet arms transfer policy indicate that arms transfers cannot merely be viewed as an economic burden on the Soviet economy. From 1974–1981 the hard currency component of Soviet arms sales to Third World countries ranged between 62 percent and 88 percent of total arms sales to developing nations during that period. The total estimated

TABLE 14.3. Estimated Hard Currency Component of Soviet Arms Sales to Third World
Countries
(in millions of US dollars and in percent)

	Hard Currency Arms Sales	Total Arms Sales	Percent Hard Currency Sales
1970	400	775	51.6
1971	400	680	58.8
1972	600	960	62.5
1973	1,600	2,100	76.2
1974	1,500	1,980	75.8
1975	1,500	1,860	80.6
1976	1,850	2,270	81.5
1977	3,220	3,810	84.5
1978	3,965	4,310	96.0
1979	3,855	4,270	90.3
1980	4,200	4,670	89.9
1981	4,200	4,960	84.7

Sources: Parpart Zoeter, "USSR Hard Currency Trade and Payments", in US
Congress, Joint Economic Committee, Soviet Economy in the 1980s:
Problems and Prospects, Washington, D.C., 1983, p. II, PP. 503–
504. Note that the data on total arms sales differ substantially
from those provided in Table 14-1.

annual hard currency income from arms sales averaged almost
$3.9 billion for the years 1977–1981 and in most years more
than covered the Soviet deficit on merchandise trade conducted
primarily with the West (see Table 14.3). Ever since the rise in
OPEC oil prices and the availability of large amounts of hard
currency in a number of Arab countries the Soviet Union has
been receiving hard currency for weapons shipped to the Middle
East. Libya, which became a major purchaser of Soviet weapons
during the last decade or so, pays for all of its purchases with
hard currency or "hard" goods, while both Syria and Iraq have
been able to cover the costs of much of their imports with hard
currency provided by other wealthy states.[36]

In an extremely interesting analysis of Soviet arms exports,
Raymond Hutchings has maintained that the fluctuations in
Soviet arms sales abroad can be understood only in the context
of internal Soviet economic forces. According to Hutchings Soviet
exports to Third World states over the past two decades have
followed a regular pattern of five-year cycles that are tied to
the planning process of the Soviet economy.[37]

What is clear from the available evidence is the fact that
arms exports to Third World states have become an important

source of hard currency and, along with petroleum and gold, comprise more than two-thirds of all Soviet hard currency exports.[38] Arms sales play a major role in covering the deficits in commodity trade on the world market. Throughout the last decade the Soviet leadership has greatly increased its imports of industrial equipment, including modern technology, in the effort to deal with problems facing the Soviet economy. However, in spite of substantial increases in the export of raw materials, the Soviet Union has continued to run a substantial deficit on trade with the industrialized West. The one area in which the Soviet Union has been able to compete effectively on the world market has been in the provision of military equipment. As we have noted above, Soviet equipment is comparable to that produced in the West and, more important, the Soviet Union has the surpluses required to enable it to export armaments to potential Third World customers.

Although the economic factor is not the most important influence determining Soviet arms transfers, it is conceivable that it increasingly comes into consideration as the Soviet leadership makes its decisions concerning the value of providing arms to various Third World customers.

An Assessment of Soviet Arms Transfer and Military Support Policy

Since a considerable portion of the discussion of Soviet involvement in the developing world that appears in the popular press tends to assume the virtually irrepressible implementation of a "grand design", it is necessary to put Soviet policy in perspective. Although the Soviet leaders have indeed greatly expanded their role in world affairs and in the Third World in particular, they have by no means been invariably successful in the accomplishment of their foreign policy goals. To a very great degree their policy initiatives and their successes and failures have depended on local developments over which they have exercised little or no control. The death of a Nasser, the seizure of power by a Mengistu, and similar developments have been extremely important for Soviet policy. The growth of arms transfer to the Third World and the ability to gain access to overseas military facilities have resulted far more from external circumstances than from Soviet policy initiatives. The expansion of regional conflicts—such as that in the Horn of Africa or the periodic explosions in Arab-Israeli relations—and the availability of surplus income in the oil-producing states have been major determinants that have added to the market for Soviet armaments, as well as for those of the Western states. The acquisition of military facilities by the Soviet forces has often been viewed by the host country as a method of enhancing its own military security against a regional opponent. This was clearly the case in both Egypt and Somalia during the height of their close relations with the Soviet Union. Yet, although the USSR has expanded its activities and capabilities in large areas of the developing world, it is still unable to dictate developments as it can, to some degree at least, in Eastern Europe.

Soviet goals in the developing world, as we have seen, have included 1) the reduction of Western, in particular American, military and political influence; 2) the containment of possible Chinese influence; 3) the establishment of a network of military facilities that will enable Soviet military forces to project power; and 4) the possible economic benefits that can be gained for the Soviet economy. In large part these goals have been accomplished—often because of the failures of American and West European policy; at other times because local developments have provided the Soviet leaders with opportunities that they were able to exploit.[39]

Soviet military assistance and arms transfer programs, as a part of overall policy toward the developing countries, are motivated primarily by political and strategic concerns. On the whole they have been related more to Soviet support for ideologically compatible allies, the search for strategic benefits, and the building of the foundations for future political influence than to economic motivations, even though the economic factor has grown in importance.

The expansion of Soviet military capabilities and of a Soviet presence throughout much of Asia and Africa have increased Soviet possibilities for influencing future political and military developments. However, it must be kept in mind that the Soviet leaders still must depend upon the good will of client states in order to maintain the network of facilities that they have constructed. As they become more involved in local affairs, as in the Horn of Africa, they will find that they cannot support two sides in a conflict and maintain favorable relations with both. As in the past, they are likely to opt for the stronger and potentially more important of the participants in a conflict. The possibility of becoming mired in local military conflicts also exists, as they are learning in both Angola and Ethiopia where Soviet-backed regimes are faced with serious internal opposition. Recent events in Afghanistan indicate the extreme situation in which the Soviet leaders felt constrained to intervene directly in order to salvage the position of a client regime and to ensure future developments compatible with Soviet interests.

The future will probably witness a continuation of Soviet policy in the developing world—or, rather, a series of policies— that differs little from what has evolved over the past two decades. The festering of the Arab-Israeli conflict and the escalating unrest in southern Africa may well provide them with expanding opportunities for involvement in both of these regions. The fact that the USSR, in spite of numerous setbacks, has been able to establish a set of political-military relationships throughout much of the Third World means that they are now able to have an impact on events and to undercut Western political and economic interests in ways that would have been impossible only a decade ago. Arms transfers have played an important part in Soviet policy in the past and will probably continue to represent the single most important Soviet instrument in relations with Third World states. As Franklyn Griffiths has argued, there is little in either Soviet political-ideological views or in Soviet perceptions of the world situation that is likely to result in a voluntary limitation on the supply of arms to potential markets in the Third World.[40]

Notes

1. United States Arms Control and Disarmament Agency (hereafter ACDA), *World Military Expenditures and Arms Transfers 1970–1979*

(Washington, D.C., 1982), p. 85; ACDA, *World Military Expenditures, 1972–1982*, Washington, D.C., 1984, p. 53.

2. *Ibid.*, pp. 86, 91.

3. ACDA, *World Military Expenditures, 1963–1973*, Washington, D.C., 1974, p. 72; ACDA, *World Military Expenditures, 1972–1982*, p. 53.

4. *Ibid.*, p. 95.

5. See Richard Lowenthal, *Model or Ally? The Communist Powers and the Developing Countries* (New York: Oxford University Press, 1977), pp. 185–186.

6. See, for example, US Department of State, Bureau of Intelligence and Research, *Communist Economic Offensive Through 1964*, Research Memorandum, RSB-65, 5 August 1965, p. 6 and US Department of State, Bureau of Intelligence and Research, *Communist Government and Developing Nations: Aid and Trade in 1965*, Research Memorandum, RSB-50, 17 June 1965, pp. 12–19.

7. For the full development of this argument see Elizabeth Kridl Valkenier, *The Soviet Union and the Third World: An Economic Bind* (New York: Praeger, 1983).

8. See, for example, the comments of Admiral S. G. Gorshkov, Commander of the Soviet Navy, in *Ogonek*, 1968 no. 6. For a Western assessment of Gorshkov's major writings see James McConnell, "The Gorshkov Articles, the New Gorshkov Book, and Their Relations to Policy", in Michael McGwire and John McDonnell, eds., *Soviet Naval Influence: Domestic and Foreign Dimensions* (New York: Praeger Publishers, 1977), pp. 565–620.

9. See, for example, Roger E. Kanet, "The Soviet Union and the Developing Countries: Policy or Policies?" *The World Today*, Vol. XXI (1975), pp. 344–345; John D. Esseks, "Soviet Economic Aid to Africa; 1959–72; An Overview", in Warren Weinstein, ed., *Chinese and Soviet Aid to Africa* (New York: Praeger Publishers, 1975), p. 114.

10. Two excellent recent books dealing with Soviet arms transfer and military policy in the Third World are Bruce D. Porter, *The USSR in Third World Conflicts: Soviet Arms and Diplomacy in Local Wars 1945–1980* (Cambridge, London and New York: Cambridge University Press, 1984); and Joachim Krause, *Die sowjetische Militärhilfepolitik gegenüber aussereuropäischen Entwicklungsländern* (Ebenhausen: Stiftung Wissenschaft und Politik, 1983).

11. Central Intelligence Agency, National Foreign Assessment Center, *Communist Aid Activities in Non-Communist Less Developed Countries 1978: A Research Paper*, ER79-104120, September 1979, p. 11.

12. See Wynfred Joshua and Stephen P. Gibert, *Arms for the Third World: Soviet Military Aid Diplomacy* (Baltimore and London: The

Johns Hopkins Press, 1969), p. 102. Also US Department of State, Bureau of Intelligence and Research, *Communist Government and Developing Nations: Aid and Trade in 1967.* Research Memorandum, RSE-120, 14 August 1968, p. 6.

13. ACDA, *World Military Expenditures, 1972–1982*, pp. 95–98.

14. See Central Intelligence Agency, National Foreign Assessment Center, *Arms Flows to LDCs: U.S.-Soviet Comparisons, 1974–1977.* ER 78–10494U, November 1978, pp. 4–6.

15. See CIA, *Communist Aid Activities in 1978*, p. 4; *Communist Aid to Less Developed Countries, 1977*, p. 3; and *Communist Aid to Less Developed Countries, 1976*, p. 4.

16. *Ibid.* See, also, Gad W. Toko, *Intervention in Uganda: The Power Struggle and Soviet Involvement* (Pittsburgh: University of Pittsburgh, University Center for International Studies, 1979), esp. pp. 105–114.

17. CIA, *Arms Flows to LDCs*, p. 5.

18. International Institute for Strategic Studies, *Strategic Survey 1978* (London, 1979), p. 98.

19. CIA, *Communist Aid Activities in 1978*, p. 20.

20. S. Nihal Singh, "Why India Goes to Moscow for Arms", *Asian Survey*, Vol. XXIV (1984), p. 709.

21. See Michael Checinski, "Structural Causes of Soviet Arms Exports," *Osteuropa-Wirtschaft*, Vol. XXIII (1977), p. 178.

22. See P. R. Chari, "Indo-Soviet Military Relations: A Comment", *India Quarterly*, Vol. XXXIII (1977), p. 456. See also Gur Ofer, "Soviet Military Aid to the Middle East: An Economic Balance Sheet", in US Congress, Joint Economic Committee, *Soviet Economic Prospects for the 1970s* (Washington, D.C.: U.S. Government Printing Office, 1973), p. 236.

23. See James M. McConnell and Bradford Dismukes, "Soviet Diplomacy of Force in the Third World", *Problems of Communism*, Vol. XXVIII no. 1 (1979), pp. 14–27.

24. Porter, *The USSR in Third World Conflicts*, p. 223.

25. For a discussion of the concept of the international correlation of forces see Haus Rissen, Internationales Institut für Politik und Wirtschaft, *Die sowjetische Konzept der Korrelation der Kräfte und seine Anwedung auf die Aussenpolitik* (Hamburg: Haus Rissen, Internationales Institut für Politik und Wirtschaft, n.d., probably 1980). See also Roger E. Kanet and Daniel R. Kempton, "Western Europe in Soviet Global Strategy: Soviet Power and the Global Correlation of Forces", in W. Kaltefleiter, ed., *Soviet Global Strategy Against Western Europe*, forthcoming.

26. See C. G. Jacobsen, *Soviet Strategic Initiatives: Challenge and Response* (New York: Praeger, 1979), pp. 51–72. See also William J. Durch, Michael D. Davidchick and Abram N. Shulsky, "Other Soviet Interventionary Forces—Military Transport Aviation and Airborne Troops", in Bradford Dismukes and James McConnel, eds. *Soviet Naval Diplomacy* (New York: Pergamon Press, 1979), pp. 336–351. In a recent article Rajan Menon cautions against the tendency to exaggerate Soviet capabilities for projecting military power in the Third World. See his "Military Power, Intervention and Soviet Policy in the Third World", in Roger E. Kanet, ed., *Soviet Foreign Policy in the 1980s* (New York: Praeger, 1982), pp. 263–284.

27. For a discussion of this issue as it related to Soviet policy see Richard B. Remnek, "The Politics of Soviet Access to Naval Support Facilities in the Mediterranean", in Dismukes and McConnell, eds. *Soviet Naval Diplomacy*, esp. pp. 357–361.

28. Robert E. Harkavy, "The New Geopolitics: Arms Transfers and the Major Powers' Competition for Overseas Bases", in Stephanie G. Neuman and Robert E. Harkavy, eds., *Arms Transfers in the Modern World* (New York: Praeger, 1979), p. 132. Harkavy's argument is expanded in his more recent study, *Great Power Competition for Overseas Bases: The Geopolitics of Access Diplomacy* (New York: Pergamon, 1982), especially pp. 175–204.

29. See "Syria-USSR: Soviets asked to Leave Syrian Naval Post", *Defense and Foreign Affairs Daily*, 14 January 1977, cited in Harkavy, "The New Geopolitics" op. cit., p. 138.

30. See the description of the Soviet basing network in "New Soviet Role in Africa Alleged", *The New York Times*, 10 December 1975, p. 11. See also Nimrod Novik, *On the Shores of Bab Al-Mandab: Soviet Dipolomacy and Regional Dynamics* (Philadelphia: Foreign Policy Research Institute, 1979).

31. See Robert O. Freedman, "The Soviet Union and Sadat's Egypt", in Michael McGwire, Ken Booth, and John McDonnell, eds., *Soviet Naval Policy: Objectives and Constraints* (New York: Praeger, 1975), pp. 211–236; and "Iraq: Defense Protocol with USSR", *Defense and Foreign Affairs Daily*, 13 October 1976, cited in Harkavy, "The New Geopolitics," p. 138.

32. Ofer, "Soviet Military Aid to the Middle East", op. cit., p. 233.

33. *Ibid.*, p. 227.

34. See Uri Ra'anan, *The USSR Arms the Third World: Case Studies in Soviet Foreign Policy* (Cambridge, Mass.: The M.I.T. Press, 1969), pp. 161–163. Singh has pointed out that the ability to pay the USSR for weapons in rupees was an important factor in the recently

completed negotiations concerning the Indian construction of MiG-31 aircraft under Soviet license. Singh, "Why India Goes to Moscow," op. cit., p. 710.

35. See Roger F. Pajak, "West European and Soviet Arms Transfer Policies in the Middle East", in Milton Leitenberg and Gabriel Sheffer, eds., *Great Power Intervention in the Middle East* (New York: Pergamon Press, 1979), p. 155.

37. Raymond Hutchings, "Regular Trends in Soviet Arms Exports to the Third World", *Osteuropa-Wirtschaft,* Vol. XXIII, no. 3 (1978), pp. 182–202.

38. In recent years arms sales for hard currency have comprised approximately 15 percent of the total of merchandise exports (including gold and arms sales). The following figures, based on data presented in Zoeter, "U.S.S.R. Hard Currency Trade and Payments", pp. 483, 503, indicate the relative importance of these three commodities in Soviet hard currency exports.

	Total Value Of Merchandise Exports, Gold Sales and Arms Sales (in million dollars)	Arms (percentage)	Gold (percentage)	Petroleum and Natural Gas (percentage)
1977	16,701	19.3	9.7	35.1
1978	19,823	20.0	12.7	34.2
1979	24,762	15.6	6.0	44.4
1980	29,264	14.3	5.4	50.2
1981	30,678	13.7	8.8	52.9

39. For a more complete discussion of this point see Porter, *The USSR in Third World Conflicts,* pp. 230–234.

40. Franklyn J. C. Griffiths, "De la justification des transferts d'armes par l'Union Soviétique", *Etudes Internationales,* Vol. VIII (1977), p. 600–617.

About the Contributors

Ronald Amann, professor of Soviet politics and director of the Centre for Russian and East European Studies, University of Birmingham, England. Recent publications: "Technical Progress and Political Change in the Soviet Union", in A. Schüller et al., *Innovationsprobleme in Ost und West*, New York, 1983; "Die politischen Hindernisse für Wirtschaftsreformen in der UdSSR", in: H.-J. Veen, ed., *Wohin entwickelt sich die Sowjetunion?* Melle, 1984; ed. with J. Cooper, *Technical Progress and Soviet Economic Development*, Oxford, 1986.

Klaus von Beyme, director of the Institute for Political Science, Heidelberg University, 1982–1985 president of the International Political Science Association. Recent publications: *Economics and Politics Within Socialist Countries*, New York, 1982; ed. with H. Zimmermann, *Policymaking in the German Democratic Republic*, New York, 1984; *Political Parties in Western Democracies*, New York, 1985.

Georg Brunner, professor in ordinary of Soviet and East European law, public law, and government and director of the Institute for Soviet and East European law, University of Cologne. Recent publications: "Die osteuropäischen Staaten im Ost-West-Konflikt", in: *Zeitschrift für Politik*, 1984, Special Edition; "Der Schutz ethnischer Minderheiten in Osteuropa", in B. Börner, H. Jahrreiss, K. Stern eds., *Jahrbuch für Ostrecht*, Vol. XXV (1984); *Das Staatsoberhaupt der DDR*, Festschrift für Karl Carstens, Cologne, 1984.

Helmut Dahm, research director at the Federal Institute for East European and International Studies, Cologne. Recent publications: "Being and Time—Creation and Development: Vasilii Zen'kovsky and His Critique of Religious Evolutionism", in: D. Cioran et al., *Studies in Honour of Louis Shein,* Ontario, 1983; "The Present State of the Marxist-Leninist Core Belief in Revolution: What Remains of Basic Marxism?" in J. J. O'Rourke et al. *Contemporary Marxism: Essays in Honour of J. M. Bocheński,* Dordrecht-Boston-Lancaster, 1984.

Christopher Davis, lecturer, Centre for Russian and East European Studies, University of Birmingham, England. Recent publications: *Opportunities in the Soviet Pharmaceutical Market in the 1980s,* Richmond (Surrey), 1985; "Zur Ökonomie des sowjetischen Gesundheitssystems," *Berichte des Osteuropa-Instituts an der FU Berlin,* No. 134 (1984); *The Health and Pharmaceutical Sectors of the Soviet Economy,* Wharton Econometric Forecasting Associates, Washington, D.C., Centrally Planned Economies Service Special Report, 1984.

Peter Frank, senior lecturer in Soviet government and politics, University of Essex. Recent publications: with R. J. Hill, *The Soviet Communist Party,* 2nd edition, London, 1983; "Foreign Policy Makers: The CPSU Local Apparat," in C. Keeble ed., *The Soviet State: The Domestic Roots of Soviet Foreign Policy,* London, 1985.

Gregory Grossman, professor of economics, University of California, Berkeley. Recent publications: "Economics of Virtuous Haste: A View of Soviet Industrialization and Institutions," in P. Desai, ed., *Marxism, Central Planning, and the Soviet Economy,* Cambridge (Mass.), 1983; "The Party as Manager and Entrepreneur," in G. Guroff and F. V. Carstensen eds., *Entrepreneurship in Imperial Russia and the Soviet Union,* Princeton, 1983.

Hans-Hermann Höhmann, senior economist at the Federal Institute for East European and International Studies, Cologne, and lecturer, University of Cologne. Recent publications: Ed.

with A. Nove and G. Seidenstecher, *The East European Economies in the 1970s*, Butterworths, London, 1982; Ed. *Die Wirtschaft Osteuropas und der VR China zu Beginn der 80er Jahre*, Verlag W. Kohlhammer, Stuttgart, 1983; Ed. with H. Vogel, *Osteuropas Wirtschaftsprobleme und die Ost-West-Beziehungen*, Baden-Baden, 1984.

Jerry F. Hough, James B. Duke professor of political science, Duke University, and staff member of the Brookings Institution. Recent publications: *The Polish Crisis: American Policy Options*, Washington, D.C., 1982; "Gorbachev's Strategy," *Foreign Affairs*, fall 1985.

Roger E. Kanet, professor and head of the Department of Political Science and member of the Russian and East European Center, University of Illinois at Urbana-Champaign. Recent publications: "The Polish Crisis and Poland's 'Allies': The Soviet and East European Response to Events in Poland," in J. Bielasiak and M. D. Simon, eds, *Polish Politics: Edge of the Abyss*, New York, 1984; "Security Issues in Soviet African Policy: The Imperatives of Soviet Security Policy in Soviet-African Relations," *Crossroads*, 1983, No. 10; "Eastern Europe and the Third World: The Expanding Relationship," in M. J. Sodaro and S. L. Wolchik, eds., *Foreign and Domestic Policy in Eastern Europe in the 1980s: Trends and Prospects*, London-New York, 1983.

Heinrich A. Machowski, senior economist at the German Institute for Economic Research, Berlin (West). Recent publications: "Aktuelle Probleme der Währungspolitik der RGW-Staaten," in H. Besters, ed., *Währungspolitik auf dem Prüfstand*, Baden-Baden, 1984; "Die Wirtschaftsbeziehungen zwischen der Bundesrepublik Duetschland und der Sowjetunion—die sowjetische Perspektive," *Osteuropa-Wirtschaft*, 1984, No. 4; "Ost-West-Handel: Entwicklung, Interessenlagen, Aussichten," in Beilage zur Wochenzeitschrift, *Das Parlament*, B5/85, 2 February 1985.

Alec Nove, emeritus professor of economics, University of Glasgow, and fellow of the British Academy. Recent publications:

The Soviet Economic System (German translation 1980), *The Economics of Feasible Socialism*, London, 1983.

Heinrich Vogel, director of the Federal Institute for East European and International Studies, Cologne. Recent publications: Ed. with H. -H. Höhmann, *Osteuropas Wirtschaftsprobleme und die Ost-West-Beziehungen,* Baden-Baden, 1984; "Politische Bestimmungsgründe in den Wirtschaftsbeziehungen zwischen Ost und West," in G. Find, ed., *East-West Economic Relations Now and in Future,* Vienna and New York, 1985; "Technology for the East—the Tiresome Issue," *Aussenpolitik,* 1985, No. 2.

Hans-Jürgen Wagener, professor of economics, Rijksuniversiteit Groningen, The Netherlands. Recent publications: "The Economics of Socialism as Economics of Shortage—A Critical Review," *De Economist,* 1982, No. 130; with J. Myusken, "Zur Verlangsamung der dynamischen Effizienz in kapitalistischen und sozialistischen Ländern," in A. Schüller, ed., *Wachstumsverlangsamung und Konjunkturzyklen in unterschiedlichen Wirtschaftssystemen,* Berlin, 1984; ed. with J. W. Drukker, *The Economic Law of Motion of Modern Society: A Marx-Keynes-Schumpeter Centennial,* Cambridge, 1985.

Peter Wiles, professor of Russian social and economic studies, University of London. Recent publications: *The New Communist Third World,* London, 1982; with M. Efrat, *The Economics of Soviet Arms,* ICERD, London School of Economics, 1985.